Peace Be With You
Christ Centered Bullying Redirect

Grades 4-8 Curriculum

Frank A. DiLallo

Thom Powers

Lisa Bartholomew

Consulting & Training Services, LLC
https://www.peacebewithyou.world

Toledo, Ohio

ISBN: 13: 978-1986037785
        10: 1986037789

Cover Design: Keith Tarjanyi

Visit https://www.peacebewithyou.world for information on professional development training, parent training, and subscription options.

Printed in the United States of America.

Table of contents

Unit 3: Love Your Neighbor

Appendices

School Community Prayer

Holy Spirit, bless our educators for their service and commitment to their educational calling. Keep them safe in their classrooms; and may all aspects of their instruction be led with your holy guidance. Father, increase creativity and innovation to teach and form students according to their needs, levels of intelligence, and learning capabilities. Let peace still any "storms" that may rage within our school community.

We pray that You will always guide our school to be a safe, Christ-centered learning environment for the formation of our students and families. We pray for supportive and strong connections between our educators and students. We pray for supportive and encouraging relationships among students. We pray for a sturdy bridge between our school and all the families we serve.

Touch the hearts of administrators to be fair, conscientious, and prayerful to the needs of teachers, students, and parents. We ask that You touch the hearts of our donors and benefactors to help sustain our school and Catholic education. Holy Spirit, increase the capacity of our students to learn, comprehend, and excel in all areas of education. Holy Spirit, like Jesus, help each student to grow in wisdom and stature. Let Your joy be their strength.

Holy Spirit, help us to always be a welcoming school that consistently models the manner of our Lord and Savior Jesus Christ. Show us all how to honor and mutually respect one another and the diversity within our school community. Holy Spirit, touch the hearts of our students and guide them to make the right choices. Touch the hearts of our educators and parents that they may see each student and one another as a Child of God. Amen

Introduction

The foundation of this current book is based on the 2011 publication of *Peace Be With You Christ Centered Bullying Solution: Teacher Manual* and student workbook accompaniment of the same title. From its inception, the groundwork of *Peace Be With You* has undergone a substantial program evolution, based on volumes of meaningful feedback from educators using the material in their classrooms. This resulted in vast refinements and enhancements to increase program effectiveness.

Many of the underpinnings of the original lessons and activities remain the same; however, each is improved for greater clarity to enrich teacher instruction. Less effective program approaches were removed and new evidence-based approaches were added to this new *Peace Be With You* curriculum. The most meaningful changes resulted in a deeper connection to Scripture in the current book.

Along with a deeper Scripture focus, a key fundamental shift occurred in our initial edition from originally trying to eliminate or move away from the problem ("anti-bullying"), to addressing bullying as an opportunity to move toward a more positive pro-peace and pro-social formative approach. In addition, the authors place much more emphasis on engaging parents in the *Peace Be With You* process. There are numerous opportunities throughout the curriculum for parents to connect with their child and create a stronger bridge between home and school through the program materials.

The authors worked prayerfully and diligently to ensure that Scripture was more intimately woven into the fabric of this current book. A meaningful part of the rewriting process continuously involved asking "What, where, when, how and why does the proposed material connect with Scripture?" which lead to a profound transformative process for the authors.

Peace Be With You is a dynamic and effective grades 4-8 Scripture-based spiritual formation curriculum. The program is prayerfully designed for Catholic/Christian classroom instruction and parent involvement. Each detailed lesson plan includes a specific purpose, learning objectives, assessment possibilities, skill building activities, facilitator scripts and more—all to assist schools in reducing peer mistreatment and guide the spiritual development of Christian leaders.

The *Peace Be With You* curriculum is based on three foundational pillars called "*Units:*"

Unit 1: Servant-Leadership (Servant-Leader Skill Building)

Unit 2: Pure in Heart (Prayer, Self-Care and Empathy Skill Building)

Unit 3: Love Your Neighbor (Supportive Peer Relationships Skill Building)

<u>Philosophy</u>
Parents as primary educators of their children, in alliance with Catholic/Christian educators, are in a prime partnership position to cooperatively foster meaningful student spiritual formation to positively impact a Christ-centered school climate, school community, and our world.

Overarching Belief

A Christ-centered school climate is a culture of reverence, whereby every student and adult is valued as a Child of God, trusting the school is steadfastly focused on a safe learning environment to grow as a whole person through academic, spiritual, and extracurricular pursuits.

Mission

In union with our Catholic/Christian Church mission, we are called to educate children on how to live out the mission of being Disciples of Jesus Christ by closely following His teachings of social justice, purity in heart, and love for our neighbor.

Vision

Through the Peace of Christ, kindness and compassion is our universal guiding principle.

Brief History

The early Peace Be With You curriculum, published by Alliance for Catholic Education (ACE) Press in 2011, is a grassroots effort originating from over a decade of extensive field-testing in hundreds of Catholic school classrooms, mostly in the Diocese of Toledo. After the initial publication, a broadened program reach has cultivated across the U.S. and abroad.

From inception, the authors have remained open—striving for continuous improvement to further enrich an already meaningful and relevant Scripture-based approach to reduce peer mistreatment and form positive Christian leaders. After close to another decade of successful implementation by an expanded network of *Peace Be With You* schools, this revised curriculum is a culmination of significant and far-reaching feedback.

Remaining true to core Christian values, *Peace Be With You* has experienced a significant spiritual renewal to further enhance the effectiveness and relevancy of the program, for elevated success and sustainability.

How to Use This Book

The *Peace Be With You Grades 4-8 Curriculum* was developed to be user-friendly to maximize effective teacher instruction and to enhance student learning. All three Unit themes (*Unit 1: Servant-Leadership, Unit 2: Pure in Heart and Unit 3: Love Your Neighbor*) are prayerfully designed and sequentially supported providing guided instruction that includes the following:

- Lesson Overview
- Lesson Purpose
- Lesson Activities
- Activity Purpose
- Learning Objectives
- Assessment Possibilities
- National Catholic Standards *(Included with all Learning Objectives and Assessments Possibilities)*
- Methodology for Each Activity

- Student Worksheets by Unit (*Appendix A-Unit 1, Appendix B-Unit 2, Appendix C-Unit 3*)
- Activity Facilitator Scripts
- Comprehensive Review by Unit
- Four Agreements by Unit

The worksheets are reproducible and provided as assessment possibilities to ensure the learning objectives are achievable and measurable. You will find student worksheets in Appendix A (Unit 1), Appendix B (Unit 2) and Appendix C (Unit 3). Worksheets are also downloadable in electronic format from our secured website at: https://www.peacebewithyou.world.

The suggested timing and application of the student worksheets is incorporated in the facilitator scripts for each activity, along with proposed approaches for teacher instruction on the implementation of each worksheet as a potential assessment tool. Multiple worksheet options are given in a conscientious effort to honor and support teacher demand to deliver diversity in their lessons for an inclusive classroom.

As educators, the authors recognize each teacher has his/her own unique teaching style and system of classroom organization. There is no requirement to adhere to the suggested curriculum approaches, such as utilizing worksheets as a part of classroom instruction vs. assigning worksheets as homework and/or how students are to hand in completed work. We encourage you to make any necessary adjustments to make the best use of the *Peace Be With You* curriculum, so that it flows with your natural teaching and organizational style.

How to Use the Audio Program
The *Peace Be With You Audio Program* is included with this curriculum to enhance teacher instruction and student learning. The audio program is a downloadable mp3 file that is incorporated into *Unit 2: Pure in Heart* activities. To obtain the free digital audio download visit https://www.peacebewithyou.world under *Peace Be With You Audio Program*. The script to the audio program is also available for download on this same website.

Teacher Curriculum Guide
Peace Be With You Teacher Curriculum Guide is a separate accompaniment that expounds on *Peace Be With You* theory and methodology. At the end of each lesson introduction in this book there are references made to specific material to support teachers in gaining a deeper understanding of the concepts and principles. The curriculum guide can be purchased in the products tab by visiting https://www.peacebewithyou.world.

Importance of Prayer
A Priest friend told Frank many years ago; "We can never pray too much." We believe in the importance and power of prayer and pray that you do too. Being a Christ-centered program, prayer is highly recommended when opening and closing each session activity. A spontaneous or recited teacher or student led prayer is appropriate. Following the closing prayer, consider concluding with a prayerful reminder for students to exit the process and classroom with a peaceful heart and mind.

Scope and Sequence

School Year Program Application

Overview

Research shows that positive impact on school climate requires consistent application of pro-social skills for the duration of the academic calendar year. Authentic application of the *Peace Be With You* curriculum ideally follows the detailed lesson plans for each activity. Each lesson plan is sequentially designed to support teacher implementation of approximately 30-45 minutes of student instruction per week. Any special student assignments completed either in or outside of class do not align with the scope & sequence timetables for each *Unit* and are based on teacher discretion.

The *Unit* timetables below represent an ideal plan for school program implementation. The Scope & Sequence for the program year will likely have to be customized and adjusted for holiday schedules and additional calendar breaks, teacher professional days or absences, and special schedules due to school delays, or any other unforeseen circumstances.

Academic Calendar	September Thru Mid November	Mid November Thru End of January	February Thru May	Weeks 21+
# of weeks	Weeks 1-7	Weeks 8-15	Weeks 16-21	Weeks 21+
Grade 4	Unit 1 Lessons 1-4 Activities 1-7	Unit 2 Lessons 5-7 Activities 8-14	Unit 3 Lessons 8-10 Activities 16-18	Teacher discretion to revisit specific lessons/activities to reinforce concepts and principles or further skill development, throughout the school year.
Grade 5				
Grade 6				
Grade 7	Special Activities Included	Unit 2 Lessons 5-7 Activities 8-15		
Grade 8				

On the evening of that first day of the week, when the doors were locked, where the disciples were, for fear of the Jews, Jesus came and stood in their midst and said to them, **"Peace be with you."**

When he had said this, he showed them his hands and his side. The disciples rejoiced when they saw the Lord. Jesus said to them again, **"Peace be with you...."**

Thomas, called Didymus, one of the Twelve, was not with them when Jesus came. So the other disciples said to him, "We have seen the Lord."

But he said to them, "Unless I see the marks of the nails in his hands and put my finger into the nailmarks and put my hand into his side, I will not believe."

Now a week later his disciples were again inside and Thomas was with them. Jesus came, although the doors were locked, and stood in their midst and said, **"Peace be with you."**

JOHN 20:19-21, 24-26

<u>Unit 1: Servant-Leadership</u>
Basic Premise

"Let no one have contempt for your youth,
but set an example for those who believe,
in speech, conduct, love, faith, and purity."

1 Timothy 4:12

The basic premise of *Unit 1: Servant-Leadership* recognizes that service to others is a foundational truth. Holy Scripture affirmatively and consistently reveals the mission and actions of Jesus unequivocally exemplify service. Steadfast in this truth, we firmly believe Jesus Christ is our perfect example of what it means to be a servant-leader.

As Christians, we are called to be Disciples of Christ, by following His teachings and living out His Word. Our humanness will cause us to stray from this path; however, with heartfelt and prayerful efforts, by following in His footsteps, there is always hope in strengthening our faith journey.

Unit 1 invites students on a faith journey to discover, examine and acknowledge that the core of their existence is to be servant-leaders. As Christian educators we are called to reveal this truth about Jesus as servant-leader with our students. This includes modeling in the manner of Christ; as well as, instruction on critical life skills to help students develop as servant-leaders.

Peace Be With You is a Scripture-led road map to support teachers in fulfilling this vital call. Each sequential lesson and activity accompaniment is prayerfully designed for teacher instruction and student learning on essential concepts and principles for the formation of Christian   servant-leaders.

Unit 1: Servant-Leadership

Scope and Sequence

Overview

You are about to embark on a journey with your students to become servant-leaders in the heart and mind of Christ. Authentic application of the *Peace Be With You curriculum* ideally follows the detailed lesson plans. Each activity requires approximately 30-45 minutes of classroom teacher instruction per week. Any special student assignments completed either in or outside of class do not align with the specified timetable below and are based on teacher discretion.

Academic Calendar	September Thru Mid November (Weeks 1-7)					Teacher discretion on revisiting lessons/activities throughout school year.	
# of Weeks	Week 1	Week 2	Week 3	Week 4	Week 5	Week 6	Week 7
Grade 4	Lesson 1 Activity 1 Who Me? A Leader? Special Assignment Possibilities	Lesson 2 Activity 2 Negative Ripples	Lesson 2 Activity 3 Positive Ripples Special Assignment Possibilities	Lesson 3 Activity 4 Safety Check Line Lesson 3 Activity 5 360° Safety Diagram	Lesson 4 Activity 6 Jesus Models Dignity for One Special Assignment Possibilities	Lesson 4 Activity 7 Jesus Models Dignity for All	Unit 1 Comp. Review Grades 4-8 - Unit 1 4 Agreements
Grade 5							
Grade 6							
Grade 7							
Grade 8							

Unit 1: Lesson One
Christ is Our Model for Servant-Leadership

*"But it shall not be so among you.
Rather whoever wishes to be great
among you will be your servant;
whoever wishes to be great
among you will be the slave of all.
For even the Son of Man
did not come to be served,
but to serve, and to give
His life as a ransom for many."*

MARK 10:43-45

Lesson One Purpose

Lesson One actively explores and examines the core of servant-leadership in the manner of Christ, in a climate that encourages, supports and cultivates student development of their unique servant-leader qualities.

Lesson One Overview

The notion of leadership, let alone being an effective leader, can be a very abstract concept for students. *Unit 1* contains very practical and meaningful involvement activities to simplify what it means to be a positive servant-leader, while lifting up Jesus as the perfect model and our highest standard for spiritual formation.

How can we empower students to become major contributors to school safety and a positive Christ-centered school climate? One key is to frequently challenge students to be aware of their call to be Christ-like servant-leaders. A second key is to remind them of the powerful role servant-leadership plays in truly making a difference in the world. A third key is to set the bar high, inspiring students to not settle for mediocrity, but to aspire them to greatness!—with Christ-like humility.

Unit 1 provides helpful ways to instruct and empower students in becoming positive servant-leaders. Each activity is an opportunity to empower and inspire students' to learn and grow as Christian servant-leaders. During the process the challenge is for them to identify and apply servant-leadership to their daily lives.

Overarching Goal

The overarching goal for students to come to a deeper understanding of Christ as our perfect model for servant-leadership and that as Children of God our sole purpose is to hear God's call for His will in our lives.

For further support in implementing the Peace Be With You Curriculum refer to:
*Unit 1: Lesson One Servant-Leader*ship in the *Teacher Curriculum Guide* for a more in-depth understanding of leadership, which discusses the misconceptions and spiritual perspectives of servant-leadership.

*"The human heart plans the way,
but the Lord directs his steps."*

Proverbs 16:9

*"Our example can be our most
persuasive influence for Christ.
Do others imitate us
because we model Him?"*

Anonymous

*"The authority by which the Christian leader leads
is not power but love, not force but example,
not coercion but reasoned persuasion.
Leaders have power, but power is safe
only in the hands of those who humble
themselves to serve."*

John Stott

Activity 1
Who Me? A Servant-Leader?

Activity 1 Purpose
To inspire the belief that as followers of Jesus Christ, students can accept their core purpose is to be servant-leaders using their God-given gifts to positively influence the school climate and beyond.

Activity 1 National Standards/Themes Correlation
Themes of Catholic Social Teachings: • Life and Dignity of the Human Person (CST-DHP) • Solidarity (CST-S) Social Studies Themes: • People, Places, and the Environment (SST-PPE) • Time, Continuity, and Change (SST-TCC) Language Arts Speaking and Listening Standards: • Prepare for and participate effectively in a range of conversations and collaborations with diverse partners, building on others' ideas and expressing their own clearly and persuasively. (CCSS.ELA-Literacy.CCRA.SL1) Language Arts Writing Standards: • Introduce claim(s) and organize the reasons and evidence clearly. (CCSS.ELA-Literacy.CCRA.W1)

	Learning Objectives Students will be able to:	Corresponding Assessment Possibilities
1	**Grades 4-8** Identify words to describe positive qualities and characteristics of servant-leadership. **_Standards_** *(CST-DHP, SST-PPE, CCSS.ELA-Literacy.CCRA.W1)*	**_#1 Worksheet_** **_Which Servant-Leader Word Fits Me Best?_** • Choose one servant-leader word and explain why that word best describes you. *Note: Print as one page and cut into a ½ worksheet.* **_#2 Worksheet_** **_What Do You Know About Servant-Leader Words?_** • Write a one-page written essay or make a 30 second-1 minute oral presentation to the class.
2	**Grades 4-8** Add to the original class generated servant-leader word list throughout the school year. **_Standards_** *(CST-DHP, SST-PPE, CCSS.ELA-Literacy.CCRA.W1)*	**_#3 Worksheet_** **_Exit Ticket: New Servant-Leader Word_** • Write a new leader word and description of why the word should be added to the servant-leader list on the **_Exit Ticket_**.

Activity 1 (continued)

3	**Grades 4-8** Apply servant-leader words to an individual they admire and explain how this individual models those qualities. ***Standards*** *(CST-S, SST-PPE, CCSS.ELA-Literacy.CCRA.W1)*	**#4 Worksheet** ***Whom Do I Admire?*** • Choose a person you admire and write about the servant-leader qualities this person models and which of these qualities are similar in the manner of Jesus.
4	**Grades 6-8** Describe the similarities and differences between servant-leader and servant-follower and the positive contribution each can make. ***Standards*** *(CST-DHP, SST-PPE, SST-TCC, CCSS.ELA-Literacy.CCRA.W1)*	**#5 Worksheet** ***Servant-Leader and Servant-Follower*** • Complete the Venn diagram comparing and contrasting servant-leader and servant-follower. **OR** **#6 Worksheet** ***Real World Servant-Leader*** • Choose a real-world servant-leader and describe the positive influence made by this individual in a 3-5 minute Power Point presentation.
5	**Grades 4-8** Identify, reflect, and write about which servant-leadership qualities reflect them and their actions with others. ***Standards*** *(CST-DHP, SST-PPE, CCSS.ELA-Literacy.CCRA.W1)*	**#7 Reflection 1** • Reflect and write about how your view of yourself as a leader has changed since the beginning of the program.

Methodology

Activity 1 instructs students to, "Stand up if you are a leader." After the teacher gives this thought-provoking directive, it is common for students to begin talking and commenting about who is and is not standing. During the activity, take mental note of who is standing, who is not standing, and who may have stood up and then sat back down. There may even be students on the edge of their seats, who begin to stand, but slowly or quickly sit down. The many reactions and responses you observe are the variety of ways your students' grapple with the notion of themselves as leaders.

One at a time, interview 5 to 10 students about their choice to stand or remain seated. You will not have time to interview every student, so randomly choose a few students to discuss their discernment process. Mention that you noticed some students did not hesitate when asked this question, while other students did hesitate.

Ask students to share their thoughts and feelings around what they experienced during the process. Ask students why they stood or didn't stand. If a student says, "Because I am on student council," take this a step further by having the student describe why he or she was chosen for student council. Ask the student to name one personal quality, trait, or characteristic to best describe him or her as a leader and how that enables actions of leadership. Listen for key words that describe positive qualities and characteristics of leadership and begin to compile a list of servant leader words on flip chart paper.

In the last 3 to 5 minutes of *Activity 1*, ask students to brainstorm (identify) as many positive leader qualities as possible and add them to create one comprehensive list. As students share a positive servant leader word, write the word down on the flipchart or hand the student an index card and marker of their choice. Ask them to print their leadership word on the card. Post the compiled servant leader words on a classroom bulletin board. As students come up with new words, they can be added to the bulletin board list. Keep the compiled positive servant leader words visible in your classroom so students can refer to them and add more positive words throughout the school year.

Activity 1 utilizes four worksheets for grades 4-8 and two additional worksheet options for grades 6-8, to support student learning, and reinforce the concepts and principles of servant-leadership.

"There are different kinds of spiritual gifts
but the same Spirit;
there are different forms of service
but the same Lord;
there are different workings
but the same Lord;
who produces all of them in everyone.
To each individual the
manifestation of the Spirit
is given form some benefit."

1 CORINTHIANS 12:4-7

"If your actions inspire others
to dream more, learn more,
do more, and become more,
you are a leader."

John Quincy Adams

Activity 1
Who Me? A Servant-Leader?

Facilitator Script

TIME/PREPARATION/LOGISTICS & PROCESS

30:00 PREPARATION/LOGISTICS
- Teachers are encouraged to post photos or the names of great leaders in advance on the classroom walls or a classroom bulletin board.
- Make copies of #'s 1-3 Worksheets, & #7 Reflection1 for grades 4-8.
- Make copies of #5 or #6 Worksheets for Grades 6-8 to be used at the teacher's discretion.
- Use a flipchart to write the servant-leader words as students share them or have students write down their leader word(s) on an index card using colorful markers.

SUPPLIES
- One flipchart and easel for teacher or one index card and colorful markers for each student.
- Two-pocket folder for each student to organize and refer to completed worksheets (or a section on an accordion-type folder or binder).

TIME   PROCESS
00:00 Say: "Without talking stand up if you are a leader!"

Note: As the teacher says this, she or he should stand tall with toes pointing straight ahead and feet shoulder width apart. Remain silent and observe what students do. (If necessary) say: "No talking, please." Or "This is a nonverbal exercise."

1:00   Say: "I am going to go around and ask you a few questions about why you stood up or why you chose not to stand."

Note: After saying you are going to ask questions, students often sit down because they think they will be less likely to be questioned and not put on the spot. Just notice this, but do not say anything to these students yet.

2:00   Ask: "Why did you stand up?" or "Why didn't you stand up?"

Note: Randomly pick students, alternating boys and girls to ask either of these two questions.

**Note: Listen carefully (and respectfully) to the responses students share. Never devalue or criticize the student's comment. Thank them and then use whatever is said as an opportunity to reinforce the positive or reframe anything negative into a positive.*

3:00   Ask: "What quality best describes you as a leader?"

Note: Ask this question of each student you randomly pick after they have shared with you why they stood up or remained seated. When you hear a positive leader word write it down on the flipchart.

TIME PROCESS

8:00   **Say:** "Thank you all for sharing, now let's brainstorm as many qualities of positive leadership as possible."

Note: In the random student questioning, you are only asking individual students for a word that describes him/her as a leader. The brainstorming session is a shift to include all students and to generate a class list of leader words. Continue to write down the positive leader words as students shout them out on the same flipchart paper or have students write down their leader word(s) on an index card. Whichever method you prefer.

Say: "Look at all the great words you came up with together that describe positive leadership. Excellent job! Remember, these are just words. It's important for us to not just say the words or just put them down on paper, but to also practice the true meaning of these words in our actions."

12:00 **Say:** "In the Sacrament of Confirmation we are asked to take a leadership role in the Church. During the preparation for this Sacrament, we are presented with the Fruits and Gifts of the Spirit. The Fruits of the Spirit are: charity, joy, peace, patience, kindness, goodness, generosity, gentleness, faithfulness, modesty, self-control, and chastity. The Gifts of the Spirit are: wisdom, understanding, counsel, fortitude, knowledge, piety, and wonder and awe."

Ask: "In our class list of servant-leader words did we use any of these words or any words similar?"

Possible Responses: Yes, we knew or understand the Fruits and Gifts. No, we did not know about these words.

14:00 **Ask:** "Could we also include the Fruits and Gifts of the Spirit with our class list of servant-leader words?"

Expected Response: "Yes"

Say: "So in addition to all your hard work to create our class list of servant-leader words we will also include the Fruits and Gifts of the Spirit to help us follow and grow in the model of Christ."

15:00 **Say:** "If you are willing to be a leader that believes, practices and will demonstrate these leader words that you came up with, please stand up! Thank you for your commitment to practice being the best leader you can be every day!"

Note: Hand out #'s 1-3 Worksheets to the class in a way that best supports the flow of the activity.

Activity 1 Facilitator Script (continued)

<u>**TIME**</u> <u>**PROCESS**</u>

Say: "Class. On *#1 Worksheet Which Servant Leader Word Fits Me Best?* write down the servant-leader word that best describes you and why." (Allow 2 minutes)

18:00: Say: "Thank you! Pass this worksheet forward. I would like to take a look at the servant-leader word you have chosen to help me get to know you a little better."

19:00 Say: "Please take a look at *#2 Worksheet: What Do You Know About Servant-Leader Words?* Your assignment is to write a one-page essay or make a 30 second to one minute oral presentation to the class on why our servant-leader words are important. Those who choose to write the one-page essay, your assignment is due_____. Those of you who choose to do a 30 second to one minute oral presentation to the class, presentations will begin on _____."

Say: "Class, please place *#3 Worksheet: Exit Ticket: New Servant-Leader Word* in your two-pocket Leader Folder (or a section on an accordion-type folder or binder). During the year when you discover a new leader word that you would like to add to our class list, write the new word and a description of why the word should be added to our servant-leader list on the *Exit Ticket.*"

*Note: Use #7 Reflection 1 at the end of Lesson One as a review and student journal reflection for Grades 4-8. If the teacher decides to utilize class time for #5 Worksheet: Servant-Leader and Servant-Follower and/or #6 Worksheet: Real World Servant-Leader, these worksheets will likely take longer for students to complete than what is indicated in the Scope & Sequence under Week 1. Therefore, it is at the discretion of the teacher if these worksheets will be completed during class time. Another option is to assign #5 and #6 worksheets as homework for grades 6-8.

Unit 1: Lesson Two
Choose Your Flavor

Lesson Two Purpose

To encourage students to make positive choices, and become more aware of how their choice of attitude and behavior influences the classroom and overall school climate.

"We are the mother of Christ when we carry Him
in our heart and body by love
and a pure and sincere conscience.
And we give birth to Him through
our holy works which ought
to shine on others by our example."

ST. FRANCIS OF ASSISI

Lesson Two Overview

Lesson Two is an opportunity to help students become more aware of how attitude and behavior impact self and others in a very profound way. Students must understand that everything they say and do has tremendous influence impacting all areas of their life—positive or negative.

Lesson Two involves two activities that call attention to how attitude affects thinking, feeling, decision-making, and actions toward others. One's choice of attitude (Choose Your Flavor) can cause a negative or positive ripple that can impact the classroom and overall school climate.

Overarching Goal

The overarching goal in *Lesson Two* is to empower students to question mistreatment and affirm positive actions among peers. Successful application of these activities promotes a positive student attitude and supports good decision-making for a thriving Christ-centered learning environment.

For further support in implementing the Peace Be With You Curriculum refer to:
Unit 1: Lesson Two Choose Your Flavor in the *Teacher Curriculum Guide* for a more in-depth understanding of how attitude impacts actions.

Activity 2
Negative Ripples

*"A negative attitude drains,
a positive attitude energizes."*

LINDSEY RIETZSCH

Activity 2 Purpose
To increase student awareness about how negative actions toward others and harmful labels such as bully, victim, or bystander can cause harsh judgments that are likely break down trust, create divisions, and limit human potential.
Activity 2 National Standards/Themes Correlation
Themes of Catholic Social Teachings: • Life and Dignity of the Human Person (CST-DHP) • Call to Family, Community and Participation (CST-CFCP) • Rights and Responsibilities (CST-RR) • Solidarity (CST-S) Social Studies Themes: • Culture (SST-C) • People, Places, and the Environment (SST-PPE) • Individual Development and Identity (SST-IDI) • Individuals, Groups, and Institutions (SST-IGI) Language Arts Speaking and Listening Standards: • Prepare for and participate effectively in a range of conversations and collaborations with diverse partners, building on others' ideas and expressing their own clearly and persuasively. (CCSS.ELA-Literacy.CCRA.SL1) Language Arts Writing Standards: • Introduce claim(s) and organize the reasons and evidence clearly. (CCSS.ELA-Literacy.CCRA.W1)

	Learning Objectives **Students will be able to:**	**Corresponding Assessment Possibilities**
1	**Grades 4-8** Analyze, understand, and describe how negative attitudes and behaviors can influence and impact self and others. **_Standards_** *(CST-DHP, CST-CFCP, SST-PPE, SST-IDI, SST-IGI, CCSS.ELA-Literacy.CCRA.W1)*	**Note: For #8 Teacher Reference, see Appendix A.* **_#9 Worksheet_** **_Negative Actions = Negative Ripples_** • Write about a putdown, the associated consequences and actions to help remediate the situation. **_#10 Worksheet_** **_Negative Ripples_** • Reflect and write how the putdown example used in #9 worksheet may have created negative ripples.

2	**Grades 4-8** Analyze, understand, and describe how the *Mistreatment Triangle* negatively impacts self and others and identify ways to positively redirect using the *Peace Be With You Triangle*. ***Standards*** *(CST-DHP, CST-RR, SST-IDI, SST-IGI, CCSS.ELA-Literacy.CCRA.SL1)*	***#11a Worksheet*** ***Triangle Talk (1)*** • Analyze the *Mistreatment Triangle* barriers. ***#11b Worksheet*** ***Triangle Talk (2)*** • Using the *Peace Be With You Triangle* identify ways to positively redirect.
3	**Grades 4-8** Draw a cartoon to describe a poor choice that may have had consequences and how they did/could turn this into a positive choice. ***Standards*** *(CST-DHP, CST-RR, SST-IDI, SST-IGI, CCSS.ELA-Literacy.CCRA.SL1)*	***#12 Worksheet*** ***Poor Choice Cartoon*** • Draw a cartoon about a poor choice and how you can turn it into a better choice with a positive outcome. **OR**
4	Describe 5 ways a "Negative Attitude" discourages others and 5 ways a "Positive Attitude" encourages others. ***Standards*** *(CST-DHP, CST-RR, SST-IDI, SST-IGI, CCSS.ELA-Literacy.CCRA.SL1)*	***#13 Worksheet*** ***Attitude Adjustment*** Practice in redirecting from negative attitude = negative ripples to positive attitude = positive ripples.

Methodology

Putdowns are common among students and routinely occur without much thought. Students often lack the ability to recognize how their actions (the ripples they make through what they say and what they do) can influence, even harm another person or group. Beginning with negative ripples questions sets up an opportunity for students to compare and contrast the positive ripples questions.

In this activity, students are asked four key questions about putdowns. The sequential order of the questions is important. The first two questions are more general and the next two questions are more specific to their actions with classmates. Each question requires students to notice in a nonthreatening way in which peers treat them. Also, the questions briefly, but honestly, examine their own individual actions toward others.

The four questions are asked with a show of hands from the entire class and directly asked of any individual students. The purpose in having students raise their hands is to increase awareness of how common putdowns are among the class.

This is in no way intended to condone or accept these actions, but rather to increase student awareness that **Negative Actions = Negative Ripples**. Most students really do want to excel; however, the negative ripples equation likely will not result in anything positive. A more likely result is that harmful conduct will place student success further out of reach.

During this exercise, it is common for the following reaction to occur:
Most hands are up during each of these four questions. When students see the unanimous response, it is glaringly apparent that put downs are very common among peers. This is important for students to notice in order to begin a shift toward positive actions.

The Four negative ripple questions include:
1. Raise your hand if you have ever been putdown (in general)?
2. Raise your hand if you have ever put someone down (in general)?
3. Raise your hand if you have ever been putdown by someone in the class?
4. Raise your hand if you have ever put someone down in the class?

Activity 2 utilizes four worksheets and two additional worksheet options with grades 4-8, to increase student awareness of the impact labels and our actions have on others.

"Trust in the Lord with all your heart,
on your own intelligence do not rely;
In all your ways be mindful of Him,
and He will make straight your paths."

Proverbs 3:5-6

Activity 2
Negative Ripples

Facilitator Script

TIME, PREPARATION, LOGISTICS, & PROCESS

15:00 PREPARATION
- Make one copy of *#8 Teacher Reference.*
- Make copies of *#'s 9-10 Worksheets*; *#11a* and *#11b Worksheets (double-sided)*.
- Make copies of the optional *#'s 12 and 13 Worksheets (teacher discretion).*

LOGISTICS
Asking Four Questions About Put-Ups
- Ask students to raise their hands if any of the four positive ripples questions apply to them. Ask each question in the order given. Pause after asking each question and follow the facilitator script to help with the flow of this lesson. The *#8 Teacher Reference: Why Do We Ask The Four (Put Down) Questions?* as a support guide when asking the four questions during this activity.

TIME   PROCESS
00:00 Say: "Let's look at some things that could get in the way of our being positive servant-leaders. I will ask some tough questions and all I expect from you is to be honest. Honesty is an important quality in a leader."

1:00   Ask: "How many of you have ever been put down? Raise your hand."

*Note: Notice how many hands are up. Most likely every hand will be raised.

     Say: "Thank you. Put your hands down."

     Say: "Here's an even tougher question."

     Ask: "How many of you have ever been put down by someone in this room? Raise your hand."

*Note: Notice how many hands are up. Usually every hand is raised.

     Say: "Look around the room and notice all the hands that are up. You're not alone."

     Say: "Thank you for being honest. Please put hands down."

2:00   Ask: "What does being put down feel like?"

*Note: Allow students time to share. When a student says a word or phrase, repeat it back to them so the student and the class hear the "echo" of the experience and they know that you heard them.

Activity 2 Facilitator Script (continued)

TIME   PROCESS
         Possible Responses: Hurt, depressed, alone, frustrated, sad, angry, like dirt, excluded, etc.

3:00 Ask: "How many of you have ever put down someone? Raise you hand."

Note: Notice how many hands are up. Usually most, if not all, hands are raised.

         Say: "Thank you. Please put hands down."

         Say: "Now, the tougher question."

         Ask: "How many of you have ever put down someone in this room? Raise your hand."

         Say: "Look around the room and notice how many hands are up. You're not alone."

4:00   Ask: "Can you think of why anyone would ever put someone down, knowing what it feels like to be put down?"

Note: Notice what students say about why someone would put someone else down. Again, "echo" their responses. In particular, notice and recognize a student who admits that put-downs are a way of getting back, getting even, getting revenge, settling the score, etc. This is a very important concept to get out into the open.

         Ask: "Is it normal and natural to want to get back, get even, or feel vengeful when we are put down?"

         Expected Response: Yes!

5:00   Say: "Yes, this is a very normal feeling!"

         Ask: "Is it ever okay to do anything to get even with someone, no matter how you feel?"

         Expected Response: No!

         Say: "You're right! Two wrongs do not make a right! It's not okay to go from any feeling to an action that could harm someone."

6:00   Say: "There were a lot of hands raised when I asked both of these tough questions. I really appreciate all of you sharing with honesty and taking the risk to raise your hands."

Note: Hand out #9 Worksheet: Negative Actions = Negative Ripples. Give students 5 minutes to complete this worksheet at their desk.

Activity 2 Facilitator Script (continued)

TIME   PROCESS

11:00 Say: "Please finish up what you are writing. If you have not yet completed this worksheet please do so at home. Please share this worksheet with your parents and have them sign it. Bring it back tomorrow and place it in the completed homework tray. Thank you!"

*Note: Hand out #10 Worksheet: Negative Ripples. Give the class 2 minutes to reflect and complete this worksheet at their desk.

13:00 Say: "Now let's take a look at *the worksheet titled 'Negative Ripples.'* In the center of the circle write in the same putdown example you used in the last worksheet (*#9 Worksheet: Negative Actions = Negative Ripples*). Please reflect and write the ripple effects your actions may have had on others in the concentric circles that apply."

Say: "Thank you!"

Ask: "Can we all agree that our actions influence others and ourselves?"

Expected Response: Yes.

Say: "You're are absolutely right! Everything we say and do has ripple effects. Negative or Positive."

Ask: "Is putting each other down the kind of standard you want to set and accept with each other?"

Expected Response: NO!

14:00 Ask: "Can we all agree to a new standard to not put others down and to put into practice our servant-leader words into actions?"

Expected Response: YES!!!

*Note: Now transition to guide students through #11a (Triangle 1) & #11b (Triangle 2) Worksheet: Triangle Talk as a group work exercise. Have students get into their existing groups or assign groups for this activity.

Say: "Please take a close look at this handout *#11a Worksheet: Triangle Talk* and discuss in your small groups the weaknesses you see in the mistreatment triangle." (Allow 2 minutes)

17:00 Ask: "What weaknesses did your group notice about the triangle itself?"
Possible Response: It's not balanced. It's not steady. It's not stable. It's top-heavy.

Say: "You're correct, an upside down triangle is top-heavy, and it is certainly unstable and will not stay in balance."

TIME   PROCESS

Ask: "What would happen if a large building were heavier on top (roof) than the bottom (floor or foundation)?"

Possible Responses: It would just topple over. It wouldn't stand up. Buildings aren't built like this. It might stand up if there were some kind of support in place to hold it up.

18:00 **Say:** "I think you're right! What I hear each of you saying is that the structure is really unstable and may even be dangerous."

Say: "Let's translate the upside down triangle to represent people and our classroom."

Ask: "How do the bully and bystander feel about 'being on top?'"

Possible Responses: Powerful. On top of the mountain. Better than someone else.

Ask: "How do you think the victim might feel being on the bottom?"

Possible Responses: Weak. Helpless. Powerless. Like dirt. Less than. Horrible. Like nothing. Worthless.

19:00 **Ask:** "Would it be possible if this negative triangle stayed this way for us to ever create a win/win/win between all three people at the points?"

Expected Response: No!

Ask: "Does this negative triangle make it more difficult for us to live out our servant-leader qualities?"

Expected Response: Yes!

Say: "I think you're absolutely right. Just like the unstable building this kind of treatment between people creates a lot of stress, anxiety, instability and even has the potential to be dangerous."

Ask: "Is it possible for changes to be made with buildings and between people?"

Expected Response: Yes.

20:00 **Ask:** "If you could, what would you do to change this unstable and negative triangle to one that is more stable and positive?"

Expected Responses: Flip it over with the heavy part on the bottom. Turn it right side up.

Say: "Great ideas!"

TIME   PROCESS

        Ask: "What did you notice about the words around the Mistreatment Triangle?"

        Expected Response: The words Bully, Bystander, and Victim.

        Ask: "Do you think these terms that describe people are helpful or harmful?"

        Possible Responses: Helpful. Harmful. What they should be called. Not sure.

21:00 Ask: "Would any of you want to be called a bully, victim, or bystander?"

        Expected Response: No.

        Ask: "Do you think it is fair for a person to be called a bully, victim or bystander?"

        Expected Response: No.

*Note: If the Expected Response is a "Yes" from students, ask the following question:

        Ask: "When put downs and other types of mistreatment are used, are there any servant-leader words from our class list that suggest that this is an acceptable way to be treated or to treat others?"

        Expected Response: NO!

        Say: "I agree. These words or terms are actually labels to describe people and can be very harmful and hurtful."

        Ask: "What were some of the servant-leader qualities we have on our list?"

        Possible response: Kind, respectful, sensitive...

*Note: Use the specific servant-leader words students say.

        Ask: "Would a kind, sensitive, respectful, sensitive leader use disrespectful words towards another?"

        Expected response: No

        Say: "Raise your hand if you would rather be called by your given name."

*Note: Notice how many hands or if all hands are up and vocalize what you notice in a positive way.

<u>**TIME**</u> <u>**PROCESS**</u>

22:00 Say: "Ok, I think most of us can agree the words bully, bystander, and victim are harmful and hurtful labels that can be used as put downs."

Ask: "Since we have agreed to set a high standard to not put others down, can we also agree not to use these harmful words to describe people?"

Expected Response: Yes.

Say: "Great!"

Say: "Now, in your small groups, discuss positive ideas you have to replace the harmful words bully, bystander and victim. Come up with a new word or phrase that shows respect for each person."

*Note: Allow 2 minutes to discuss the labels around the Mistreatment Triangle (1).

23:00 Say: "Group leaders, please report in on what your group came up with."

*Note: There will most likely be a number of positive ("Person who...") and may even be some negative (Brat, jerk, etc.) responses to replace the terms bully, bystander, and victim. Please listen and not react to what students come up with. Pay more attention to the positive replacements and reframe any negative ones by saying that replacing a harmful word or label with another harmful word or label is not helpful and will not make things better. Also, where appropriate, emphasize that a label is a judgment of the person, and we should focus only on the actions of the person.

Say: "Thank you for the many different words and ways you came up with that we could use to replace these harmful ones with a positive term to shift things in a positive direction?"

Say: "Go to the word 'Bully' on your worksheet and cross off this term. From what I heard you say, the best replacement would be a 'Person who mistreated.' Please write 'Person who mistreated' on the line above the crossed out term bully."

24:00 Say: "Now go to the word 'Bystander.' From what I heard you say, the best replacement would be a 'Person who witnessed mistreatment.' On the line above it, please write 'Person who witnessed mistreatment' on the line above the crossed out term 'bystander.'"

Say: "Now go to the word 'Victim'" From what I heard you say, the best replacement would be a 'Person who was mistreated.' On the line above it, please write 'Person who was mistreated' on the line above the crossed out term victim."

*Note: Use your best discretion—If you think the students have come up with something even more positive than "Person who...." there may be more student "buy-in" if you use their replacements.

Activity 2 Facilitator Script (continued)

<u>TIME</u> <u>PROCESS</u>

25:00 **Say:** "Great work groups! I notice it only took a few simple changes to make a huge difference in something very negative. You flipped the unstable triangle to make it stable and you changed the language on some hurtful terms encouraging us to remember that first and foremost we are all people. We are all children of God. By making this language shift we are able to move in a more helpful, hopeful, and positive direction. Way to go!"

Say: "Now, turn your worksheet over to look closely at *#11b Worksheet Triangle Talk* with the *Peace Be With You Triangle* on the other side. Take a few moments with your small groups to reflect and discuss what you notice about this triangle."

*Note: Allow 2 minutes to discuss the Peace Be With You Triangle 2.

27:00 **Ask:** "What about this triangle is helpful/hopeful?"

Possible Responses: Focuses on the Trinity. Looks at the positive. Looks steady. Looks stable. Looks balanced.

Say: "Yes, it is focused on positive ways we can care for ourselves and each other."

Say: "Does anyone know what the ancient symbol of the Holy Trinity is?"

Expected Response: No.

Say: "The ancient symbol of the Holy Trinity is an upright triangle."

Say: "By using this ancient symbol, we focus on the Trinity."

Ask: "Why is this focus on the Trinity so helpful in how we think and act?"

Possible Responses: "We look to God, Jesus, and the Holy Spirit to guide us. We are guided by the model of Jesus."

Say: "Yes, we can model our behaviors in the manner of Jesus."

Ask: "What about this triangle gives it strength?"

Possible Responses: "It is balanced. Won't topple over. It's on a strong foundation.

30:00 **Say:** "Yes, it is much more balanced and much stronger than the mistreatment triangle."

Ask: "Does this *Peace Be With You* upright triangle help us live out our servant-leader qualities?"

Expected (Possible) Responses: Yes!

Ask: "Could this triangle be used as our guide?"

Activity 2 Facilitator Script (continued)

TIME **PROCESS**

    Expected (Possible) Responses: Yes!

    Say: "Excellent! Thank you!"

    Say: "Let me summarize what we have accomplished so far: 1. You changed the negative language and labels in the mistreatment triangle to more positive and hopeful language. 2. You shifted a low standard of putdowns and mistreatment to a higher standard for how we should treat each other, and 3. We agree to use the *Peace Be With You Triangle* as our guide for how we should treat each other."

    Say: "Awesome work!"

32:00 **Ask:** "Based on our change to positive language, setting a higher standard, and looking to the *Peace Be With You Triangle* as our guide, how should we expect of ourselves and how would you expect to be treated by others?"

    Possible Responses: Give each other put-ups. Kindness. Respect. Cooperation. Helpfulness.

    Say: "Yes! Thank you! I think this is a very realistic expectation and standard we have set for each other and certainly one that will make a positive ripple in our classroom and school!"

*Note: If teacher decides to use this option, hand out #'s 12 or 13 Worksheets, and continue with the following facilitator script:

33:00 **Say:** "Please complete these two worksheets at home. The first handout *#12 Worksheet: Poor Choice Cartoon*, asks you to draw about a poor choice and how you did or could turn it into a positive choice. The second handout *#13 Worksheet: Attitude Adjustment,* asks you to write several examples of a negative attitude and to turn it into a positive attitude. Please only choose one of the two worksheets and follow the directions to complete the worksheet of your choice. When completed, please share your worksheet with a parent. Ask one or both parents for an example of a poor choice or negative attitude in which they were able to turn their poor choice or negative attitude into something positive. Please place your choice of one of these two worksheets signed by a parent in the completed homework tray by _____."

<u>Positive Ripples</u>

*"Each time a person
stands up for an ideal,
or acts to improve the lot of others,
or strikes out against injustice,
he or she sends forth
a tiny ripple of hope.
And crossing each other
from a million different centers of
energy and daring,
those ripples build
a current that can
sweep down the mightiest
walls of oppression."*

ROBERT KENNEDY

Activity 3
Positive Ripples

Activity 3 Purpose
Through self-reflection and small group collaboration to actively engage students in creative and meaningful approaches to generate positivity in the school community.
Activity 3 National Standards/Themes Correlation

Themes of Catholic Social Teachings:
- Life and Dignity of the Human Person (CST-DHP)
- Call to Family, Community and Participation (CST-CFCP)
- Rights and Responsibilities (CST-RR)
- Solidarity (CST-S)

Social Studies Themes:
- Culture (SST-C)
- People, Places, and the Environment (SST-PPE)
- Individual Development and Identity (SST-IDI)
- Individuals, Groups, and Institutions (SST-IGI)

Language Arts Speaking and Listening Standards:
- Prepare for and participate effectively in a range of conversations and collaborations with diverse partners, building on others' ideas and expressing their own clearly and persuasively. (CCSS.ELA-Literacy.CCRA.SL1)

Language Arts Writing Standards:
- Introduce claim(s) and organize the reasons and evidence clearly. (CCSS.ELA-Literacy.CCRA.W1)

	Learning Objectives Students will be able to:	**Corresponding Assessment Possibilities**
1	**Grades 4-8** Define attitude. ***Standards*** *(CST-DHP, SST-PPE, SST-IDI, CCSS.ELA-Literacy.CCRA.SL1, CCSS.ELA-Literacy.CCRA.W1)*	****Note: For #14 Teacher Reference, see Appendix A.*** ***#15 Worksheet*** ***My definition of ATTITUDE*** • Define **A-T-T-I-T-U-D-E** using each letter of the word to write an associated positive word.
2	**Grades 4-8** Describe how put-ups (compliments) can influence and impact self and others. ***Standards*** *(CST-DHP, SST-PPE, SST-IDI, CCSS.ELA-Literacy.CCRA.SL1, CCSS.ELA-Literacy.CCRA.W1)*	***#16 Worksheet*** ***Cool Compliments*** • Generating positivity among students by encouraging put-ups and positive ripple effects.

3	**Grades 4-8** Identify, understand and apply peer support strategies. **_Standards_** *(CST-DHP, CST-RR, CST-CFCP, SST-PPE, SST-IDI, SST-IGI, CCSS.ELA-Literacy.CCRA.SL1, CCSS.ELA-Literacy.CCRA.W1)*	**_#17 Worksheet_** **_YVP Peer Support Strategies_** • Focus on YVP Peer Support Strategies that are proven effective in creating a positive school climate. **_*Note: For #18 Teacher Reference, see Appendix A._**
4	**Grades 4-8** Hypothesize what their school would be like with only positive ripples. **_Standards_** *(CST-DHP, CST-S, CST-CFCP, CST-RR, SST-PPE, SST-IDI, CCSS.ELA-Literacy.CCRA.SL1, CCSS.ELA-Literacy.CCRA.W1)*	**_#19 Worksheet_** **_My Dream School_** • Spend time envisioning our dream school.
5	**Grades 6-8** Discuss the positive actions of a biblical character and the outcome of those choices. **_Standards_** *(CST-DHP, CST-S, CST-CFCP, CST-RR, SST-C, SST-PPE, SST-IDI, SST-IGI, CCSS.ELA-Literacy.CCRA.SL1, CCSS.ELA-Literacy.CCRA.W1)*	**_#20 Worksheet_** **_Positive Ripples in the Bible_** • Identify the positive actions of the biblical characters found in Scripture.
6	**Grades 6-8** Identify creative ways to turn problems or something negative into something positive. **_Standards_** *(CST-DHP, SST-PPE, SST-IDI, CCSS.ELA-Literacy.CCRA.SL1, CCSS.ELA-Literacy.CCRA.W1)*	**_#21 Worksheet_** **_Choose Your Flavor_** • Exploring ways to turn problems or something negative into a positive.
7	**Grades 4-8** Describe one positive action they can do in the school and recognize the positive ripples resulting from this action. **_Standards_** *(CST-DHP, CST-RR, CST-CFCP, SST-PPE, SST-IDI, SST-IGI, CCSS.ELA-Literacy.CCRA.SL1, CCSS.ELA-Literacy.CCRA.W1)*	**_#22 Worksheet_** **_Positive Actions = Positive Ripples_** • Review of *Lesson 2* and practice in cause and effect.

Methodology

Put ups require a higher order of thinking and a level of compassion that is not as common among students. Students have the ability, but often fail to recognize the tremendous impact their positive actions (the ripples they make through what they say and what they do) have on self/other and a positive school climate. Extending kindness to a classmate goes a long way in building trust and a safe and thriving learning environment. The last activity on negative ripples, sets up an opportunity for students to compare and contrast positive ripples for this activity.

It is important to compare and contrast "Negative Ripples" with "Positive Ripples" for students to come to the awareness that positivity is a more generative and sustainable result for self/others, and the school.

In this activity the first two questions ask students if they have ever put someone up or received a put-up from someone in general, and in the second two questions, if these actions have occurred for them with a classmate. During this exercise, one or more of the following reactions will occur:

1. When most hands are up during these four questions, students are pleasantly surprised to discover that they do put each other up. Teachers can use this as an opportunity to acknowledge students for their courage and reinforce taking even more initiative to put up their classmates.
2. Students notice that not many hands are up when asked the four questions. This is an opportunity for teachers to encourage students to take more risks to put up a classmate and reinforce how important this action is for relationship building and a positive school climate.

This activity sets up an invitation and challenge for students to raise their standard—making a shift to **Positive Actions = Positive Ripples** among peers—for the classroom and the school.

Having students notice and appreciate their positive actions inside and outside of the classroom, is important feedback to reinforce more like actions. It also is an opportunity for you to acknowledge and reinforce their positive actions with peers.

The Four Positive Ripples questions include:
1. Have you ever been put-up (felt complimented, encouraged, and supported) by someone?
2. Have you ever put someone up (complimented, encouraged, and supported) someone?
3. Have you ever been put-up (complimented, encouraged, and supported) by someone in the class?
4. Have you ever put (complimented, encouraged, and supported) someone up in the class?

Activity 3 utilizes five worksheets for grades 4-8 and two additional worksheet options with grades 6-8, to promote positive ripples.

Activity 3
Positive Ripples

Facilitator Script

TIME, PREPARATION, LOGISTICS, & PROCESS

15:00 PREPARATION
- Make one copy of *#14 Teacher Reference* and *#18 Teacher Reference*.
- Make copies of *#'s 15, 16, 17, 19 & 22 Worksheets* for grades 4-8.
- Make copies of *#'s 20 and 21 Worksheets* for grades 6-8 *(teacher discretion)*.
- Teachers are encouraged to have pictures or slogans of positive messages posted around the classroom and in particular a graphic image of ripples in water.
- On blackboard, poster or Smartboard post *#18 Teacher Reference: YVP* Peer Support Strategies.

LOGISTICS
Asking Four Questions About Put-Ups
- Ask students to raise their hands if any of the four positive ripples questions apply to them. Ask each question in the order given. Pause after asking each question and follow the facilitator script to help with the flow of this lesson. Download: *#14 Teacher Reference: Why Do We Ask The Four (Put-Up) Questions?* as a support guide when asking the four questions during *Activity 3* Positive Ripples.

Note: Please see the Teacher Curriculum Guide for the rationale and more suggestions on facilitating the four questions.

TIME   PROCESS
00:00 Say: "There are probably at least 100 flavors of ice cream. Today we only have two flavors available: chocolate and vanilla."

Ask: "Who are chocolate lovers? Who are vanilla lovers? Who raised their hand twice?" Laugh out loud!

1:00 Ask: "If attitude came in two flavors, what would those two flavors be?"

Possible Responses: Good and bad. Okay and not okay. Right and wrong. Helpful and not helpful. Delicious and disgusting. Positive and negative, etc. All answers are correct. Go with Positive/Negative.

Say: "That's right! Positive and negative."

Ask: "If the flavor you choose is negative, just like throwing a pebble in a pond, what kind of ripples will you make in the school?"

Expected Response: Negative.

TIME   PROCESS

2:00   Say: "That's right! Choosing a negative flavor of attitude affects everyone in a negative way. Negative Actions = Negative Ripples."

Ask: "If the flavor you choose is positive, just like throwing a pebble in a pond, what kind of ripples will you make in the school?"

Expected Response: POSITIVE!!!

Say: "That's right! Positive Actions = Positive Ripples!"

3:00   Say: "You have the power to influence the classroom and our school environment every moment of every day with the attitude you choose. Positive or negative."

Note: Handout #15 Worksheet: My definition of ATTITUDE. It is at the teacher's discretion whether or not to do this worksheet in class or as a homework assignment. The script below instructs students on the later.

Say: "Please place this handout *#15 Worksheet: My definition of ATTITUDE* in your Leader Folder. Take this handout home and complete it with one of your parents. Have your parent sign the handout and place it back in your Leader Folder and bring it to class tomorrow. Thank you!"

4:00   Say: "I think we must continuously ask ourselves the question; 'What kind of ripple do I want to make in my school?' Please choose wisely! You can and do make a difference!"

Say: "Now let's look at some ways we can encourage each other to be positive servant-leaders!"

Say: "One way to help us all choose a positive flavor of attitude and stay positive is by giving each other put-ups (compliments)."

Note: Handout #16 Worksheet: Cool Compliments. Give students 2 minutes to complete this worksheet at their desks. It is at the teacher's discretion whether or not to collect this worksheet from students.

Say: "Please reflect on and answer the questions in this handout #16 Worksheet: Cool Compliments."

6:00   Say: "Time. Thank you."

Say: "In the last activity you raised your hands for four questions. What I noticed is that all of you have received or have given put downs and all of you agreed that put downs can be harmful and can create negative ripples."

Say: "I will ask you four more questions and all I expect is that you respond/answer honestly. As I mentioned, honesty is an important quality in a leader."

Activity 3 Facilitator Script (continued)

TIME   PROCESS

   Ask: "Raise your hand if you've ever been put-up."

*Note: Notice how many hands are up. Most likely every hand is raised.

   Say: "Take a look around the room and notice all the hands up. Awesome!"

7:00   Say: "Thank you. Put your hands down."

   Say: "Raise your hand if you've been put-up by someone in this room?"

*Note: Notice how many hands are up. Usually every hand is raised.

   Say: "Look around the room and notice all the hands that are up. Awesome! This tells me that many positive servant-leader qualities are happening among all of you."

   Say: "Thank you for being honest. Put your hands down."

8:00   Ask: "What does being put-up feel like?"

*Note: Allow the class time to share. When a student says a word or phrase, repeat it back to them so the student and the class hear the "echo" of the experience and that you heard them.

   Possible Responses: Happy, loved, worth something, included, good, great, I want to dance, sing, etc.

9:00   Say: "Raise your hand if you've ever put-up someone."

*Note: Notice how many hands are up. Usually most, if not all, hands are raised.

   Say: "Look around the room and notice all the hands that are up. Awesome!"

   Say: "Thank you. Put your hands down."

   Say: "Raise your hand if you've ever put-up someone in this room."

   Say: "Look around the room and notice how many hands are up. Awesome! Celebrate all the servant-leader qualities that are happening among yourselves and the positive ripple effects these positive actions are creating. This truly makes a positive difference in our classroom and school!"

10:00 Ask: "How does putting up someone make you feel?"

   Possible Responses: Good. Great. Wow! Happy. Excited. Joyous. Joyful. My stomach does flip flops.

Activity 3 Facilitator Script (continued)

Note: Notice what is said. Again, "echo" student responses.

<u>TIME</u> <u>PROCESS</u>

Say: "We all know receiving put-ups and giving put-ups to others feels great."

> **Ask:** "Why don't we do this more often?"

> **Possible Responses:** Too afraid. It's hard to do. I don't know. We forget. I might get putdown for putting up someone.

> **Say:** "I know it is a risk to put-up each other."

11:00 Ask: "Can we agree though, that giving and receiving put-ups is how we all want to be treated?"

> **Expected Response:** YES!

> **Ask:** "Can we also agree that put-ups will help us to have a safer, more positive, more supportive, and even more caring school?"

> **Expected Response:** YES!!!

> **Ask:** "What servant-leader words from our list might give us the courage to give and receive put-ups and practice our servant-leader gifts?"

Note: Listen to the class as they say out loud the leader words. List them on the board (flipchart, Smartboard, etc.,) to acknowledge and reinforce the servant-leader words that they believe will be of support.

12:00 Say: "Great Job! This is an awesome list of leader words from out list that will be of support to all of us."

> **Say:** "I have one more thing that I think will help us to be even more positive and supportive as leaders in our school."

Note: Hand out #17 Youth Voice Project Peer Support Strategies. Place #18 Teacher Reference: Peer Support Strategies on the blackboard, Smartboard or flipchart.

> **Say:** "There was a survey done with thousands of students in grades 5-12 called the *Youth Voice Project*. The students in the survey that were mistreated reported some very specific actions by their classmates called Peer Support Strategies, really helped make things better for them and their schools."

13:00 Say: "Let's look at this handout which has the most helpful Peer Support Strategies the students in the Youth Voice Project came up with. I also have these on the (blackboard, Smartboard, flipchart)."

> **Say:** "Let's read these action strategies together."

TIME   PROCESS

Class Reads Together
- Spent time, sat with me, hung out with me.
- Talked to me at school to encourage me.
- Listened to me.
- Gave me advice (hope).
- Helped me tell an adult (about a problem).
- Helped me get away; made a distraction.
- Called (or texted) me at home to encourage me."

14:00 Say: "Check all of the action strategies on the worksheet that you have used with your classmates. Choose one that you checked and answer the questions below the strategies."

Note: Allow 2 minutes for this exercise.

Say: "Time. I am really happy to see all the checked action strategies on your handouts. This tells me you are practicing servant-leadership. I am very proud of you all!"

15:00 Ask: "Are there any Peer Support Strategies you can add to the list that you think will help?"

Note: Allow the class time to share. When a student says a word or phrase, repeat it back, so the student and class can hear the "echo" to let them know that you have heard them. Ask the class if they agree if this additional Peer Support Strategy will help. With enough agreement, add it to the list of Peer Support Strategies. Please post the list in your classroom.

17:00 Say: "I applaud (commend, or praise, or thank) you all for your willingness and courage to be a part of our effort to put each other up and support each other more often. This will take some effort, but I am confident that together we can do this!"

Say: "The *Peer Support Strategies* from the *Youth Voice Project* along with the ones you have added are very powerful and supportive actions. Each action strategy contains servant-leader qualities and that I am confident each of you are capable of doing in our classroom. I want to see all of you practicing these important actions with each other often."

18:00 Say: "Let me summarize what we have accomplished so far:
- First of all, I think I could have guessed this, but I now know that you all like ice cream!
- We all have a choice in our flavor of attitude every day. Negative Attitudes = Negative Ripples and Positive Attitudes = Positive Ripples. Choose wisely!—because your attitude and actions make a powerful difference in our classroom and school.
- We all agree that giving and receiving put-ups is how we want to be treated and that put-ups can help us to have a safer, more positive, more supportive, and more caring school and
- We now have tools in the list of servant-leader words and Peer Support Strategies to help each other be positive and supportive servant-leaders."

Activity 3 Facilitator Script (continued)

<u>TIME</u>   <u>PROCESS</u>

20:00 Say: "If you are willing to be a positive and supportive leader that chooses to make a positive ripple in our school, stand up!"

> ***Optional:*** *Three-Step Commitment process:*

> ***Say:*** "If you are willing to commit to this goal, 1. Raise your hand 2. Stand up and 3. Take one step forward.

*Note: If any student does not stand up, ask him/her (in private) to share concerns and explain why committing to this step is difficult. This is not a time to shame or humiliate a student into compliance. By listening you will honor the students' concerns and model compassionate servant-leadership.

*Important Reminder: We are not asking students to individually accomplish this goal, but rather to make a commitment to work together at it.

21:00 Ask: "What kind of choice do you want to make as a leader in this school?"

> **Say:** "Choose your flavor! But, choose the one that reflects the kind of school you want to be a part of. Choose wisely!"

> **Say:** "Now raise your hand (stand up, take one step forward) if you want to be part of a higher standard to encourage put-ups and other supportive actions among each other in our classroom and school."

22:00 Say: "Notice the hands up (all of you standing and have taken one step forward) in the room. I am very proud of all of you!"

> **Say:** "Together we can create a positive and respectful school just by using put-ups and supporting each other daily! Together you have the power to create an amazing school!"

23:00 Say: "Please take some time to complete this *handout #19 Worksheet: My Dream School.*"

*Note: Give the class 3 minutes to complete this worksheet at their desks. Collect the completed handout and pull out any positive themes that you notice and share these positive themes with students when you are ready.

24:00 Say: "Thank you! Please place your Dream School handout on my desk before you leave today."

*Note: If the teacher decides to assign #20 Worksheet: Positive Ripples in the Bible and #21 Worksheet: Choose Your Flavor, these assignments will likely take longer for students to complete than what is allotted in the Scope & Sequence under Week 3. Therefore, these worksheets are to be introduced and assigned to Grades 6-8 at the discretion of the teacher.

<u>**TIME**</u> <u>**PROCESS**</u>

25:00 Say: "Please take these two handouts home with you in your Leader Folder to share with your parents. The first handout *is #20 Worksheet: Positive Ripples in the Bible*, which asks you to use the provided Scripture and biblical characters to identify their positive actions.

Say: "The second handout is *#21 Worksheet: Choose Your Flavor*, is an opportunity to write about ways you can turn problems or something negative into a positive choice or action. Please complete one of the two handouts, have a parent sign it and place it in the homework tray by _____."

26:00 Say: "Let's look at *#22 Worksheet: Positive Ripples = Positive School* for the remainder of our class time together. In the center circle write a positive servant-leader action you will do here at school. In the outlining circles, write down what positive ripples you believe your positive action will make. Also, in each circle write how you will involve other students in this same action to increase the ripple effects."

*Note: Allow 5 minutes for this worksheet.

31:00 Say: "Time. Thank you."

35:00 Ask: "Would anyone like to share their positive action and the positive ripple you believe your action will make in our school?" (The ending time indicated will be shorter or longer depending on how interactive the class is in sharing their positive action and positive ripple.)

*Note: Pause after you ask this question. Even after the pause you may not have any student share. That's ok. If you have one or a number of students share their positive ripple, please take the time to "echo" what each says and recognize the stated positive action by writing it down on the board. You will know best if follow up questions can be asked about the impact of their positive action and how the student plans to involve others in this same action.

Unit 1: Lesson Three
Safe at School

"I have told you this
so that you might have peace in Me.
In the world you have trouble,
but take courage,
I have conquered the world."

John 16:33

Lesson Three Purpose

To closely examine what it means to be "safe" to increase awareness of what is "unsafe" and to develop skills that support and encourage students to take personal responsibility for their safety.

Lesson Three Overview

Feeling safe in one's environment is a basic human need. A school can be a thriving learning environment only when adults and students create a solid foundation of personal safety. A safe school climate is essential for teacher instruction and student learning. The level of formative success is predicated on degree that students feel safe.

The two activities in this lesson define four generalized areas of safety, increases awareness, and creates a common language to help communicate personal safety in a non-threatening way. Lesson Three also provides an opportunity for adults at school to hear student perception of safety at school.

Lesson Three Activity 4: Safety Check Line asks students (Grades 4/5) to place a numerical value on a continuum between 0-10 that best represents their overall level of safety (physical, mental/emotional, social and spiritual) at school. Through reflection and class discussion, students develop skills in taking personal responsibility to advance any number on the continuum toward a 10 (Safest).

Lesson Three Activity 5: 360° Safety Diagram asks students (Grades 6-8) to closely examine each of the four areas of personal (physical, mental/emotional, social and spiritual) safety. Numerical values are given to each concentric circle for students to identify their personal level of *360° Safety.* Students use critical thinking using the numerical values in a math calculation to arrive at their *360° Safety* number. Through reflection and class discussion, students develop skills in taking personal responsibility to advance any number on the continuum toward a 10 (Safest).

Overarching Goals

The overarching goals in *Lesson Three* are to define safety, increase awareness of safety for self and others, and develop important skills in taking personal responsibility for one's safety toward ensuring a safe Christ-centered learning environment for all.

For further support in implementing the Peace Be With You Curriculum refer to:

Unit 1: Lesson Three: Safe At School in the *Teacher Curriculum Guide* for a more in-depth understanding of the importance of a safe learning environment.

<u>**Activity 4**</u>
<u>**Safety Check**</u>

Activity 4 Purpose
To recognize and define four generalized areas of safety and utilize a self-assessment tool to determine personal and interpersonal safety in the classroom, school, and beyond.
Activity 4 National Standards/Themes Correlation
Themes of Catholic Social Teachings: • Life and Dignity of the Human Person (CST-DHP) • Call to Family, Community and Participation (CST-CFCP) Social Studies Themes: • People, Places, and the Environment (SST-PPE) • Individual Development and Identity (SST-IDI) • Individuals, Groups, and Institutions (SST-IGI) Language Arts Speaking and Listening Standards: • Prepare for and participate effectively in a range of conversations and collaborations with diverse partners, building on others' ideas and expressing their own clearly and persuasively. (CCSS.ELA-Literacy.CCRA.SL1) Language Arts Writing Standards: • Introduce claim(s) and organize the reasons and evidence clearly. (CCSS.ELA-Literacy.CCRA.W1)

	<u>**Learning Objectives**</u> **Students will be able to:**	**Corresponding Assessment Possibilities**
1	<u>**Grades 4-8**</u> Define safety through the use of Web-mapping. <u>***Standards***</u> *(CST-DHP, SST-PPE, SST-IDI, SST-IGI, CCSS.ELA-Literacy.CCRA.SL1, CCSS.ELA-Literacy.CCRA.W1)*	<u>***#23 Worksheet***</u> ***Safe to Be Me*** • Complete the web listing all the words, phrases, ideas, etc. that are associated with feeling safe. *****Take this activity a step further by having students use the web to write a paragraph about what it means to be safe.***
2	<u>**Grades 4-8**</u> Identify and define four key areas of safety: Physical, Mental/Emotional, Social and Spiritual. <u>***Standards***</u> *(CST-DHP, SST-PPE, SST-IDI, SST-IGI, CCSS.ELA-Literacy.CCRA.SL1, CCSS.ELA-Literacy.CCRA.W1)*	**Note: For #24 Teacher Reference, see Appendix <u>A</u>.* <u>***#25 Worksheet***</u> ***The Four Areas of Safety Defined*** • List and write a definition for each of the four areas of safety. <u>***OR***</u> <u>***#26 Worksheet***</u> ***Examples of The Four Areas of Safety*** • Give an example for each of the four key areas of safety.

Activity 4 (continued)

| 3 | **Grades 4-8**
Apply Safety Check Line self-assessment tool to help determine personal and interpersonal safety.

Standards:
(CST-DHP, CST-CFCP, SST-PPE, SST-IDI, SST-IGI, CCSS.ELA-Literacy.CCRA.SL1, CCSS.ELA-Literacy.CCRA.W1) | **#27 Worksheet**
Safety Check Line
• Identify a number on the Safety Check Line that best represents you and journal about the steps you will take to get closer to a 10 (See Methodology). |

Methodology

Adults at school must continuously assess and evaluate student safety and take prudent steps to respond accordingly. Identifying a number on the *Safety Check Line* between 0-10 helps gives students and teachers a communication tool to assess and communicate the level of perceived severity of concern for physical, mental/emotional, social, and spiritual safety.

Although subjective, the *Safety Check Line* is a simple, yet helpful student measurement for self-identification, observation, decision-making, and clear communication about personal safety. It is best for teachers to not judge student numbers or themselves during this process. Use this communication tool as an opportunity to strengthen student/teacher relationships, responsiveness to students, and ultimately to build and sustain a safe learning environment.

SAFETY CHECK LINE

| 0 | 1 | 2 | 3 | 4 | 5 | 6 | 7 | 8 | 9 | 10 |

LEAST SAFE   **SAFEST**

Figure 1

At the far left of the Safety Check continuum is "0" which represents *"Least Safe"*—*absence* of civility and the possible *presence* of threat of harm or actual harm. At the far right "10" represents *"Safest"*—*presence* of civility and the *absence* of threat of harm or actual harm.

Any numbers in between represent the varying degrees of personal safety for the student. A "0" or any number lower than 5 indicate the absence of safety and possible presence of threat of harm or actual harm. Any number above 5 and closer to 10 indicates the presence of civility and possible absence of threat of harm or actual harm.

Use *#24 Teacher Reference: Four Areas of Safety,* and four *Activity 4* worksheets to support teacher instruction and student learning to gain a better understanding of safety.

Overarching Goal

The *Safety Check Line* establishes a fundamental working goal throughout the school year. It is critical that students commit to and are reminded of this goal; *"I help myself and others get closer to a 10."*

<u>IMPORTANT!</u>
Our classroom is only as safe as our lowest number!

Activity 4
Safety Check

Facilitator Script

TIME, PREPARATION, LOGISTICS, & PROCESS

10:00 PREPARATION
- Make one copy of *#24 Teacher Reference: Four Areas of Safety* as a support for instruction. The reference can also be posted on the classroom wall, Smartboard, or flipchart.
- Make copies of *#23, #25 or #26, and #27 Worksheets* for grades 4-8.

LOGISTICS
Instruction on the Four Areas of Safety
- Draw a *Safety Check Line (Fig. 1)* on the board, Smartboard, or flipchart (See *Safety Check Methodology* Figure 1).
- Students should have a sheet of paper, index card, or post-it note, and pencil.

*Note: Hand out #23 Worksheet: Safe to Be Me.

TIME   PROCESS
0:00   **Say:** "Class, as we begin this next part of servant-leadership and how to create positive ripples, we need to understand the importance of safety and what it means to feel safe. Please complete the web worksheet in front of you by filling in the circles provided. Add circles to include additional words, phrases, ideas, etc. that you associate with feeling safe."

*Note: Once students are ready with paper and pencil, give them at least 5 minutes to complete this exercise.

Ask: "What does safety mean to you?"

*Note: Teacher would know best about whether or not to open this question up to the entire class. If you believe doing so would make students too vulnerable, please do open this question up to class discussion.

Possible Responses: To feel like no one will hurt me. To not have to worry about people saying "bad" things about me. To feel like nothing "bad" is going to happen today, etc.

8:00   **Say:** "I think all that you have said is correct! I would like you to use your web and write a paragraph tonight describing your definition of feeling safe. Please attach your paragraph to the web worksheet you just completed and turn it in tomorrow. Thank you!"

*Note: Post #24 Teacher Reference: Four Areas of Safety.

__TIME__ __PROCESS__

Say: "Let's go over Physical, Mental/Emotional, Social, and Spiritual Safety, one at a time."

Say: "Let's begin with physical safety."

Ask: "How would students act to keep each other physically safe?"

Possible Responses: No punching, kicking, etc. Respecting my space.

Say: "Thank you."

9:00 **Say:** "*Physical safety* means we are all making every reasonable effort to protect the human body. All students should be reasonably free from any type of harm or threat of harm. No adult or student should enter another's personal space in any way that may cause, or threaten to cause physical harm, or interfere with learning."

Say: "A '10' for *Physical Safety* means no one would punch, push, pinch, kick, slap, scratch, poke, choke, trip, bite, pull hair, flick, or any other form of physical mistreatment. A "10" also means we are respecting each other's personal space."

Ask: "How would students act to keep each other mentally/emotionally safe?"

Possible Responses. I don't know. No putdowns. Only use put-ups.

10:00 **Say:** "Thank you. *Mental/Emotional safety* means we are all making every reasonable effort to protect the mental and emotional wellbeing of each person. Together we are creating a school climate where students feel comfortable being themselves and expressing their views, without fear of being judged. A school where all students feel respected and accepted."

Ask: "How would students act to keep each other safe socially?"

Possible Responses. I don't know. No rumors. No negative social media.

11:00 **Say:** "Thank you. *Social Safety* means we are making every reasonable effort to protect each other from harm or danger in face-to-face settings or in our electronic communications, including social media. This means we do not start rumors or keep them going. We do start or contribute to any negative texts, or posts on social media. We do not talk behind someone's back. We do not laugh at or ridicule. We do not ignore or exclude others."

Ask: "How would students act to keep each other safe spiritually?"

Possible Responses. I don't know. No putdowns of a person's religion. Respect people when they pray or worship.

Activity 4 Facilitator Script (continued)

<u>TIME</u> <u>PROCESS</u>

12:00 **Say:** "Thank you. *Spiritual safety* means, to be free from harm or danger to worship, to express and be respected for my religious beliefs. To not be made a target of prejudice or racial, cultural, or religious slurs."

Say: "Let's focus on a tool we can use called the *Safety Check Line*. This will help us throughout the school year to make sure everyone feels safe, and it's a way we can work together to create positive ripples in our classroom and school."

Say: "Please take a look at the *Safety Check Line* (on the board or flipchart)."

13:00 **Say:** "On this continuum (point to the board or flipchart) 0 means 'Least Safe' and 10 means 'Safest.'"

Say: "Now, close your eyes for a brief moment and ask yourself 'how safe do I feel in our classroom?'"

*Note: This is an important reflective moment even though you will only allow for about 30 seconds.

14:00 **Say:** "Based on the definitions you heard for physical, mental/emotional, social and spiritual safety, choose one number on the *Safety Check Line* continuum that best represents how safe you feel in our classroom."

Say: "When you have your *Safety Check Line* number, write it down on the index card (or post-it) that I have given you. Do not write your names on this card (or post-it). When completed, raise your hand and I will collect the cards 9 (or post-its). I will not be looking at what you have written down to identify you, but only to come up with a range of *Safety Check Line* numbers."

*Note: As students finish, collect their cards. Look at each card, taking note of the lowest and highest numbers. The lowest and highest Safety Check Line numbers becomes the range that you will share with the class. For example: "Class, you have reported that the Safety Check Line as a class represents a range from 3 to 10."

16:00 **Say:** "Thank you for sharing your numbers with me. I have looked at each card (or post-it) and found the range is *Safety Check Line* numbers. Class, you have reported that the Safety Check Line as a class represents a range from _____ to _____."

Important: If for any reason a student requests to speak with you or the school counselor in private about their Safety Check Line number, please ensure that their request is honored. Ask the student to share their number in private or to write their name on a post-it note or index card for you to share with the school counselor. Please do not take a low number by one of your students personally or as a reflection on you. Rather view this approach as an opportunity and vehicle for students to share their concern(s), when they might not otherwise do so. If a student shares his/her Safety Check Line number with you in private or writes down their name and Safety Check Line number after your invitation, he/she trust coming to you on this.

TIME   PROCESS

Ask: "What message does this *Safety Check Line* class number range mean to you?"

Possible Responses: We're not all feeling safe. Some of us feel safe, some of us don't.

17:00 Say: "You're correct. Those are all very good explanations for what those *Safety Check Line* numbers tell us. So now that we know the range of safety we feel as a class, what can we do to get everyone in our class closer to a 10?"

Possible Responses: Work on using more put ups with each other. Practice the servant-leadership words more. Cooperate with each other more, etc.

18:00 Say: "Those are great insights. Can we agree to work together as a class to practice these behaviors so we can spread positive ripples in our classroom and help our class to get closer to a 10?"

Expected Response: Yes

Say: "Thank you for your honesty and for sharing your *Safety Check Line* numbers and working together so we can help everyone in our class feel physically, mentally/emotionally, socially and spiritually safe."

Note: Students do not usually bring up the obvious and what is most important about this exercise; "Not everyone is a 10 in our class."

19:00 Ask: "What would be the ideal *Safety Check Line* number for us all to have?"

Expected Response: 10!

Say: "Thank you! This is our goal today and throughout the school year; that we help ourselves and each other move closer to a 10."

20:00 Say: "Repeat and mirror after me: *I will help myself* (gesture to yourself) *and others* (gesture to others) *get closer to a 10* (hold up 10 fingers)."

Activity 4 Facilitator Script (continued)

*Note. If students are not in sync with this first "repeat after me" do it again so they will feel more unified around the goal. You can also have one student lead a third round to solidify the goal with the entire class.

TIME   PROCESS

21:00   Ask: "If you are willing to commit to this goal, raise your hand."

           Optional: *Three-Step Commitment process:*

           Say: "If you are willing to commit to this goal, 1. Raise your hand 2. Stand up and 3. Take one step forward.

*Note: If any student does not stand up, ask him/her (in private) to share concerns and explain why committing to this step is difficult. By listening you will honor the students' concerns and model compassionate servant-leadership.

Important Reminder

We are not asking students to individually accomplish the goal of helping self and others to get closer to a 10, but rather to make a commitment to work together at it.

Activity 5
360° Safety Diagram

Activity 5 Purpose
To recognize and define each of the four generalized areas of safety using a self-assessment tool requiring critical thinking skills to determine personal and interpersonal safety in the classroom, school, and beyond.

Activity 5 National Standards/Themes Correlation
Themes of Catholic Social Teachings: • Life and Dignity of the Human Person (CST-DHP) • Call to Family, Community and Participation (CST-CFCP) Social Studies Themes: • People, Places, and the Environment (SST-PPE) • Individual Development and Identity (SST-IDI) • Individuals, Groups, and Institutions (SST-IGI) Language Arts Speaking and Listening Standards: • Prepare for and participate effectively in a range of conversations and collaborations with diverse partners, building on others' ideas and expressing their own clearly and persuasively. (CCSS.ELA-Literacy.CCRA.SL1) Language Arts Writing Standards: • Introduce claim(s) and organize the reasons and evidence clearly. (CCSS.ELA-Literacy.CCRA.W1)

	Learning Objectives Students will be able to:	Corresponding Assessment Possibilities
1	**Grades 6-8** Apply 360° self-assessment tool to help determine personal and interpersonal safety. ***Standards*** (CST-DHP, SST-PPE, SST-IDI, SST-IGI, CCSS.ELA-Literacy.CCRA.SL1, CCSS.ELA-Literacy.CCRA.W1)	***#28 Worksheet*** ***360° Safety Diagram*** • Choose a number that best represents you for each of the four areas of safety. Add the four numbers and divide to find your average number of safety.
2	**Grade 6-8** Reflect on their 360° Safety to increase awareness and responsibility for personal safety. ***Standards*** (CST-DHP, SST-PPE, SST-IDI, SST-IGI, CCSS.ELA-Literacy.CCRA.SL1, CCSS.ELA-Literacy.CCRA.W1)	***#29 Reflection 2*** ***360° Safety*** • Students will reflect on their 360° safety and identify ways to shift their 360° Safety number upward to the desired number.

Activity 5
360° Safety Diagram

Methodology

Similar to the Safety Check Line, Activity 5 asks to identify a number between 0-10 to help students and teachers assess and communicate the level of perceived severity of concern for physical, mental/emotional, social, and spiritual safety. The 360° Safety Diagram adds critical thinking steps to identify one number for each of the four areas (quadrants) of safety. The values arrived at then become a solvable math problem in determining one that represents overall personal safety.

At the center of the 360° Safety Diagram is "0" which represents "Least Safe"—absence of civility and the possible presence of threat of harm or actual harm. At the outside of the circle "10" represents "Safest"—presence of civility and the absence of threat of harm or actual harm.

Grade 6-8 students will identify and shade one safety number that best represents their level of personal safety in each of the four safety categories: 1. Physical 2. Mental/Emotional 3. Social and 4. Spiritual Safety. After the four 360° Safety Diagram numbers are identified and shaded, students add their individual numbers and divide by four to determine their overall level of personal safety. Students should not be required to show this worksheet or reveal their safety number to the class.

To determine the average range of class safety, ask students to anonymously place their total 360° Safety Diagram number on a post-it or index card. The post-its or index cards will reveal the range of class safety (lowest student number to highest student number) or each number can be added and divided by the total number of students to determine the average of the safety number for the entire class.

Although subjective, the 360° Safety Diagram helps increase students skills in self-identification, observation, decision-making, and clear communication about their personal safety. When used as a communication tool, adults at school can better assess and evaluate student safety and take the most prudent next steps to respond accordingly. It is best for teachers to not judge student numbers or themselves during this process. Use the results as an opportunity to strengthen student/teacher relationships, responsiveness to students, and ultimately to build and sustain a safe learning environment.

Reuse *#24 Teacher Reference: Four Areas of Safety* and two *Activity 5* worksheets to support teacher instruction for grades 6-8 to gain a better understanding of safety and servant-leadership.

Overarching Goal

The 360° Safety Check Diagram helps to establish a fundamental working goal throughout the school year. It is critical that students commit to and are reminded of the goal; "I will help myself and others get closer to a 10.

Activity 5
360° Safety Diagram

Facilitator Script

TIME, PREPARATION, LOGISTICS, & PROCESS

10:00 PREPARATION/LOGISTICS
- Make copies of *#28 and #29 Worksheets* for grades 6-8.
- Make one copy of *#24 Teacher Reference: Four Areas of Safety* as a support for instruction. This reference can also be posted on the classroom wall, Smartboard, or flipchart.

Note: Activity 4 is a prerequisite to implementing this activity with any grade.

TIME   PROCESS
0:00   **Say:** "Class. Let's review what you have learned about safety from the last activity."

Ask: "What does safety mean to you?"

Note: Teacher would know best about whether or not to open this question up to the entire class. If you believe doing so would make students too vulnerable, please do open this question up to class discussion.

Possible Responses: To feel like no one will hurt me, to not have to worry about people saying "bad" things about me, to feel like nothing "bad" is going to happen today, etc.

8:00   **Say:** "I think all that you have said is correct!"

Say: "Let's go over Physical, Mental/Emotional, Social, and Spiritual Safety again."

Say: "Let's begin with physical safety."

Ask: "How would students act to keep each other physically safe?"

Possible Responses: No punching, kicking, etc. Respecting personal space.

Say: "Thank you."

9:00   **Say:** "*Physical Safety* means we are all making every reasonable effort to protect the human body. All students should be reasonably free from any type of harm or threat of harm. No adult or student should enter another's personal space in any way that may cause or threaten to cause physical harm, or interfere with learning."

Say: "A '10' for *Physical Safety* means no one would punch, push, pinch, kick, slap, scratch, poke, choke, trip, bite, pull hair, flick, or any other form of physical mistreatment. A "10" also means we are respecting each other's personal space."

Activity 5 Facilitator Script (continued)

<u>TIME</u> <u>PROCESS</u>

Ask: "How would students act to keep each other mentally/emotionally safe?"

Possible Responses. I don't know. No putdowns. Only use put-ups.

10:00 Say: "Thank you. *Mental/Emotional Safety* means we are all making every reasonable effort to protect the mental and emotional wellbeing of each person. Together we are creating a school climate where students feel comfortable being themselves and expressing their views, without fear of being judged. A school where all students feel respected and accepted."

Ask: "How would students act to keep each other safe socially?"

Possible Responses. I don't know. No rumors. No negative social media.

11:00 Say: "Thank you. *Social Safety* means we are making every reasonable effort to protect each other from harm or danger in face-to-face settings or in our electronic communications, including social media. This means we do not start rumors or keep them going. We do start or contribute to any negative texts, or posts on social media. We do not talk behind someone's back. We do not laugh at or ridicule. We do not ignore or exclude."

Ask: "How would students act to keep each other safe spiritually?"

Possible Responses. I don't know. No putdowns of a person's religion. Respect people when they pray or worship.

12:00 Say: "Thank you. *Spiritual Safety* means, to be free from harm or danger to worship, to express and respected for my religious beliefs. To not be made a target of prejudice or racial, cultural, or religious slurs."

Say: "Let's focus on a tool we can use called the *360° Safety Diagram*. This will help us throughout the school year to make sure everyone feels safe and a way we can work together to create positive ripples in our classroom and school."

*Note: Hand out #29 Reflection 2: 360° Safety

Say: "Please take a look at the *360° Safety Diagram* handout."

13:00 Say: "This diagram has concentric circles. Each circle represents a number from 0 which means 'Least Safe' the last concentric circle 10, which means 'Safest.'"

Say: "Now, close your eyes for a brief moment and ask yourself 'how safe do I feel in our classroom?'"

*Note: This is an important reflective moment even though you may only allow for about 30 seconds.

Activity 5 Facilitator Script (continued)

TIME   PROCESS

14:00   Say: "Based on the definitions you heard, shade to the number in each of the four areas of safety that best represents you for how safe you feel in our classroom. For example: If you are a six for physical safety, you would shade from the first concentric circle of zero to the sixth concentric circle."

Say: "You may begin shading each area of personal safety; physical, mental/emotional, social and spiritual to a number that best represents you."

*Note: Give students 3 minutes to shade in the four safety numbers.

17:00   Say: "Now, add each of your four *360° Safety* numbers, and divide by four to come up with your overall 360° Safety number. For example: If my physical safety is at a 6, my mental/emotional safety at a 5, my social safety is at a 7 and my spiritual safety at a 9, the numbers add up to 27. I divide 27 by four = 6.75, which is my *360° Safety Diagram* number."

*Note: Give students an additional 3 minutes to calculate their four safety numbers.

**Important Note: If for any reason a student requests to speak with you or the school counselor in private about their 360° Safety Diagram number, please ensure that their request is honored. Ask the student to confidentially share their number with you in private or anonymously write their name on a post-it note or index card and fold it up for you to share with the school counselor. Please do not take a low number by one of your students personally or as a reflection on you. Rather, view this exercise as an opportunity and vehicle for students to share their concern(s), when they might not otherwise do so. If a student shares his/her 360° Safety Diagram number with you in private or anonymously writes down their name and 360° Safety Diagram number after your invitation, he/she trusted coming to you on this.

Say: "When you have your *360° Safety Diagram* number, write it down on the index card (or post-it) that I have given you. Do not write your names on this card (or post-it). When completed, raise your hand and I will collect the cards (or post-its). I will not be looking at what you have written down to identify you, but only to come up with a range of *360° Safety Diagram* numbers."

*Note: As students finish, collect their cards. Look at each card, taking note of the lowest and highest numbers. The lowest and highest 360° Safety Diagram numbers becomes the range that you will share with the class. For example: "Class, you have reported that as a class on the 360° Safety Diagram we are a range from 3 to 10."

20:00   Say: "Thank you for sharing your numbers with me. I have looked at each card (or post-it) and found the range is *360° Safety Diagram* numbers. Class, you have reported that we are a range from _____ to _____."

Ask: "What message does our class *360° Safety Diagram* number range mean to you?"

TIME   PROCESS

Possible Responses: We're not all feeling safe. Some of us feel safe, some of us don't.

21:00   Say: "You're correct. Those are all very good explanations for what those *360° Safety Diagram* numbers tell us. So now that we know the range of safety we feel as a class, what can we do to get everyone in our class closer to a 10?"

Possible Responses: Work on using more put ups with each other. Remind myself of the servant-leader words. Cooperate with each other more.

22:00   Say: "Those are great insights. Can we agree to work together as a class to practice these behaviors so we can spread positive ripples, helping our class to get closer to a 10?"

Expected Response: Yes

Say: "Thank you for your honesty and fort sharing your 360° Safety numbers and working together so we can help everyone in our class feel physically, mentally/emotionally, socially and spiritually safe."

Note: Students do not usually bring up the obvious and what is most important about this exercise; "Not everyone is a 10 in our class."

23:00   Ask: "What would be the ideal *360° Safety Diagram* number for us all to have?"

Expected Response: 10!

Say: "Thank you! This is our goal today and throughout the school year; that we help ourselves and each other move closer to a 10."

Ask: "If you are willing to commit to this goal, please raise your hand."

Optional: Three-Step Commitment process:

Say: "If you are willing to commit to this goal, 1. Raise your hand 2. Stand up and 3. Take one step forward.

Note: If any student does not stand up, ask him/her (in private) to share concerns and explain why committing to this step is difficult. This is not a time to shame or humiliate a student into compliance. By listening you will honor the students' concerns and model compassionate servant-leadership.

Important Reminder: We are not asking students to individually accomplish this goal, but rather to make a commitment to work together at it.

Activity 5 Facilitator Script (continued)

TIME   PROCESS
24:00 Say: "Repeat and mirror after me: *I will help myself* (gesture to yourself) *and others* (gesture to others) *get closer to a 10* (hold up 10 fingers)."

*Note. If students are not in sync with this first "repeat after me" do it again so they will feel more united around the goal. You can also have one of your students lead a third round to solidify the goal with the class.

   Say: "Thank you! I am very proud of you for committing to this goal to help ourselves and others move closer to a 10!"

   Say: "Please take time to reflect and write on *#29 Reflection 2: 360° Safety Diagram* about how you will help yourself and others move closer to a 10."

*Note: Give students 5 minutes to complete this exercise in class. Another option, would be for students to take this worksheet home and return it to class on the required date.

30:00 Say: "That's time. Please pass this worksheet forward so that I can take a look at what you have written. I will return this worksheet for you to keep in your Leader Folder (or section in an accordion-type folder or binder)."

IMPORTANT:
Our classroom is only as safe as our lowest number!

Unit 1: Lesson Four
Discovering the Compassion of Christ

"Can you find out the depths of God?
or find out the perfection of the Almighty?"

Job 11:7

Lesson Four Purpose

To closely examining the virtuous actions of Jesus as our perfect model for servant-leadership by immersing students in Scripture.

Lesson Four Overview

By making Scripture relevant, and examining Jesus as our perfect model of servant-leadership, students are encouraged to practice and apply Christ-like actions in their everyday lives. At a profound level the compassion of Christ and a menu of positive responses are available to students when faced with challenging situations.

This lesson deepens compare and contrast analysis with common forms of current day peer mistreatment placed next to the servant-leadership of Jesus and others to inspire positive and relevant responses among peers. Such analysis fosters thoughtful (objective) and heartfelt (compassionate) choices to reduce harmful actions and enhance supportive actions that create a positive ripple in the classroom, school, and beyond.

The two activities and nine worksheets that accompany *Lessons Six* and *Seven* support teacher instruction and student learning for an enriching Scripture-based experience and ultimately spiritual formation.

<u>Overarching Goal</u>

The overarching goal of *Lesson Four is* by deeply immersing students in Scripture they will come to know Jesus in a more intimate and relevant way as their perfect model of servant-leadership.

For further support in implementing the Peace Be With You Curriculum refer to:

The Teacher Curriculum Guide for more information about the common forms of mistreatment, a detailed understanding of physical and emotional mistreatment, and compare and contrast as an important process for developing critical thinking skills to identify options that emphasize positive choices.

Activity 6
Jesus Models Dignity for One

Activity 6 Purpose
Through the use of select Scripture, students actively engage in compare and contrast between common forms of peer mistreatment and the virtuous behaviors of Jesus for important skill acquisition in servant-leadership.

Activity 6 National Standards/Themes Correlation
Themes of Catholic Social Teachings: • Life and Dignity of the Human Person (CST-DHP) • Call to Family, Community and Participation (CST-CFCP) • Rights and Responsibility (CST-RR) • Solidarity (CST-S) Social Studies Themes: • Culture (SST-C) • People, Places, and the Environment (SST-PPE) • Individual Development and Identity (SST-IDI) • Individuals, Groups, and Institutions (SST-IGI) Language Arts Speaking and Listening Standards: • Prepare for and participate effectively in a range of conversations and collaborations with diverse partners, building on others' ideas and expressing their own clearly and persuasively. (CCSS.ELA-Literacy.CCRA.SL1) Language Arts Writing Standards: • Introduce claim(s) and organize the reasons and evidence clearly. (CCSS.ELA-Literacy.CCRA.W1)

	Learning Objectives Students will be able to:	Corresponding Assessment Possibilities
1	**Grades 4-8** Role-play selected Scripture passages to examine the actions of Jesus and how they can follow His model. ***Standards*** *(CST-DHP, CST-CFCP, CST-RR, CST-S, SST-C, SST-PPE, SST-IDI, SST-IGI, CCSS.ELA-Literacy.CCRA.SL1, CCSS.ELA-Literacy.CCRA.W1)*	***#30 Scripture Connection 1*** ***(Luke 19: 1-10)*** • Scripture reading for Role-Play 1: Dignity for One. ***#31 Role-Play 1*** • Use the Role-Play 1 script to enact the Scripture and discuss what was learned from the actions of Jesus.

| 2 | **Grades 4-8**
Use selected Scripture passages to analyze common forms of peer mistreatment to compare and contrast with the virtuous actions of Jesus/Others.

Standards
(CST-DHP, CST-CFCP, CST-RR, CST-S, SST-C, SST-PPE, SST-IDI, SST-IGI, CCSS.ELA-Literacy.CCRA.SL1, CCSS.ELA-Literacy.CCRA.W1) | **#32 Scripture Analysis 1**
• Small group work to analyze and discuss peer mistreatment and Jesus' actions in the context of this Scripture.

#33 Debate
(Grades 6-8)
• Debate the Virtuous Actions of Jesus versus Peer Mistreatment to analyze the similarities and differences between common forms of peer mistreatment and virtuous actions of Jesus/Others. |
| 3 | **Grades 4-8**
Reflect on the Scripture passage and how it relates to personal experience.

Standards
(CST-DHP, CST-CFCP, CST-RR, CST-S, SST-C, SST-PPE, SST-IDI, SST-IGI, CCSS.ELA-Literacy.CCRA.SL1, CCSS.ELA-Literacy.CCRA.W1) | **#34 Reflection 3**
Jesus Models Dignity for One
• Students reflect on how this Scripture passage is relevant to their lives and connect this to the biblical characters and servant-leader words. |

Methodology

Activity 6 immerses students in the Scripture of Luke 19: 1-10, to actively engage them in a compare and contrast critical thinking process, using common forms of mistreatment and the virtuous actions of Jesus and Others. This Scripture from Luke parallels common current day group dynamics in which youth and adults feel justified in mistreatment, because they judge another as "different," e.g., loud, annoying, needy, odd/quirky mannerisms, too short, too tall, wears eccentric clothing, etc.

The compare and contrast analysis gives students an opportunity to examine the purity of Jesus' actions and the stark contrast of the wrongful actions of those who mistreated Zacchaeus. The goal of this exercise is to help students become more aware of their actions and how our actions impact others, using Jesus as our perfect model for servant-leadership. Activity 6 utilizes four worksheets for grades 4-8 and one additional worksheet for grades 6-8 to support teacher instruction and student learning on the virtuous actions of Jesus.

IMPORTANT CAUTION!
When addressing any form of peer mistreatment, we must remain alert to not unwittingly model, teach or encourage mistreating behaviors among students. Using scripted role-plays to compare and contrast peer mistreatment next to the virtuous behaviors of Jesus can be very effective in positively influencing student behavior; however, depicting peer mistreatment can also be mimicked, contributing to a negative contagion problem that is difficult to undo. Thus, the implementation of the following activities should be used with caution. Always default to the virtuous actions of Jesus.

Activity 6
Jesus Models Dignity for One

Facilitator Script
Scripture Connection 1

TIME/PREPARATION/LOGISTICS & PROCESS

10:00 PREPARATION
- Make copies of *#30 Scripture Connection 1 and #32 Scripture Analysis 1* for grades 4-8.
- Make copies of *#33 Worksheet* for Grades 6-8 only.
- Make six copies of *#31 Role-Play 1*, one each of the six select students involved in the role-play.

LOGISTICS
- A chair or spot for Zacchaeus to be in the tree
- Class reads silently Scripture from Luke 19: 1-10 (*#30 Scripture Connection 1*).
- Select one or more students to read the Scripture (Luke 19: 1-10) out loud to the class.
- Optional: Ask students to read the Scripture passage out loud together as a class.
- Select students to role-play using the script provided.
- Room large enough for the "crowd" to gather.

Stage Directions for Role-Play 1:

- A member of the crowd will call out "Jesus is coming."
- Jesus comes into the town with a crowd following.
- Zacchaeus is in the "tree" trying to see Jesus.
- People around Zacchaeus will not listen to him or interact with him, but continue to stand around him trying to prevent him from seeing Jesus.
- The Narrator stands off to the side and directs most of the action from the narration in the script (with teacher guidance if necessary).

TIME PROCESS
0:00 Say: "I am very proud of the work we have accomplished together over the last three lessons taking a close look at how we can create a positive school community by being positive servant-leaders."

Say: "Remember: <u>P</u>ositive <u>S</u>ervant-<u>L</u>eaders (PSL) + Other <u>P</u>ositive <u>S</u>ervant-<u>L</u>eaders (PSL) = A Positive School!"

1:00 Say: "Today let's take a close look at Scripture and Jesus as our perfect model of servant-leadership."

Say: "We will read and have fun role-playing Scripture from Luke19: 1-10. Please pay close attention to what we all can learn from the actions of Jesus to help guide our lives today."

Activity 6 Facilitator Script (continued)

TIME   PROCESS

2:00   **Say:** "To begin our faith journey into Scripture, we are going to complete a series of steps to examine a passage from the Holy Gospel according to Luke: Chapter 19 vs. 1-10."

Note: Hand out #30 Scripture Connection 1 (Luke 19: 1-10), so all students have an opportunity to read the passage.

   Say: "First, silently read this Scripture passage from Luke. When you are finished reading, please give me thumbs up, so I will know when everyone is ready to continue. Please begin reading."

4:00   **Say:** "Thank you for your thumbs up. Now, let's have some fun role-playing this Scripture passage."

   Say: "Do I have six volunteers willing to play the roles?"

   Expected Response: Many students will raise their hands. Select six students—one narrator, Zacchaeus, Jesus, and three students to represent the rest of the class as the "Grumbling Crowd.

Note: Hand out one #31 Role-Play 1 to each of the six select students.

Note: Set-Up: Once the six students have #31 Role-Play 1, set-up a chair to be the sycamore tree for Zacchaeus to "climb up" or a spot for Zacchaeus to stand. Briefly instruct the students involved in the role-play on where they should be set-up using the stage directions found at the beginning of the script.

6:00   **Say:** "The three students playing the "grumbling crowd" will lead the rest of the class during the role-play in becoming a part of the "grumbling crowd.""

   Say: "Now that everyone is set, let's begin with the narrator in the role-play script."

Note: Students will act out the role-play as found on the role-play script they have been given.

10:00   **Say:** "Now let's take a moment to reflect on the passage and role-play. As you silently reflect, think about the actions of the characters involved in this passage and in particular about what Jesus does."

12:00   **Say:** "Please form your small groups to complete the worksheet (*#32 Scripture Analysis 1*) being handed out. When your group is completed with the worksheet, please raise your hands."

Note: Give students a minute or so to get into their small group.

13:00   **Say:** "Thank you for getting into your small groups so quickly. Please begin to work together in your small groups on this worksheet. If you like you can have one person in your group re-read the Scripture passage out loud to help your group answer the worksheet questions together."

Activity 6 Facilitator Script (continued)

<u>**TIME**</u> <u>**PROCESS**</u>
18:00 Say: "Now let's discuss as a class how your group responded to the worksheet questions."

Ask: "Who is being mistreated?"

Expected response: Zacchaeus

Ask: "How is he being mistreated?"

Expected response: The crowd is making it difficult for Zacchaeus to see Jesus, so he climbs a Sycamore tree. Hateful grumbling at him.

19:00 Ask: "Why is Zacchaeus being mistreated?"

Possible responses: Zacchaeus is a tax collector and people do not trust him and despise him because he has cheated them.

Ask: "What feelings might Zacchaeus have?"

Possible responses: Zacchaeus may feel angry or upset since the crowd will not move for him. He also may feel unwanted or excluded."

Ask: "Who is mistreating?"

Expected responses: The crowd

20:00 Ask: "What feelings might some of the crowd have when they were mistreating Zacchaeus?"

Possible responses: They might have felt vengeance, powerful, or justified in their choice.

Ask: "Do people 'deserve' to be mistreated, even when it seems justified?"

Expected response: No. Yes, because they did something wrong.

*Note: This is a good time to take a few minutes to discuss with the class about how no one "deserves" to be mistreated whether they have done something wrong or not. This is also a good time to reiterate that there are consequences for classroom/school infractions and that we are not to appoint ourselves the judge and jury on the actions of others.

22:00 Ask: "Who is witnessing the mistreatment?"

Expected responses: Jesus, the crowd, and the disciples.

TIME/PROCESS

    Ask: "What kind of mistreatment might some of the crowd be witnessing? "

    Possible Responses: Watching Zacchaeus struggle to see Jesus. They see Zacchaeus climb up a tree."

    Ask: "What feelings might some of the crowd have as they witness Zacchaeus being mistreated?"

    Possible responses: Angry, upset, guilty, don't know what to do.

    Ask: "Which characters in this scripture created a negative ripple?"

    Possible responses: The crowd, Zacchaeus (possibly due to his actions when he was a tax collector).

23:00   **Ask:** "How was a negative ripple created?"

    Possible responses: The crowd when they excluded or hated Zacchaeus. Zacchaeus when he cheated people out of their money.

    Ask: "Why do you think these characters created a negative ripple?"

    Possible responses: By being angry and spreading hate. Trying to gain revenge over how they had been treated by Zacchaeus.

    Ask: "What was the result of the negative ripple of the crowd?"

    Possible responses: Zacchaeus was excluded and he climbs a tree. The crowd spread hate.

24:00   **Ask:** "Which characters created a positive ripple in this passage?"

    Possible responses: Jesus. Zacchaeus.

    Ask: "How did these characters create a positive ripple?"

    Possible responses: Jesus told Zacchaeus he was going to his house. Zacchaeus when he said he would care for the poor and pay back what he had stolen from people.

    Ask: "What was the result of the positive ripple?"

    Possible responses: Zacchaeus changed (conversion as a result of his contact with Jesus) his ways by caring for others. Jesus modeled how to reach out to others. Others were blessed.

Activity 6 Facilitator Script (continued)

<u>TIME</u> <u>PROCESS</u>

25:00 Ask: "Did Jesus respond the way we would expect people to respond in a situation like this? Why or why not?"

Possible responses: Students may say no because most people would have said Zacchaeus was a "sinner" and we don't want to have anything to do with him. If they did invite Zacchaeus anywhere it would have not been to their house. Or they may say yes because Jesus was a visitor in the village/town and he needed to stay somewhere, or students may say yes because He is Jesus.

Ask: "What did you feel as you role played this skit?" (*Echo students' feelings as you hear them.*)

Ask: "What can you learn about yourself from these feelings?" (*Echo what you hear students saying.*)

26:00 Ask: "What situations in our school are similar to actions role played in this skit?"

Possible responses: When we don't include others at our lunch table. When we tell people they can't be on our team. When we tell people they don't belong. When we don't choose someone for our team, etc.

Ask: "What can we learn about Jesus' actions?"

Possible responses: If we truly want people to feel included and show we care, we should go to them first, and go to their house, lunch table, etc. to help them feel included.

Ask: "What positive servant-leader qualities did Jesus demonstrate?"

Possible responses: Listening. Kindness. Caring. Generosity. Made the first move to reach out.

27:00 Say: "Class, let's take a moment and summarize what we learned from the actions of Jesus."

Ask: "How can we apply what we learned in this role-play to create positive ripples and help strengthen our classroom community?"

Possible Responses: Jesus reached out to Zacchaeus and went to his house and called Zacchaeus by his name. We can reach out in the same way in support of a classmate, by going to their (home, locker, lunch table, etc.). We can walk with a classmate. We can call our classmates by their name. We can call or text them after school hours. We can include every classmate in our activities, so no one feels left out.

28:00 Say: "Thank you for your hard work. Now take a few minutes to reflect to write on *#34 Reflection 3: Jesus Models Dignity for One* what you have learned from this scripture passage."

33:00 Say: "Thank you for being respectful of each other during quiet reflection."

Activity 6 Facilitator Script (continued)

<u>**TIME   PROCESS**</u>

Ask: "What did you learn from this activity that you could use in your everyday life?"

Possible responses: To not exclude or label others. To treat others with respect, kindness, and to reach out to others, etc. Be kind to even not so kind people.

34:00 Say: "Class, thank you for your participation in this role-play and discussion to help us find more ways to build a positive community in our classroom! You have worked really hard today. Thank you!"

Activity 7
Jesus Models Dignity for All

Activity 7 Purpose
Through the use of select Scripture, students actively engage in compare and contrast between common forms of peer mistreatment and the virtuous behaviors of Jesus for important skill acquisition in servant-leadership.

Activity 7 National Standards/Themes Correlation
Themes of Catholic Social Teachings: • Life and Dignity of the Human Person (CST-DHP) • Call to Family, Community and Participation (CST-CFCP) • Rights and Responsibility (CST-RR) • Solidarity (CST-S) Social Studies Themes: • Culture (SST-C) • People, Places, and the Environment (SST-PPE) • Individual Development and Identity (SST-IDI) • Individuals, Groups, and Institutions (SST-IGI) Language Arts Speaking and Listening Standards: • Prepare for and participate effectively in a range of conversations and collaborations with diverse partners, building on others' ideas and expressing their own clearly and persuasively. (CCSS.ELA-Literacy.CCRA.SL1) Language Arts Writing Standards: • Introduce claim(s) and organize the reasons and evidence clearly. (CCSS.ELA-Literacy.CCRA.W1)

	Learning Objectives **Students will be able to:**	**Corresponding Assessment Possibilities**
1	**Grades 4-8** Review Scripture Connection 1. **Standards** (CST-CFHP, SST-IDI, CCSS.ELA-Literacy.CCRA.SL1)	• The facilitator Script for *Scripture Connection 2: Jesus Models Dignity for All,* guides the review of *Scripture Connection 1: Dignity for One.*
2	**Grades 4-8** Role-play selected Scripture passages to examine the actions of Jesus and how they can follow His model.	***#35 Scripture Connection 2*** ***(John 8: 1-11)*** • Scripture reading for the Role-Play 2: *Dignity for All.*

	Standards (CST-DHP, CST-CFCP, CST-RR, CST-S, SST-C, SST-PPE, SST-IDI, SST-IGI, CCSS.ELA-Literacy.CCRA.SL1, CCSS.ELA-Literacy.CCRA.W1)	***#36 Role-Play 2*** ***Jesus Models Dignity for All*** • Use Role-Play 2 script to enact the Scripture and discuss what was learned from the actions of Jesus.
3	**Grades 4-8** Use selected Scripture passages to analyze common forms of peer mistreatment to compare and contrast with the virtuous actions of Jesus/Others. *Standards* (CST-DHP, CST-CFCP, CST-RR, CST-S, SST-C, SST-PPE, SST-IDI, SST-IGI, CCSS.ELA-Literacy.CCRA.SL1, CCSS.ELA-Literacy.CCRA.W1)	***#37 Scripture Analysis 2*** • Small group work to analyze and discuss peer mistreatment and Jesus' actions in the context of this Scripture.
4	**Grades 4-8** Reflect on the Scripture passage and how it relates to personal experience. *Standards* (CST-DHP, CST-CFCP, CST-RR, CST-S, SST-PPE, SST-IDI, SST-IGI, CCSS.ELA-Literacy.CCRA.SL1)	***#38 Reflection 4*** ***Jesus Models Dignity for All*** • Students reflect on how this Scripture passage is relevant to their lives and connect this to the biblical characters and servant-leader words.

Methodology

Activity 7 further immerses students using Scripture from John 8: 1-11 to actively engage them in a compare and contrast critical thinking process, using common forms of mistreatment and the virtuous actions of Jesus. This Scripture from John is another example of common current day group dynamics in which social contagion causes youth and adults to often feel justified in mistreating others, hiding behind the power imbalance of the group. Although there is no physical mistreatment in this Scripture, the threat of harm is looming, making it an extremely volatile situation.

Power and manipulation are another form of mistreatment that is captured in this Scripture. The Scribes and Pharisees clearly have an agenda to get their own way and misuse their power (Power Imbalance) by controlling the woman and enflame a social contagion with the crowd in an attempt to manipulate Jesus. The compare and contrast analysis gives students an opportunity to examine the purity of Jesus' actions, in spite of the active social contagion, with the stark contrast of the intended wrongful actions of the crowd. The goal of this exercise is to help students become more aware of their actions and how our actions impact others, using Jesus as our perfect model for servant-leadership.

Activity 7 utilizes four worksheets for grades 4-8 to support teacher instruction and student learning on the virtuous actions of Jesus.

IMPORTANT CAUTION!

When addressing any form of peer mistreatment, we must remain alert to not unwittingly model, teach or encourage mistreating behaviors among students. Using scripted role-plays to compare and contrast peer mistreatment next to the virtuous behaviors of Jesus can be very effective in positively influencing student behavior; however, depicting peer mistreatment can also be mimicked, contributing to a negative contagion problem that is difficult to undo. Thus, implementation of the following activities should be used with caution. Always default to the virtuous actions of Jesus.

For further support in implementing the Peace Be With You Curriculum refer to:
The *Teacher Curriculum Guide* for more information about the common forms of mistreatment, a detailed understanding of physical and emotional mistreatment, and compare and contrast as an important process for developing critical thinking skills to identify options that emphasize positive choices.

But when they continued asking Him,
He straightened up and said to them,
"Let the one among you who is without sin
be the first to throw a stone at her."

John 8:7

Activity 7
Jesus Models Dignity for All

Facilitator Script
Scripture Connection 2

TIME, PREPARATION, LOGISTICS, & PROCESS

10:00 PREPARATION
- Make copies of *#35 Scripture Connection 2, #37 Scripture Analysis 2, and #38 Reflection 4* for grades 4-8.
- Make five copies of *#36 Role-Play 2*, one for six select students involved in the role-play.
- One sheet of paper for each student to make a "stone."

LOGISTICS
- Class reads silently Scripture from John 8: 1-11. (*#35 Scripture Connection 2*).
- Select one or more students to read the Scripture (John 8: 1-11) out loud to the class.
- Optional: Ask students to read the Scripture passage out loud together as a class.
- Select students to role-play using the script provided.
- Room large enough for the "crowd" to gather.

Characters:
1. Narrator
2. Jesus
3. Woman
4. Leader of the Pharisees
5. Crowd

Stage Directions for Role-play 2:

- The Leader of the Pharisees walks in with the woman (female student) next to him, as the narrator begins reading from the script.
- Jesus is teaching the group as the Leader of the Pharisees and the Woman enters.
- The Crowd is part of the group being taught by Jesus (some students sit down when Jesus sits to teach them and the remaining students stand around witnessing the action taking place). The "stones" will be dispersed on the floor so they are available for the "crowd (students)" to pick up.
- The Narrator will stand off to the side. While reading, the script will guide the action of the characters.

TIME **PROCESS**

0:00 **Ask:** "Class. What do you remember about the role-play and Scripture analysis we completed last week from the Gospel of Luke where Jesus modeled dignity and value for one?"

Expected Responses: Jesus showed kindness to Zacchaeus. Jesus went to Zacchaeus' house. Zacchaeus was mistreated. Zacchaeus was mistreated when the crowd would not let him see Jesus. Jesus showed how to spread a positive ripples, etc. (Echo and acknowledge student responses.)

1:00 **Ask:** "What leader words apply to the virtuous actions of Jesus in this Scripture?

Expected Responses: Students will likely recall and recite several words from their leader word list such as humility, patience, compassion, kindness, etc. (Echo and acknowledge student responses.)

Ask: "What positive ripples did Jesus spread and how did He spread them in this Scripture?"

Expected Responses: Jesus created positive ripples by treating Zacchaeus with kindness and caring. He wanted to be with Zacchaeus and eat dinner with him in his home.

Ask: "How did Jesus' positive actions influence the actions of Zacchaeus?

Expected Response: Zacchaeus spread positive ripples when he told Jesus that he would pay back all he had taken fourfold.

Ask: "What does 'fourfold' mean?" (If students bring up the word 'fourfold.')

Expected Response: Pay back what he took from the people times four.

Say: "Yes! Thank you!"

3:00 **Ask:** "What action steps did Jesus or Zacchaeus take to help themselves or others get to a 10?"

Expected Responses: Jesus went to Zacchaeus' house for dinner. Jesus was kind and caring to Zacchaeus. Zacchaeus told Jesus he would repay all that he took fourfold.

5:00 **Say:** "Class. Today we're going to take another close look at the actions of Jesus, by role-playing and analyzing a new Scripture passage. We can all learn more about, and be reminded of, the actions of Jesus to help guide our lives today."

Say: "To continue our faith journey, we are going to complete a series of steps to examine a Scripture passage from the Holy Gospel according to John: Chapter 8 verses 1-11."

Say: "Silently read the Scripture passage in front of you. When you have read the passage, give me a thumbs up so I will know when everyone is ready to continue."

Activity 7 Facilitator Script (continued)

TIME PROCESS

6:00 Say: "Please begin reading." (Allow 1 minute)

7:00 Say: "Thank you for your thumbs up."

Say: "Let's continue by role playing the Scripture passage. In order to accurately role-play this situation, we need to create some props. In our role-play, Jesus helps a woman who is about to be stoned."

Ask: "What do you think these stones represent in our life?"

Possible Responses: The stones represent things that can go wrong in our lives or mistakes we've made. Ways that we may have wronged self and others. Situations that may cause jealousy, power, pride, etc. (Echo student responses.)

*Note: Provide or have students take out one sheet of paper.

8:00 Say: "On the sheet of paper in front of you, list things that are "stones" in your life. When you've finished your list, give me a thumbs-up so I know we are ready for the next step."

10:00 Say: "I can see by your thumbs up that you have all finished your lists. Thank you! Now, crumble up your list into a "stone." Have your stone ready. You will need it for this role -play."

12:00 Say: "In today's role-play, everyone will play a role as you did last week. We are going to reenact an event from Scripture in which Jesus creates positive ripples from a situation that began in a very negative way. I will select students to take specific roles. If you'd like to play one of the parts, please raise your hand when I request for volunteers. Everyone who does not have a specific role will become a member of the crowd. The crowd and Pharisees will need their "stones" for the role-play. Jesus and the woman will leave their stones at their seat because they won't need them."

*Note: After you have invited the students to participate in the skit, select students to play the characters listed at the beginning of this facilitator script. All other students will become members of the crowd.

13:00 Say: "Looks like everyone is ready, so everyone take their places please."

Say: (Once everyone is in their places.) "Please begin." Or "Action!"

15:00 Say: "Class, let's discuss the role-play and scripture you have all just read and participated in."

Ask: "Who was mistreated in this Scripture story?"

Expected Response: Jesus. The woman

Ask: "Who was mistreating others?"

TIME   PROCESS

Expected Response: The Scribes and Pharisees.

16:00 Ask: "Who witnessed the mistreatment and what did they do?"

Expected Response: The crowd witnessed. The crowd was preparing to stone the woman, then walked away after Jesus made the statement; "Let he who is without sin throw the first stone."

Ask: "What were Jesus's actions in this situation?"

Expected Response: He stood up to the crowd (Scribes/Pharisees). He showed compassion. He wrote in the sand. He bent (knelt) down. He listened. He was patient, kind, and open to the naysayer's rants.

Ask: "Why do you think the crowd put down their stones and left?"

Possible Response: They realized that they also have sinned. They should not judge others when they have made mistakes too.

17:00 Ask: "Did Jesus respond the way we would expect people to respond in a situation like this? Why or why not?"

Possible Response: Students may respond 'no,' because they don't know of anyone who would act that way, or they may say 'yes' because He is Jesus.

Ask: "How did you feel during the role-play?"

Possible Responses: Nervous, anxious, like I wanted to throw a stone, etc.

18:00 Ask: "What can we learn from our feelings?"

Possible Responses: To listen to our feelings and use them to guide our actions. To take time and listen to our conscience before we act, etc. To pray before we act.

Say: "Sometimes and some days our 'stones' feel heavier than others. Sometimes they are so heavy that we take them out on others."

Ask: "Is it okay to take out our burdens on others?"

Expected Response: No!

Say: "I agree!"

19:00 Ask: "So if it's not okay to take our burdens out on others, what can we do with these burdens to not bring any harm on ourselves or others?"

Activity 7 Facilitator Script (continued)

<u>TIME</u>   <u>PROCESS</u>

Possible Responses: Talk to someone about it (friend, parent, school counselor, trusted adult). Take a walk. Pray. Sing. Dance. Read a good book. Play a video game. Focus on a hobby.

Say: "I like the positive choices you've suggested as ways we all can take care of ourselves."

20:00   **Say:** "Please pick up your 'stone. Feel the weight of it. Now, one at a time, I would like each of you to walk to the wastebasket and (cast, throw, toss) your burdens (what weighs you down) into the trash."

Say: "After you 'let go' (or turn our burdens over to Jesus) of your burdens, let yourself feel lighter and freer."

Say: "Let's begin with the back (front) row, one person at a time please."

Note: Teacher can model this action by going first or last to toss her/his 'burdens' into the trash.

25:00   **Say:** "It's good to let go of (or turn our burdens over to Jesus). Notice that no one was harmed when you did this. Thank you!"

Ask: "What can we learn from what Jesus models for us in this situation?"

Possible Responses: We can learn that by being patient, understanding and not judging others, people are able to respond peacefully (under even harsh conditions). When we treat people as equals we show love for our neighbor.

26:00   **Ask:** "What positive servant-leader qualities did Jesus demonstrate?"

Possible Responses: Patience, kindness, compassion, listening, etc.

Ask: "What situations in our lives are similar to the situation that we just read about in this Scripture?"

Possible Responses: A group of students gathering together to intimidate another student. Students who use insults and threats to make another student feel worthless, etc. Making fun of someone, mocking students or even the teacher.

27:00   **Say:** "Class, let's take a moment and summarize what we learned from the actions of Jesus."

Possible Responses: Jesus did not criticize anyone for their choices. The only direction Jesus gave was to tell the woman "to go and sin no more." Other than that, Jesus treated everyone with patience and understanding.

28:00   **Say:** "How can we apply what we learned through role-playing the parts in this story to our classroom and be ones who spread positive ripples into our classroom community (in other words, what have we learned to help build a more positive classroom community?)"

Activity 7 Facilitator Script (continued)

<u>**TIME**</u> <u>**PROCESS**</u>

Possible Responses: We can treat each other with kindness and not judge each other. We can practice patience with our classmates instead of becoming angry or frustrated when our classmates do things that bother us, etc. Reach out to defend others.

29:00 Say: "Class, please take a few minutes and reflect on the work we have just accomplished by completing the journal reflection."

31:00 Say: "Class, thank you for participating today in the role-play and discussion to help us find more ways to build a positive environment in our classroom! You worked really hard today. Thank you for your commitment to participate in building a safer classroom and school community."

Unit 1
Comprehensive Review and Four Agreements

Purpose	
To reinforce the concepts and principles learned to promote positive actions and encourage positive ripple effects in school and at home.	
1	**Grades 4-8** Recall and recite Unit 1 concepts by completing a comprehensive review. **Standards** *(CST-DHP, CST-CFCP, CST-RR, CST-S, SST-C, SST-PPE, SST-IDI, SST-IGI, CCSS.ELA-Literacy.CCRA.SL1, CCSS.ELA-Literacy.CCRA.W1)*	***#39 Unit 1: Comprehensive Review***
2	**Grades 4-8** Reflect, process, and agree to *Unit 1* principles by signing the Four Agreements. **Standards** *(CST-DHP, CST-RR, CST-S, SST-C, SST-PPE, SST-IDI, SST-IGI, CCSS.ELA-Literacy.CCRA.W1)*	***#40 Unit 1: Four Agreements*** • If the student agrees, he/she is to sign the *Servant-Leader Four Agreements* along with the teacher, principal and a parent.

Unit 1
Comprehensive Review and Four Agreements

Facilitator Script

TIME/PREPARATION/LOGISTICS & PROCESS

10:00 PREPARATION/LOGISTICS
- Make copies and hand out *#39 Unit 1: Comprehensive Review and #40 Unit 1: Four Agreements* for grades 4-8.
- Use *#39 for instruction* written reflections on the entire unit.
- Invite students to take completed *#39 and #40* home to share with a parent.
- Ask students to return the signed agreements to class and hand into the teacher.

TIME PROCESS

0:00 **Say:** "We have learned many new things in this first Unit. Let's review what we've learned by completing a student reflection activity. Please let me know you have finished, by giving me a thumbs-up."

5:00 **Say:** "Thank you for completing this reflection. Now that you have reviewed some of what you have learned, please look over the *Four Agreements* that have just been handed out."

Say: "Let's read the *Four Agreements* out loud together."

6:00 **Say:** "Thank you!"

Ask: "Do you think you can agree to these statements?"

Expected Response: Yes!

Say: "If you agree, please sign the *Servant-Leader Four Agreements (#40 Unit 3: Four Agreements)*. I will come around and sign each of yours after you have signed it. Take the worksheet and *Four Agreements* home to share with your parents. Return both tomorrow signed by a parent. Thank you for your commitment to working together to create positive ripples and build up our classroom and school community!"

PEACE BE WITH YOU!

Unit 2
PURE IN HEART

While you are proclaiming peace with your lips, be careful to have it even more fully in your heart.

ST. FRANCIS OF ASSISI

Unit 2: Pure in Heart
Basic Premise

"Blessed are the clean of heart,
for they will see God."

Matthew 5:8

The basic premise of *Unit 2: Pure in Heart* is that Christ-like actions emanate from a benevolent heart. Nurturing one's inner life and following Jesus' example is an essential part of an open benevolent heart and a fruitful faith journey. Unfortunately, a barrage of daily distractions, onslaughts of immoral atrocities, and a mainstream society that does not embrace introspection, make sustaining a benevolent heart extremely difficult. The only saving grace is a family and faith community that models and encourages prayer, quiet meditation, and Christ-like compassion.

The absence of healthy introspection and prayer can result in negative emotional states (irritability, intolerance, impatience, etc.) that could lead to thoughtlessness, heartlessness, even the mistreatment of self and others. Mistreatment is not behavior just reserved for "bullies." All of us have said or done mean and hurtful things, which are a sign pointing to the importance of taking a prayerful pause to examine our conscience in an effort to restore our sense of compassion.

Actively engaging our youth in a faith community is critical for their moral guidance, as it is certain they will face many challenges that will test their moral compass. When we urge students to follow Christ and honor their Christian-call to servant-leadership, we also must support and equip them with the necessary tools for the journey. Having the proper tools for self-care is vital for nurturing one's spiritual journey and sustaining a benevolent heart.

Genuine self-care requires a disciplined practice of quiet meditation and prayer to healthily meet one's physical, mental, emotional, social, and spiritual needs. Mindful, thoughtful, Christ-like actions of peace and compassion are built on an intimate relationship with Jesus, who consistently models a perfect union with His Heavenly Father is an inward contemplative process of prayer, meditation, and reflection.

"Then he made the disciples get into the boat
and precede him to the other side,
while he dismissed the crowds.
After doing so, he went up on the mountain
by himself to pray.
When it was evening he was there alone."

Matthew 14: 22-23

Recognizing, accessing, and living out the true nature of one's God-given servant-leader qualities is an "inside job." *Unit 2* emphasizes important practical skills to prepare and support students in their daily spiritual care to nurture and strengthen their faith. This includes practical approaches for countering daily distractions, leading a balanced lifestyle, and underscoring the importance of belonging to a faith community.

Regular contemplative practice can strengthen intrapersonal skills that build resiliency, self-efficacy, and support the spiritual formation of a positive contributing Christian servant-leader. As Christian educators we are called to follow and teach Jesus' example as the true road map to learn about spreading pure peace and compassion toward self and others and how to be—Pure in Heart.

"May the eyes of (your)
hearts be enlightened,
that you may know
what is the hope
that belongs to His call,
what are the riches of the glory
in His inheritance
among the holy ones,"

Ephesians 1:18

"Be doers of the word and
not hearers only,
deluding yourselves."

James 1:22

Unit 2: Pure in Heart

Scope & Sequence

Overview
Authentic application of the *Peace Be With You* curriculum ideally follows the detailed lesson plans. Allow approximately 30-45 minutes per activity of classroom teacher instruction per week. Teachers are encouraged to continue *Unit 2* stress management and meditation practice throughout the school year to help students further integrate these life skills and to reinforce the importance of self-care.

Academic Calendar	Mid November Thru End of January (Weeks 8-15)				Teacher discretion on revisiting lessons/activities throughout school year.		
	Week 8	Week 9	Week 10	Week 11	Week 12	Week 13	Week 14	Week 15
Grade 4	Lesson 5 Activity 8 Living in Fast Forward Part 1	Lesson 5 Activity 8 Living in Fast Forward Part 2	Lesson 5 Activity 9 Under-standing Stress	Lesson 6 Activity 10 Stress √ — Activity 10a Medita-tion 1 — Activity 10b Post-Stress √ -	Lesson 6 Activity 11 Stress Manage-ment Skills — Activity 12 Medita-tion 2	Lesson 7 Activity 13 Affirma-tions for the Heart	Lesson 7 Activity 14 Peace Prayer St. Francis — Activity 15 Medita-tion 3	Unit 2 Comp. Review Grades 4-8 — Unit 2 4 Agreements
Grade 5								
Grade 6								
Grade 7								
Grade 8								

<u>Unit 2: Lesson Five</u>
Distracted from the Call

*"It's amazing how confused and distracted
and misdirected so many people are."*

Stephen Covey

Lesson Five Purpose

To increase awareness of how distractions and high stress can obscure our ability to "hear the call."

Lesson Five Overview

Life is full of unceasing distractions—a kaleidoscope of external and internal "noise" pushing and pulling us in ways that can overwhelm and consume our time and energy. To name a few, the unyielding entrapments of commercialism, materialism, and the irresistibility of electronic devices can split us off from the true nature of who we are called to be as Christians.

Such distractedness appears to result in a hurried, overstretched, stress-induced culture with little time or patience for contemplative practice. Contemplative practice and acquiring intrapersonal skills, such as stillness, silence, meditation, reflection or prayer, have become infrequent, even foreign. Lacking or lagging skills in this area could cause a person to experience difficulties with priorities, problem solving, and overall self-care, which in turn could result in physical, mental, emotional, social, and spiritual imbalances.

Servant-leadership can be stressful and exhausting. *Lesson Five* is an opportunity to take an honest look at our busyness and the negative consequences that can result from such a stressful pace.

Overarching Goal

The overarching goal is to become aware of when students are distracted and encourage taking time to slow down enough to hear God's call for them on their faith journey.

For further support in implementing the Peace Be With You Curriculum refer to:
Unit 2: Lesson Five Distracted from the Call in the *Teacher Curriculum Guide* for a more in-depth understanding of the importance of contemplative and intrapersonal skill building for forming successful servant-leaders.

Activity 8
Life in Fast Forward

"Desire without knowledge is not good;
and whoever acts hastily, blunders."

PROVERBS 19:2

Activity 8 Purpose
To increase awareness of how hurrying and busyness can lead to physical, mental, emotional, social, and spiritual imbalances, high-risk choices, that distract us from our call as servant-leaders and contrasting this with how a prayerful, centered, and balanced lifestyle in these five areas is more aligned with a call to Christ-centered, compassionate servant-leadership; creating positive and generative ripples in the school and beyond.

Activity 8 National Standards/Themes Correlation
Themes of Catholic Social Teachings: • Life and Dignity of the Human Person (CST-DHP) • Solidarity (CST-S) Social Studies Themes: • People, Places, and the Environment (SST-PPE) • Individual Development and Identity (SST-IDI) • Individuals, Groups, and Institutions (SST-IGI) Language Arts Speaking and Listening Standards: • Prepare for and participate effectively in a range of conversations and collaborations with diverse partners, building on others' ideas and expressing their own clearly and persuasively. (CCSS.ELA-Literacy.CCRA.SL1) Language Arts Writing Standards: • Introduce claim(s) and organize the reasons and evidence clearly. (CCSS.ELA-Literacy.CCRA.W1)

	Learning Objectives Students will be able to:	Corresponding Assessment Possibilities
1	**Grades 4-8** Recognize and list the signs of negative stress from a busy and hurried lifestyle and compare and contrast with the positive signs of a balanced life. **_Standards_** CST-DHP, SST-PPE, SST-IDI, CCSS.ELA-Literacy.CCRA.SL.1, CCSS.ELA-Literacy.CCRA.W.1	**_#41 Worksheet_** **_Living in "Fast Forward"_** • Students will complete the Living in Fast Forward worksheet, followed up by working collaboratively with a partner and class discussion.

	Learning Objectives Students will be able to:	Corresponding Assessment Possibilities
2	**Grades 4-8** Pray or recite a poem to assist in reflecting about technology. ***Standards*** CST-DHP, CST-S, SST-PPE, SST-IDI, SST-IGI, CCSS.ELA-Literacy.CCRA.SL.1	***#42 Prayers and Poem Options*** • Teacher will choose one of two prayers or a poem option that can be prayed or recited during class.
3	**Grades 4-8** Explore the upsides, downsides, and impact technology has on their stress level. ***Standards*** CST-DHP, CST-S,SST-PPE, SST-IDI, SST-IGI, CCSS.ELA-Literacy.CCRA.SL.1, CCSS.ELA-Literacy.CCRA.W1	***#43 Worksheet*** ***Jesus & Technology*** • Analyze if and how Jesus would have used electronic devices if available to spread his message.

Methodology

No doubt the pace of our world is speeding up at an exponential rate causing rapid and unprecedented change. For instance, technological advances that once took centuries, decades, or years, now occur in very short periods of time—minutes or less. Technology has exponentially increased the speed of calculations from decades to minutes and communication from months to nanoseconds. The phrase "Life in Fast Forward" is used in this context to describe how easy it is for all of us to be captivated, consumed and distracted by this accelerated pace. Life in fast-forward has become normative, forcing us into overdrive and constantly pushing us to the brink of exhaustion.

Overwhelmed by life's demands can cause an emotional cascade of irritability, agitation, intolerance, impatience, meanness, nastiness, cruelty, rudeness, anger, frustration, and so on. When we take the time to go inward to listen, these negative emotional states could be useful behavioral indicators—a "red alert" informing us that we are out of balance and should exercise self-care to restore balance. A chronic state of exhaustion however, leaves us with little energy or space for prayer and meditation to rejuvenate our spirit. Consequently, the absence of contemplative practice makes it is easy to ignore the signs and can cause one to lose their way.

Activities 8 and *9* are designed to help students take an honest look at what causes potential imbalances and the resulting consequences. This sets the stage to introduce students to skills that will help them get beyond the distractions that can interfere with hearing their call. *The Peace Be With You Program Audio* accompaniment is provided to enhance teacher instruction and student learning.

Activity 8 utilizes three worksheets for grades 4-8 to support teacher instruction and student learning on how we can become distracted from our calling. This activity is divided into Part 1 and Part 2 for two separate class periods of instruction. *Track 1* of the *Peace Be With You Program Audio* is offered as a helpful accompaniment to this activity.

For further support in implementing the Peace Be With You Curriculum refer to:
Unit 2: Lesson Five Activity 8: Living in "Fast Forward" in the *Teacher Curriculum Guide* for a more in-depth understanding of the importance of contemplative and intrapersonal skill building for forming successful servant-leaders.

Activity 8
Living in "Fast Forward"

"Some of the secret joys of living are not found
by rushing from point A to point B,
but by inventing some imaginary letters along the way."

Douglas Pagels

Facilitator Script

TIME/PREPARATION/LOGISTICS & PROCESS

ACTIVITY 8—PART 1

15:00 PREPARATION/LOGISTICS
- Download the *Peace Be With You Program Audio* to your computer or electronic device.
- Cue up Track 1 of the audio program.
- Make copies of *#41 Worksheet: "Living in "Fast Forward"* for each student.
- Pre-determine how students will pair up to create a "working team."

*Note: This activity is chunked into 2 separate class periods for expanded discussion and reflection on this important topic. Worksheets #41 and #43 for this activity can be used during class, as well as sent home, to encourage parent-child connection and bridged discussions between home and school.

TIME   PROCESS—Part 1

00:00 Say: "Class, please raise your hand if you have ever been so hurried and busy that your mood (cranky, irritable, grouchy, overwhelmed) or health (you got sick from being run down and exhausted) paid a negative price."

Expected Response: All hands will most likely be raised.

1:00   Say: "Thank you. From all of the hands raised, I can tell this is an important topic for us to focus on.

Say: "Class, let's take some time to listen to a brief lesson about how a hurried and busy pace can negatively impact our lives. Please listen carefully to this audio track and write down any thoughts about what you hear."

*(Play Track 1 of Audio Program—5:17 minutes)

7:00   Say: "Thank you for being such good listeners."

*Note: Hand out #41 Worksheet: Living in "Fast Forward" to students.

<u>TIME</u> <u>PROCESS—Part 1</u>

Say: "Class, on the worksheet being handed out, please read the prompts in the first column and list your responses to each prompt in the next column under 'My Thoughts.'
You have 10 minutes to work on this. When you are finished please sit quietly until everyone has completed their worksheet."

17:00 Say: "Now class, pair up with your team partner and decide between the two of you who will be the listener and who will be the speaker."

Say: "Listeners raise your hands. Thank you!"

Say: "Speakers raise your hands. Thank you!"

18:00 Say: "Speakers you have 2 minutes to share your worksheet responses with your partner. I will let you know when to switch. You may begin."

20:00 Say: "Thank you, that's time. Listeners thank your partner for sharing. Now the Speakers become the listeners and the listeners the speakers. You may begin."

22:00 Say: "That's time. Listeners, thank your partner for sharing."

Say: "Everyone quietly please stand. Stretch to the right. Now stretch to the left. Good! You may be seated."

23:00 Say: "Please remain in your teams. Discuss with you partner the unique ways you are similar to each other from your responses to the prompts. Fill-in your responses in the next column on your worksheet under 'Ways We Are Similar.' If you like, you can also add your partners' responses in this column along with your own. You will each have 2 minutes to complete this task. Please begin."

25:00 Say: "Thank you, that's time. Thank your partner for working with you to accomplish this task."

26:00 Say: "In your same teams, now discuss any unique differences there might be between you and your partner. Please fill-in your responses in the next column on your worksheet under 'Ways We Are Different.' Again, if you like, you can add your partners' responses in this column along with your own. You each have two minutes to complete this task. Please begin."

28:00 Say: "Thank you, that's time. Thank your partner for working with you to accomplish this task."

Say: "Thank you all for sharing in your teams and being such kind and thoughtful listeners."

Say: "Now, let's open your team discussions to the entire class. Please refer to your worksheet if you need to when your team shares with the class."

Activity 8—Part 1 Facilitator Script (continued)

TIME   PROCESS—Part 1

29:00   Ask: "What team would like to start us off to share with the class what interesting things you have learned about yourself or about your partner?"

30:00   Expected Response: A lot of enthusiasm from a number of teams to begin this class discussion.

*Note: How many teams you permit to share and the timeframe on this class discussion is at the teacher's discretion.

**Note: Ask "what, why, when, where and how" questions with entire class to help facilitate class discussion.

Say: "Thank you (Student Name) and (Student Name) for beginning our class discussion."

40:00   Say: "Teams, thank you for sharing your interesting thoughts and ideas with the class."

*Note: Depending on how many teams you permit to share, class time will vary for this activity.

Ask: "Class, overall, what have you learned about what it means to live in 'fast forward?'"

Possible Responses: Slow down! A hectic life has consequences. Being hurried and busy is stressful.

42:00   Say: "Thank you class. We will soon be learning some ways that will help us slow down to take better care of ourselves."

43:00   Say: "Hand in your worksheets, so that I can take a look at your responses to the questions and the process between you and your partner."

ACTIVITY 8—PART 2

10:00 PREPARATION/LOGISTICS
- Make one copy *#42 Prayers and Poem Options*.
- Make copies of *#43 Worksheet: Jesus & Technology* for each student.
- Pre-determine if students will pair up in the same "working team" or if you will mix it up by assigning new partners.

TIME   PROCESS—Part 2

0:00   **Say:** "Class, last week we discussed of how a hurried and busy life can cause high stress that can have many consequences that affect our lives. Technology is a wonderful tool for our lives. The use of technology can also have a downside that can contribute to the stress in our lives. Today, we are going to reflect on our use of technology and have some fun with considering what it might have been like if Jesus had technology."

*Note: From #42 Prayers and Poem Options, the teacher or a student will pray the Prayer for a Peaceful Internet, or Serenity Prayer for Technology, or recite the poem, Christ Has No Presence but Yours. Feel free to use a prayer or poem of your own.

1:00   **Say:** "Let us pray (or listen to this poem)."
        Say: "Please quietly pair up with your assigned partner."

3:00   **Say:** "You and your partner will have 10 minutes choose five of the questions and answer them together on the worksheet being handed out. When you receive your worksheet, please begin."

*Note: Handout #43 Worksheet: Jesus and Technology.

13:00   **Say:** "Time's Up! Please return to your seats."

14:00   **Say:** "Let's discuss the questions on this worksheet. As we go through the questions as a class, if you and your partner did not choose or discuss a particular question, you may still share your thoughts with the class."

*Note: It is teacher discretion on whether or not you take class time to go through each of the questions on this worksheet. Have the students share their thoughts on how Jesus may have used today's technology if it had existed during his time. Encourage all possible responses. If the students are not participating as much as you would like, share your own thoughts or use your own system of student participation.

24:00   **Say:** "Thank you for all of your wonderful discussion around this fascinating topic! I really liked the _____ tweet or the _____ #hashtag. I think those really sum-up Jesus's message while here on earth and truly reflect how Jesus may have used technology."

25:00   **Say:** "Please take this worksheet home and choose at least two questions to discuss with one of your family members. Please record what was discussed on the worksheet. I will be interested to take a look at what you and your family member think about Jesus using technology. Please hand in your worksheet tomorrow."

Activity 8—Part 2 Facilitator Script (continued)

<u>TIME</u> <u>PROCESS—Part 1</u>
26:00 Say: "Any questions? Thanks for thinking about and discussing how Jesus might have used technology! I really enjoyed our discussion and all of your wonderful, positive and creative ideas."

"Have no anxiety at all, but in everything,
by prayer and petition, with thanksgiving,
make your requests known to God."

Philippians 4:6

Activity 9
Understanding Stress

"Let nothing disturb you. Let nothing frighten you.
All things are passing. God never changes.
Patience gains all things. Who has God wants nothing.
God alone suffices."

Prayer of St. Teresa of Avila

Activity 9 Purpose
To increase awareness and understanding of the causes and effects of stress on the body, mind, spirit, and implications on one's thoughts, words and actions as a servant-leader.

Activity 9 National Standards/Themes Correlation
Themes of Catholic Social Teachings: • Life and Dignity of the Human Person (CST-DHP) • Call to Family, Community, and Participation (CST-FCP) • Solidarity (CST-S) Social Studies Themes: • People, Places, and the Environment (SST-PPE) • Individual Development and Identity (SST-IDI) • Individuals, Groups, and Institutions (SST-IGI) Language Arts Speaking and Listening Standards: • Prepare for and participate effectively in a range of conversations and collaborations with diverse partners, building on others' ideas and expressing their own clearly and persuasively. (CCSS.ELA-Literacy.CCRA.SL1) Language Arts Writing Standards: • Introduce claim(s) and organize the reasons and evidence clearly. (CCSS.ELA-Literacy.CCRA.W1) • Use technology, including the Internet, to produce and publish writing and to interact and collaborate with others. (CCSS.ELA-Literacy.CCRA.W6)

	Learning Objectives Students will be able to:	Corresponding Assessment Possibilities
1	**Grades 4-8** Compare and contrast negative and positive stress and the ripple effects each have for the classroom and school. **Standards** CST-DHP, SST-PPE, SST-IDI, SST-IGI, CCSS.ELA-Literacy.CCRA.SL.1, CCSS.ELA-Literacy.CCRA.W1	***#44 Poster Directions*** ***Negative/Positive Stress*** • Cut out five or more pictures from a magazine that represent negative stress and five or more pictures that represent positive stress. Place the negative stress pictures on half of a poster board and positive stress pictures on the other half. Share your poster with the class during a gallery walk. ***#45 Grading Rubric*** ***Neg./Pos. Stress Poster***

	Learning Objectives Students will be able to:	Corresponding Assessment Possibilities
2	**Grades 4-8** Use the guitar analogy to define stress. **_Standards_** CST-DHP, CST-FCP, SST-PPE, SST-IDI, SST-IGI, CCSS.ELA-Literacy.CCRA.SL.1, CCSS.ELA-Literacy.CCRA.W.1, CCSS.ELA-Literacy.CCRA.W.6	**_#46 Video Production_** **_Guitar Analogy Video_** • Create a Guitar Analogy Video to demonstrate low stress, high stress and perfect harmony.

Methodology

Stressors are common, especially for those who honor their call to servant-leadership. Schools rarely if ever uses class time as an opportunity to teach students about the nature of stress and important coping strategies. As a result, stress is often assumed to be a negative state we all just have to live with, rather than something we can actively manage and positively use to accomplish various tasks—such as tests, and extracurricular pursuits.

Activity 9: Understanding Stress is an opportunity to assist students in becoming more aware of, and better understand the causes and effects of, stress on the body, mind, and spirit. Using compare and contrast, students can better understand how negative and positive stress influences our thoughts, words and actions that cause ripple effects.

This activity utilizes two worksheets for grades 4-8 and a grading rubric to support teacher instruction and student learning in understanding stress. Track 2 of the *Peace Be With You Program Audio* is used as a helpful accompaniment to this activity.

For further support in implementing the Peace Be With You Curriculum refer to:
Unit 2: Lesson Five Activity 9: Understanding Stress in the *Teacher Curriculum Guide* for a more in-depth understanding of the importance of contemplative and intrapersonal skill building for forming successful servant-leaders.

Facilitator Script

Activity 9
Understanding Stress

TIME/PREPARATION/LOGISTICS & PROCESS

10:00 PREPARATION/LOGISTICS
- Cue up Track 2 of the *Peace Be With You Program Audio* from your computer or electronic device.
- Make copies of the *#44 Poster Directions* for each student.
- Make Copies of *#45 Grading Rubric: Negative/Positive Stress Poster* to assess each student.
- Make copies of the *#46 Video Production* for each student.

TIME   PROCESS
00:00 Say: "Class, we are about to listen to a brief lesson about how stress impacts our lives in both good and bad ways. Please listen carefully to this audio track and write down any thoughts about what you hear in your journal or on a piece of loose-leaf paper."

*(Play Track 2 of Audio Program—2:11 minutes)

3:00   Say: "Thank you for being such good listeners. Let's see if you can use what you have learned about stress over the past couple of weeks, including what we heard today, to create a Negative/Positive Stress Poster. Please come up to the front of the class to pick up one sheet of poster paper and one worksheet."

*Note: Use your best organizational system for each student to receive one sheet of poster paper and one hand out.

5:00   Say: "Please follow the directions to create your poster. You have 20 minutes to prepare your poster. When finished, please place your completed poster at eye level around the classroom. I will be excited to see your posters."

24:00 Say: "Please take one minute to finish up your poster and hang it up if you have not already done so."

25:00 Say: "Please stand in front of your poster (*Pause for students to stand in front of their poster*). Now step to the poster on your right. Every time I ring the bell (clap my hands, snap my fingers, etc.) you will move to the next poster on your right until you return back to your own poster. Take some time to admire each poster and remember to read the captions."

Ask: "Is everyone ready to take a gallery walk?"

Expected Response: Yes!

30:00 Say: "Thank you for creating such awesome posters and for participating in our gallery walk. Let's take a moment and see what we learned about stress in our class."

Activity 9 Facilitator Script (continued)

<u>TIME</u> <u>PROCESS</u>

Ask: "Would anyone like to share something they admired about a particular Negative/Positive Stress Poster?"

*Note: Teacher discretion on how many and how long you permit students to share what they admire about each other's poster which will cause script times to vary.

Possible responses: I have the same/similar negative stress. I didn't realize how many things can cause stress. I discovered some new ways to have positive stress in my life.

33:00 Say: "Thank you for sharing what you admire and learned during the gallery walk."

Ask: "From what you learned, what can we do to help reduce stress in our classroom and create positive ripples?

Possible responses: We can be aware of things that cause our classmates stress and try not to do those things. We can work to bring things that create positive stress for our classmates instead of negative stress. We can work to help calm each other and encourage positive deep breaths.

35:00 Say: "Thank you for all your great thoughts and ideas! Let's work on reducing negative stress and increasing positive stress together!"

Say: "Class, please take a look at this final handout for today."

*Note: Hand out #46 Video Production to students.

Say: "Please have fun with working on the Guitar Analogy Video with your assigned group. You have two weeks from today to complete this video. Do share your video with your parents before bringing it to share with the class. I look forward to seeing all of your creative work reflected in the videos. As we have time, I will share the videos I feel addressed the guidelines with the class. Thank you for your focus on how we all can reduce stress."

36:00 Say: "Thanks again for sharing your posters today. That was a lot of fun!

*Note: Teachers—it is highly recommended that you prescreen all student videos prior to classroom viewing.

Unit 2: Lesson Six
Self-Care Strategies

*"Beloved, I hope you are prospering
in every respect and are in good health,
just as your soul is prospering."*

3 John 2

Lesson Six Purpose

Students are supported in making a commitment to meditation and prayer in developing essential intrapersonal skills for self-regulation, focus, and inner peace toward becoming important agents of a safe and Christ-centered school climate.

Lesson Six Overview

In the previous unit, students are invited to recognize, examine, and develop their Christian-call to servant-leadership. As we invite and encourage students to become servant-leaders, we must acknowledge that high stress often accompanies servant-leadership. In order to fully embrace their call, it is imperative that students are taught the necessary skills for their formation in becoming positive effective Christian servant-leaders.

Lesson Six begins the process of examining, developing, and strengthening "inner assets" to develop intrapersonal skills that equip students with deeper understanding and increased capacity for self-care. Intrapersonal skill acquisition is essential in building important foundational tools to help shape, guide and strengthen one's moral compass.

Lesson Six includes multiple self-care strategies to identify, assess, and mitigate daily distractions, and high stress. Through prayerfully designed activities, teacher instruction helps students recognize and contrast distractions and personal imbalances with inner peace in personal mind, body, and spirit balance. Activities include: a baseline measurement to identify and assess their current stress level, a practice meditation, and four stress management skills to help reduce high stress.

These and similar skills are critical for self-care to recognize and become more aware of how to healthily meet physical, mental, emotional, social, and spiritual needs. Affording class time and also encouraging time outside of class in this area will bolster students' self-confidence in mind, body and spirit for a fortified and sustained role in servant-leadership. By providing frequent opportunities for student practice in self-care, we can increase the likelihood of Christ-like compassion toward self and others to create positive rippling effects for a safe and positive school climate.

Overarching Goal

With regular practice students can become more proficient and build on self-care strategies to strengthen their intrapersonal skills and contemplative discipline. Self-care strategies will also help students build resiliency, self-efficacy, and support their spiritual formation as a positive contributing servant-leader.

It is important to note that any of the meditations or prayers offered in the *Peace Be With You Christ Centered Bullying Redirect* program are not intended to replace Mass or any other Christian worship services. Part of our evangelization is to encourage and support our students' to attend at least one Mass a week to be in community and to partake in the Eucharist.

The stress management strategies in this lesson are more secular in nature; however, these skills should be taught as tools to center, focus and find a quiet, still interior for personal reflection, prayer and meditation throughout the week. Developing a stronger personal spiritual life permits a student to bring a spiritually stronger self to Liturgy and Sacraments.

For further support in implementing the Peace Be With You Curriculum refer to:
Unit 2: Lesson Six Self-Care Strategies in the *Teacher Curriculum Guide* for a more in-depth understanding of the importance of contemplative and intrapersonal skill building for forming successful servant-leaders.

> *"Rely on the mighty Lord;*
> *Constantly seek His face."*
>
> *1 Chronicles 16:11*

Activity 10
Stress Check

Activity 10 Purpose
To increase student awareness through the use of a self-assessment baseline measurement to help identify their current level of stress and in response apply the most appropriate self-care strategy.

Activity 10 National Standards/Themes Correlation
Themes of Catholic Social Teachings: • Life and Dignity of the Human Person (CST-DHP) • Rights and Responsibilities (CST-RR) Social Studies Themes: • People, Places, and the Environment (SST-PPE) • Individual Development and Identity (SST-IDI) • Individuals, Groups, and Institutions (SST-IGI) Language Arts Speaking and Listening Standards: • Prepare for and participate effectively in a range of conversations and collaborations with diverse partners, building on others' ideas and expressing their own clearly and persuasively. (CCSS.ELA-Literacy.CCRA.SL1) Language Arts Writing Standards: • Introduce claim(s) and organize the reasons and evidence clearly. (CCSS.ELA-Literacy.CCRA.W1)

	Learning Objectives Students will be able to:	Corresponding Assessment Possibilities
1	**Grades 4-8** Apply a self-assessment baseline measurement as a strategy for identifying their personal level of stress. **Standard** (CST-DHP,CST-RR, SST-PPE, SST-IDI, SST-IGI, CCCSS.ELA-Literacy.CCRA.SL1, CCSS.ELA-Literacy.CCRA.W1)	***#47 Stress Check Log*** • On the Pre-Stress Check line, students circle a number that best represents their current level of stress based on a continuum ranging from 0-10 prior to the short meditation.

Methodology

For the purposes of this curriculum, a *Stress Check* is *Self-Care Strategy #1*. The *Stress Check* is a very simple and practical self-care strategy for students to reflectively recognize personal levels of stress at any given moment. As a standalone tool, this strategy helps support the effective navigation of the many expected and unexpected circumstances students face throughout any given day.

With practice, students are able to quickly recognize their current stress level and if needed, choose from a menu of self-care strategies to help them adjust their stress level for optimum success. For instance, prior to taking a test a student uses the Stress Check and identifies being at an 8 or 9 (feels anxious—high stress).

With this awareness, the student can then apply a self-care strategy (such as the *Breath Check*) to help reduce high stress to a more manageable level that will best support him/her during the test.

The *Stress Check* can also be used as a *Pre-Post-Stress Check* for students to measure their progress toward the development and integration of this life skill. Teacher instruction uses a four-step *Stress Check* application that is detailed in *Activity 10, 10a and 10b* below.

- *Activity 10*—asks students to identify a *Pre-Stress Check* number prior to Meditation 1.

- *Activity 10a*—students experience *Meditation 1* on Track 3 *Peace Be With You Audio Program*.

- *Activity 10b*—Immediately following *Meditation 1*, students identify a *Post-Stress Check* number and apply the *Pre-Post-Stress Check Formula* to measure progress.

For example, prior to the meditation a 7th grader named "James" circles a *Pre-Stress Check* number of 7 on the continuum. Immediately following the meditation, while James is still in a relaxed state, he circles a *Post-Stress Check* number of 4. The applicable numbers are then inserted into a *Pre-Post-Stress Check Formula* to increase cognitive skill development and to integrate this self-care strategy. This very simple four-step process is shown on the next page, using "James" as an example.

EXAMPLE PRE-POST-STRESS CHECK
FIVE SIMPLE APPLICATIONS

"James—7ᵗʰ grader"

1. **PRE-STRESS CHECK (Prior to Meditation)**

   0   1   2   3   4   5   6   (7)   8   9   10
   LOW   **HIGH**

2. **MEDITATION EXPERIENCE**

3. **POST-STRESS CHECK (After Meditation)**

   0   1   2   3   (4)   5   6   7   8   9   10
   LOW   **HIGH**

4. **Applying PRE-POST-STRESS CHECK FORMULA**

   Pre-Stress Check (7) – Post-Stress Check (4) = Stress Reduction Score (3)

5. **James journals or draws about his meditation experience in class or as a homework assignment.**

These five simple applications to the *Pre-Post-Stress Check* reinforce this process as a self-care strategy, by rewarding students with a confidence-boosting experience when stress reduction is achieved. If for any reason stress reduction is not achieved during the initial pre-post-experiences, encourage continued practice to help students make progress toward the goal.

This activity utilizes one worksheet for grades 4-8 to support teacher instruction and student learning on *Skill #1 Stress Check*.

"Come to Me,
All you who labor
and are burdened,
and I will give you rest."

Matthew 11:28

Activity 10
(Pre-)Stress Check

Facilitator Script

TIME/PREPARATION/LOGISTICS & PROCESS

10:00 PREPARATION/LOGISTICS
- Draw Stress Check continuum on (board, flipchart or Smartboard).
- Make copies of *#47 Stress Check Log* for each student.
- Complete *Activity 10, 10-A, & 10-B* in sequence during one class period for a total of approximately 36-40 minutes.

TIME   PROCESS

00:00 Say: "Class, let's take a look at the *Stress Check*, which I have placed on the (board, flipchart, Smartboard).

Ask: "Does this remind you of anything we used earlier this year?"

Expected Response: Yes. The *Safety Check Line.*

Say: "You're right. This does look like our *Safety Check Line.*"

Ask: "What did the 0 and 10 represent on the *Safety Check Line*?"

Expected Response: 0 is least safe and 10 is for safest.

1:00   Say: "Yes, that's right. The numbers on the *Stress Check line* are used in a similar way. Let's take a closer look."

Say: "Class, let's take a look at the *Stress Check*, which you can see here on the (point to the *Stress Check* on the board, flipchart, Smartboard)."

2:00   Say: "This is a simple continuum line, similar to the *Safety Check Line*. On the far left (point to zero) the zero represents the lowest level of stress that you personally have ever experienced and on the far right (point to 10) is a 10 that represents the highest level of stress that you personally have ever experienced,"

NOTE: Hand out #47 Stress Check Log.

4:00   Say: "On your worksheet under the *Pre-Stress Check*, circle one number between 0 and 10 that best represents your current level of stress. Raise your hand when you have circled a number."

Say: "Thank you!"

5:00   Say: "This is your personal *Stress Check* number and you do not have to share it with anyone."

Note: Transition to the next activity: Activity 10a: Meditation 1

"For no one
can lay a foundation
other than the one
that is there,
namely, Jesus Christ."

1 Corinthians 3:11

Activity 10a
Meditation 1

Activity 10a Purpose
To increase awareness of self-regulation, by practicing quiet and stillness, while listening to a meditation that opens hearts and minds for students to hear God's call for them to servant-leadership.

Activity 10a National Standards/Themes Correlation
Themes of Catholic Social Teachings: • Life and Dignity of the Human Person (CST-DHP) • Rights and Responsibilities (CST-RR) Social Studies Themes: • People, Places, and the Environment (SST-PPE) • Individual Development and Identity (SST-IDI) • Individuals, Groups, and Institutions (SST-IGI) Language Arts Speaking and Listening Standards: • Prepare for and participate effectively in a range of conversations and collaborations with diverse partners, building on others' ideas and expressing their own clearly and persuasively. (CCSS.ELA-Literacy.CCRA.SL1)

	Learning Objectives Students will be able to:	Corresponding Assessment Possibilities
1	**Grades 4-8** Practice self-regulation by listening to an audio meditation, to reinforce stress reduction as a self-care strategy and then journal about their experience. ***Standards*** (CST-DHP, CST-RR, SST-PPE, SST-IDI, SST-IGI, CCSS.ELA-Literacy.CCRA.SL1)	***None***

Methodology

Listening to this short meditation is an exercise to encourage quiet and stillness. With practice, students can achieve a relaxed state, inner peace, and increased awareness that stress can be managed for self-control and emotional regulation. Most students have a very favorable experience; however, it is not uncommon for some students to feel a level of anxiety with this strategy because the process and experience of finding a peaceful state is so foreign.

Remember, taking time for quiet and/or stillness is not generally encouraged in our culture, which is all the more reason educators should teach this concept. By emphasizing and encouraging practice in quiet and stillness as self-care strategies, students can achieve a deep relaxed state, inner peace, and greater confidence.

There are no worksheets needed specifically for *Activity 10a Meditation 1*; however, the worksheets that precede and follow this activity are important for teacher instruction and student learning. Track 3 of the *Peace Be With You Program Audio* is an essential accompaniment to this activity.

Activity 10a
Meditation 1

Facilitator Script

TIME/PREPARATION/LOGISTICS & PROCESS

15:00 PREPARATION/LOGISTICS
- Teacher is encouraged to listen to Track 3 ahead of time (12:27 minutes).
- Cue audio to Track 3.
- Settle students prior to playing Track 3.
- Room lights are dimmed or turned off if there is enough natural light.

TIME PROCESS

6:00 Say: "Class. There are two important rules when listening to this meditation:"

*Note: Teacher discretion whether or not to post these two rules in the classroom.

Rule # 1: No talking.

Rule # 2: Do Not Disturb Your Neighbor.

Say: "Raise your hand if you agree to these rules. Thank You."

7:00 Say: "Sit comfortably in your seats during this exercise. No need to write. I invite you to just relax and listen carefully to this audio track of a person calmly guiding you through a peaceful experience, which is accompanied by gentle music. When the track is over please sit quietly without talking, until I give you the next direction."

*(Play Track 3 of Audio Program—12:27 minutes)

20:00 Say: "Welcome back. Without talking, please refer to your worksheet and circle a number on the Post-Stress Check that best represents your level of stress right now.

*Note: Teachers are encouraged to play gentle music of your choice as background when working on tasks following the audio tracks. The Peace Project: The Music, is an option.

Activity 10b
(Post-) Stress Check

Activity 10b Purpose
To increase awareness of stress by utilizing a baseline measurement tool to identify current stress level to help determine subsequent self-care strategies.

Activity 10b National Standards/Themes Correlation
Themes of Catholic Social Teachings: • Life and Dignity of the Human Person (CST-DHP) • Rights and Responsibilities (CST-RR) Social Studies Themes: • People, Places, and the Environment (SST-PPE) • Individual Development and Identity (SST-IDI) • Individuals, Groups, and Institutions (SST-IGI) Language Arts Speaking and Listening Standards: • Prepare for and participate effectively in a range of conversations and collaborations with diverse partners, building on others' ideas and expressing their own clearly and persuasively. (CCSS.ELA-Literacy.CCRA.SL1) Language Arts Writing Standards: • Introduce claim(s) and organize the reasons and evidence clearly. (CCSS.ELA-Literacy.CCRA.W1)

	Learning Objectives Students will be able to:	Corresponding Assessment Possibilities
1	**Grades 4-8** Apply a self-assessment baseline measurement to determine their personal stress level following a short meditation. ***Standards*** (CST-RR, CST-DHP, SST-PPE, SST-IDI, SST-IGI, CCSS.ELA-Literacy, CCRA.SL1, CCSS.ELA-Literacy.CCRA.W1)	***#47 Stress Check Log*** • Students refer back to this worksheet to circle a *Post-Stress Check* number that best represents their level of stress following the meditation.
2	**Grades 4-8** Reflect on the meditation through journaling or drawing about their experience. ***Standards*** (CST-RR, CST-DHP, SST-PPE, SST-IDI, SST-IGI, CCSS.ELA-Literacy, CCRA.SL1, CCSS.ELA-Literacy.CCRA.W1)	***#48 Meditation 1 Journal 1*** • Students use the worksheet to journal about their meditation experience. ****Note: Copy these worksheets back to back to allow for student option.*** ***#49 PeaceScape Drawing 1*** • Students draw an image of what peace means to them following the meditation.

Methodology

Activity 10b utilizes three worksheets. First, direct students to return to *#47 Stress Check Log*, to record their *Post-Stress Check* number following *Activity 10a Meditation 1*. The *Post-Stress Check* is applied following the meditation to compare and contrast the *Pre-Stress Check*. Following this up with the *Pre-Post-Stress Check Formula helps to* promote critical thinking.

Following Track 3 of the *Peace Be With You Program Audio*, allow time for reflection, journaling or drawing, to further nurture the experience.

Second, the next two worksheets are copied as a double-sided handout for students to select between *#48 Meditation 1 Journal 1* and *#49 PeaceScape Drawing 1*, to help them best describe their meditation experience. Encouraging journaling and/or drawing helps to build empathy skills.

Third, refer students back to *#47 Stress Check Log*, to record their *Post-Stress Check* number following *Activity 15 Meditation 3*. The *Stress Check Log* can be kept in the Leader Folder.

Thank you for opening up your heart and classroom for this important work! Permit yourself to enjoy this *Peace Be With You Program Audio* track with your students. By doing so you will benefit; and they will too from your modeling.

"When cares increase within me,
your comfort gives me joy."

Psalm 94: 19

"Do not conform yourselves to this age
but be transformed by the renewal of your mind,
that you may discern what is the will of God,
what is good and pleasing and perfect."

Romans 12:2

Activity 10b
Post-Stress Check

Facilitator Script

TIME/PREPARATION/LOGISTICS & PROCESS

15:00 PREPARATION/LOGISTICS
- Make copies of *#48 Meditation 1 Journal 1 and #49 PeaceScape Drawing 1 for students to journal or draw on.*
- Draw *Stress Check* continuum on (board, flipchart or Smartboard) for *Post-Stress Check.*
- Students refer back to *#47 Stress Check Log* to enter *Post-Stress Check* and work the *Pre-Post-Stress Check Formula.*
- Place *Pre-Post-Check Formula* on the (board, flipchart, Smartboard).

TIME   PROCESS

Say: "Class, on your worksheet under the *Post-Stress Check*, please circle one number between 0 and 10 that best represents your level of stress after the meditation. Raise your hand when you have circled a number."

28:00 Say: "Thank you! Again, this is your personal *Stress Check* number, so you do not have to share it with anyone."

Say: "Now class, take a look at the *Pre-Post-Check Formula* on the (board, flipchart, Smartboard). The formula is also on this same worksheet below the *Pre- and Post-Stress Checks.*"

Say: "Enter your *Pre-and Post-Stress Check* numbers in the formula and subtract to find your total."

29:00 Say: "Hopefully you were able to come down on your *Stress Check* number to show you have reduced your stress. If you didn't come down at all or even went up from your Pre-Stress Check number, that's okay. With practice you can reduce your stress level using this series of exercises."

30:00 Say: "There is no right or wrong answer. These are your personal *Stress Check* numbers. Everyone did super on this exercise and with practice, I am confident you will all get better and better!"

Say: "Take about 5 minutes to journal or draw) about your experience on the journal (or *PeaceScape*) worksheet."

35:00 Say: "Please finish writing your last sentence (or pause your drawing). If you would like to journal (or draw) more, please feel free to do so at home."

36:00 Say: "Thank you class!"

Activity 11
Stress Management Skills

Activity 11 Purpose
To further develop intrapersonal skills with additional stress management tools that increase awareness to support student focus, self-regulation and peace building.

Activity 11 National Standards/Themes Correlation
Themes of Catholic Social Teachings: • Life and Dignity of the Human Person (CST-DHP) • Solidarity (CST-S) Social Studies Themes: • People, Places, and the Environment (SST-PPE) • Time, Continuity, and Change (SST-TCC) Language Arts Speaking and Listening Standards: • Prepare for and participate effectively in a range of conversations and collaborations with diverse partners, building on others' ideas and expressing their own clearly and persuasively. (CCSS.ELA-Literacy.CCRA.SL1) Language Arts Writing Standards: • Introduce claim(s) and organize the reasons and evidence clearly. (CCSS.ELA-Literacy.CCRA.W1)

	Learning Objectives Students will be able to:	Corresponding Assessment Possibilities
1	**Grades 4-8** *Apply four skills as self-care strategies to increase awareness or stress reduction for better focus and self-regulation to enhance academic and extra-curricular pursuits.* ***Standards*** (CST-S, SST-PPE, CCSS.ELA-Literacy.CCRA.W1)	***#50 Worksheet*** ***Stress Management Skills*** • Apply four skills to build self-care strategies for managing stress.
2	**Grades 4-8** *List four self-care strategies and explain how one or more can be used daily to support intrapersonal skill development.* ***Standards*** <ins>(CST-S, SST-PPE, CCSS.ELA-Literacy.CCRA.W1)</ins>	***#51 Worksheet*** ***Taking Good Care of Myself*** • List four self-care strategies and write about using one or more on a daily basis to support inner peace and self-care.

Methodology

Activity 11 instructs students on three additional strategies for further support in stress management and intrapersonal skill development. In the preceding *Activity 10, 10a* and *10b*, students received instruction on **Skill #1: Stress Check**.

To introduce students to the three remaining stress management strategies, *Activity 11* is chunked into three skills; **Skill #2: Breath Check, Skill #3: Tension Check** and **Skill #4: Balance Check**. The facilitator script for this activity incorporates the three skills as one instructed activity, during one class period, for a total of approximately 30 minutes. Self-care skills #2, #3, and #4 are discussed below.

With increased awareness of personal stress patterns, students can successfully apply all four of the stress management strategies (*Stress Check, Breath Check, Tension Check, & Balance Check*) to support their mental, physical, emotional, social, and spiritual growth.

Activity 11 utilizes two worksheets to support teacher instruction and student learning on essential skills in stress management. Track 4 of the *Peace Be With You Program Audio* is a helpful accompaniment to this activity.

Activity 11
Stress Management Skills

Prayer of St. Augustine

Breathe into me, Holy Spirit,
that my thoughts may all be holy.

Move in me, Holy Spirit,
that my work, too, may be holy.

Attract my heart, Holy Spirit,
that I may love only what is holy.

Strengthen me, Holy Spirit,
that I may defend all that is holy.

Protect me, Holy Spirit,
that I may always be holy.

*Note: Reminder—The __STRESS CHECK__ is __SKILL #1__.

BREATH CHECK—SKILL #2

Conscious and intentional breathing is simply breathing low into the diaphragm or low abdomen. This low breathing—often called "belly breaths"—helps students increase serotonin levels and other calming chemicals to obtain a more relaxed state.

Breath and Spirituality

Theologian and storyteller John Shea has a wonderful story where he asks the question: What is the most important part of our body? Invite students to answer this question letting them know that all their answers are correct. The most common answers will be the soul, the heart, or the mind. Thank students for their input.

Share with students that the most important part of their body for today is their nose! After the laughter has subsided, ask them why the nose might be the most important part of their body. Share that all answers are correct. The most important response will be "without breathing, we will die."

Then share Scripture verse, Genesis 2:7, "The Lord God formed man out of the clay of the ground and blew into his nostrils the breath of life, and so man became a living being." This Scripture recalls the sacred touch of God's mouth to man's nostrils. Invite the students to sit up straight with their feet firmly on the ground. Have them close their eyes and breathe deeply through the nose. Now have them imagine God's mouth is blowing air into their nostrils filling their lungs with His breath. As they exhale, have them imagine they are breathing out God's love around the classroom, the school, the community, and the world.

TENSION CHECK—SKILL #3

Everyone experiences tension in a variety of places on the body at various times throughout the day. During times of increased stress or distress these "tension spots" can become even more pronounced. Mostly subjective, tension spots are commonly reported to show up in such areas as the head (temples, forehead or back of head) jaw, neck, shoulders, and low back. Becoming more attuned to the body by listening to personal "stress cues" or "stress indicators" makes these tension spots important messengers for self-care.

This "Tense and Release" exercise can help students become more aware of physical stress. When overly tight or tense (high stress), one is likely experience a decrease in academic or extra-curricular performance. When overly loose (low stress), performance in these areas can decrease. Tension can be an important signal to help gain insight and awareness about the body and how to apply self-care strategies for improved performance. By tracking or listening these tension spots, one can communicate the encouragement to let go or get moving! By ignoring or medicating tension spots; hoping they will "go away" we kill the messenger.

With the *Tension Check* strategy students practice intentional tensing and releasing to become more aware of how to mitigate tension spots that may inhibit successful academic and extra-curricular performance. Tensing and releasing in an exaggerated way brings a focused attention to how a particular area of the body is supporting or inhibiting overall performance. Students will increase body and tension awareness by holding and exaggerating the tension for 10-20 seconds and then releasing to experience a more relaxed state of "letting go" with that area of the body.

By juxtaposing the two physical states (tension and relaxation), students experience a dramatic contrast, which is recorded consciously and unconsciously as "muscle memory." With practice, students will become more aware of where they hold tension.

BALANCE CHECK—SKILL #4

The *Balance Check* compares and contrasts balance and imbalance. This exercise uses the body as a metaphor to first demonstrate how high stress can cause our lives to get out of balance, often leading to negative consequences for the mind, body and spirit. Secondly, the metaphor demonstrates mind, body, and spirit benefits to balance. Instruction on the metaphor of physical imbalance juxtaposed with the metaphor of physical balance results in "muscle memory" to increase awareness of personal stress, reinforcing the importance of maintaining a balanced lifestyle for physical, emotional, social, and spiritual well-being.

In this exercise, students are directed to stand with feet shoulder width apart and toes pointing straight ahead. The spine is straight and long. With hands and arms at their side, this "base position" is a powerful leader posture that can give students a feeling of strength, confidence and balance. In Yoga, base position is often called the "Mountain Pose." When students are in base position or Mountain Pose, emphasize the importance of leading a balanced life.

When balanced, the body is more immune to illness, more resistant to peer pressure, more likely to use good judgment and more likely to have better academic and extracurricular outcomes.

To juxtapose base position, students are asked to lift one leg to represent imbalance. Begin by asking students to only slightly lift one leg and eventually progress to a higher more difficult leg lift. This action symbolizes that most of us can manage small amounts of stress, which may even be helpful in performing tasks. However, with increased stress, one is more at risk for a potential "fall" (real and metaphoric).

A "fall" for the purposes of this exercise means a person is more susceptible to negative peer pressure and poor decision making. When students are in the imbalanced position, emphasize that when our lives are out of balance, we are much more susceptible to illness, negative peer pressure, poor decision making, as well as poor academic and extracurricular outcomes.

PRECAUTION: The object of the Balance Check exercise is not intended to get students to actually fall. The object is only to have them experience a very brief period of being off balance to demonstrate the lesson. Let students know that you do not want anyone to fall or get hurt from this exercise. If at any time you see a student struggling with lifting their leg to any height in which they appear to be losing balance that could in a way that could result in a fall, immediately ask the entire class to come back to base position.

Activity 11
Stress Management Skills

Facilitator Script

TIME/PREPARATION/LOGISTICS & PROCESS

20:00 PREPARATION/LOGISTICS
- Download the *Peace Be With You Program Audio* to your computer or electronic device.
- Cue up Track 4 of the audio program.
- Make copies of *#50 & #51 Worksheets* for each student.
- Post the *Prayer of St. Augustine* or one or more of the following quotes as visuals for your classroom:

    1. *"Smile, breathe and go slowly."*
         THICH NHAT HANH
    2. *"Focusing on the act of breathing clears the mind of all daily distractions and clears our energy enabling us to better connect with the Spirit within."*
         AUTHOR UNKNOWN
    3. *"For breath is life, and if you breathe well you will live long on earth."*
         SANSKRIT PROVERB
    4. *"Tension is who you think you should be. Relaxation is who you are."*
         CHINESE PROVERB
    5. *"If your teeth are clenched and your fists are clenched, your lifespan is probably clenched."*
         ADABELLA RADICI
    6. *"Be aware of wonder. Live a balanced life—learn some and think some and draw and paint and sing and dance and play and work every day some."*
         ROBERT FULGHUM

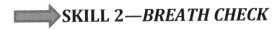 **SKILL 2—BREATH CHECK**

TIME   PROCESS
00:00 Say: "When stressed out, anxious or worried, we often breathe way up here." (With an open hand, motion across your upper chest.)

Say: "This is called high or shallow breathing. This kind of breathing releases what are called fight or flight chemicals that signal to the brain that we are in some danger."

1:00 Say: "Fight or flight is very important if there were actually a real danger present. If we were threatened by an animal, person, or a situation that could cause us harm, fight or flight is activated to help us survive."

Say: "Fight or flight helps us run faster, jump higher, or do whatever we need to do to take care of ourselves and survive the danger."

<u>**TIME**</u> <u>**PROCESS—Skill 2-*Breath Check***</u>

2:00   **Say:** "Most of the time we are safe. When we breathe high or shallow because of stress, it can trick our brain into believing there is danger and trigger fight or flight even though no danger is present. This 'false alarm' causes even more stress!"

Say: "This means that we can actually cause ourselves to feel stressed out, anxious, and worried when we really don't need to. In a previous lesson we talked about how business and being hurried can increase stress. This state can also trigger fight or flight."

3:00   **Say:** "One of the things we can do is practice breathing in a way that can help us reduce stress."

Say: "We learned that high or shallow breathing can cause us to feel more stressed."

Ask: "How can our breath be used to reduce stress and slow down?"

Possible Responses: Don't know. Breathe slower. Breathe into the abdomen/belly/stomach.

4:00   **Say:** "Very good! The kind of breathing we are going to practice is a slow, intentional breath that helps slow us down. For fun, we can call these 'belly breaths.'"

Say: "Place a hand on your belly and breathe in with me slow and low." (As you say this, place one or two of your open hands on your low abdomen.)

Say: "Hold it….Hold it….Hold it….and exhale slowly and completely."

5:00   **Say:** "Let's try it again. Take in another slow belly breath in. Notice your hand rise when you inhale. Now exhale noticing your hand fall with your breathe out."

Say: "If your hands do not rise and fall with your breath, it may mean that you are breathing high or shallow into the upper chest."

6:00   **Say:** "Breathing low takes some practice, but I noticed that you all did very well with this."

*Note: Transition to the Tension Check

**Note: Students can stand or be seated for this activity.

➡ SKILL 3—*TENSION CHECK*

TIME   PROCESS (continued)

Say: "When stressed we hold tension in different places in the body— like the jaw, shoulders, and low back."

7:00   **Say:** "If we ignore this tension, it can hurt our body and hurt our performance on test and in other activities."

Say: "It's important to learn how to relax the body to help improve our performance on test and other activities, and be more open to God."

Say: "Let's practice to help our body to know the difference between tension and relaxation."

8:00   **Say:** "Hold your two hands straight out in front of you without bothering your neighbor." (Demonstrate as you say this.)

Say: "Now make two fists and feel the tension in your hands. Really exaggerate and hold the tension in your hands. Make a mental note: 'This is tension in my hands.' Look at your fist. See and feel the tension."

9:00   **Ask:** "What do you notice as you look at your hands?"

Possible Responses: Hands and fingers are discolored. Feel a tingling sensation in hands. Hands get sweaty.

10:00 **Say:** "Continue to look at your fists. Now, very slowly and gently open both hands—like a flower unfolding—notice the releasing sensation. Notice how your hands feel as you let go of the tension."

Say: "Wiggle your fingers (hold two hands up palms out wiggling 10 fingers) to exaggerate the release and freedom from the tension."

11:00 **Say:** "Now say to yourself, 'This is relaxation!'"

Ask: "What do you notice in your hands now?"

Possible Responses: Aaahhh! Better! Not so tight! More comfortable. More relaxed.

12:00 **Say:** "This letting go sensation is relaxation! That's all relaxation is—just letting go!—loosening the grip!"

Say: "Let's do another tension release exercise."

<u>TIME</u>   <u>PROCESS—Skill 3-*Tension Check*</u>

Say: "Shrug your shoulders." (Demonstrate as you say this.) Hold this tension in your neck and shoulders making a mental note that this is tension I am holding in my neck and shoulders."

13:00 Say: "Hold the shrug a little longer noticing the tension."

Ask: "What do you notice in your neck and shoulders?"

Possible Responses: Feel a tingling sensation. Feels tight. Feels uncomfortable.

14:00 Say: "Now slowly and gently drop your shoulders to their normal base position and notice the releasing sensation. Observe how your neck and shoulders feel as you let go of the tension."

Say: "Make a mental note: 'This is relaxation!' Gently roll your head from side to side allowing yourself to feel the freedom from the release of tension." (Demonstrate as you say this.)

15:00 Say: "Good job!"

*Optional. Have students tense the entire body from head to toe and then release. Discuss how this option compares with exercises one and two.

*Note: Transition to the Balance Check.

➡️ SKILL 4—BALANCE CHECK

<u>00:00</u>   <u>PREPARATION/LOGISTICS</u>
- Predetermine if this activity will work in your classroom or should be moved to another suitable space.
- If necessary prearrange the classroom for an open space or for another space free of any hazardous obstacles.
- Make sure there is ample space between students.
- If you move the class to another location allow for transition time.
- Ensure students are physically safe, especially when demonstrating imbalance.
- Create an environment conducive to playfulness and learning, yet emphasizing safety.

<u>TIME</u>   <u>PROCESS (continued)</u>

Say: "Balance is like having both feet firmly planted on the ground while standing straight and tall."

*Note: If you have any students who cannot stand or for whom balancing may be a safety concern, include them in this exercise from a seated position. This will model inclusiveness to the class.

Activity 11 Facilitator Script (Continued)

TIME   PROCESS—Skill 4-Balance Check

16:00 Say: "Balance is also sitting up straight and tall with feet firmly planted on the floor."

Note: If needed, facilitator can demonstrate balance in both standing and seated positions.

Say: "This is balance! (Demonstrate as you say this.) This is called 'base position,' which is both feet planted firmly, standing as straight as possible or for those that need to remain seated sitting up straight and tall with feet firmly planted on the ground." (*Have students get into base position.*)

17:00 Say: "Allow yourself to quietly feel the strength and confidence of this posture." (Pause for a moment to allow students to experience base position. Suggest to students the option of closing their eyes to eliminate distractions and to connect fully.)

Say: "Whenever you want to feel strength and confidence go to your base position."

18:00 Say: "Stress is like lifting one foot off the floor." (If needed; say to students seated): "Stress is like tilting your head to one side or the other."

Note. If needed, facilitator can demonstrate imbalance in both the standing and seated positions.

Say: "Notice how lifting your foot is different from base position."

19:00 Ask: "What do you notice?" Echo their responses.

Possible Responses: More stress on the leg holding up the other. Body shifts to the right or the left. Head feels heavier. Feel off balance. (You will get a variety of responses).

20:00 Ask: "If we had to keep our foot off the floor or our head tilted for a long period of time (a sustained stressful event), what would we do to adapt to this situation?"

Possible responses: Hold on to something or someone. Physically adjust our balance by leaning to one side. Live with the discomfort/pain or try to get back to base position.

21:00 Say: "Whatever the adjustment, there are many problems that could occur."

Ask: "What might some of these problems be?"

Possible responses: Relying on an object or person for support. Physical problems in parts of the body may show up. Turning to alcohol, tobacco, or other drugs to medicate the pain. Having to work harder to get back to base position, because of lots of stress.

22:00 Ask: "What is the price we pay for ignoring our signs of stress?"

Possible response: Things get worse, not better.

TIME   PROCESS—Skill 4-Balance Check

Say: "Lift one foot/leg even higher off the floor and notice the difference between this and base position."

23:00 Say: "Those of you that are seated, tilt your head to one side along with your body and notice the difference between this and your base position."

Say: "Increasing stress is like having to lift your foot higher off the ground or your body begins to move with the head."

24:00 Say: "Come back to base position."

Ask: "How long can we realistically maintain one foot off the floor or keep our head tilted to one side?

*Note. Allow students to safely struggle with the imbalance while you discuss this point for greater impact.

Say: "Notice the difference between balance and being off balance."

Say: "Come back to base position."

25:00 Say: "This may not seem hard at first, but if we had to hold this position for a period of time it only gets harder."

Ask: "How is this like real life stress?" (*Echo their responses.*)

26:00 Say: "We can't be out of balance very long before we start paying a price." The bigger the stress and the longer it lasts, the greater the price we pay."

Say: "This is why it is so important that we take care of ourselves everyday and do our best to maintain a balanced life!"

Ask: "While you were off balance, would it be harder or easier for someone or something to push you over all the way?"

Expected Response: Very easy.

27:00 Ask: "Would it be harder or easier to push you over in base position?"

Expected Response: Harder.

Say: "When a person is off balance, what are some negative influences that might seep in?" Possible responses: Abuse of alcohol, tobacco, other drugs, peer pressure, more susceptible to colds, flu, infections, disease.

TIME PROCESS—Skill 4-Balance Check

28:00 Ask: "In what physical position are we more prepared to deal with these outside influences?"

Expected response: Base position.

Ask: "Why?" (*Echo their responses.*)

Say: "When we are balanced in mind, body, and spirit, we are less susceptible to outside influences that can be harmful to us."

29:00 Ask: "Who can tell me what 'inoculation' means?" (If students do not know, have them look it up in the dictionary.)

Ask: "How can maintaining balance inoculate us from these outside influences?"

Possible responses: Boost the immune system, happier, less negative conflict, lower blood pressure, etc.

30:00 Say: "If you are feeling out of sorts on any given day, get into base position for a minute or so, to help yourself find balance."

"Come to me, all you who labor and are burdened,[b] and I will give you rest. 29 [c]Take my yoke upon you and learn from me, for I am meek and humble of heart; and you will find rest for yourselves.

"Come to me,
all you who labor and are burdened,
and I will give you rest.
Take my yoke upon you and learn from me,
for I am meek and humble in heart;
and you will find rest for yourselves."

Matthew 11: 28-29

Activity 12
Mediation 2

Activity 12 Purpose
To experience a meditation for the application and reinforcement of four stress management strategies from previous activities, to further integrate intrapersonal skill development.

Activity 12 National Standards/Themes Correlation

Themes of Catholic Social Teachings:
   • Life and Dignity of the Human Person (CST-DHP)
   • Solidarity (CST-S)
Social Studies Themes:
   • People, Places, and the Environment (SST-PPE)
   • Time, Continuity, and Change (SST-TCC)
Language Arts Speaking and Listening Standards:
   • Prepare for and participate effectively in a range of conversations and collaborations with diverse partners, building on others' ideas and expressing their own clearly and persuasively. (CCSS.ELA-Literacy.CCRA.SL1)
Language Arts Writing Standards:
   • Introduce claim(s) and organize the reasons and evidence clearly. (CCSS.ELA-Literacy.CCRA.W1)

	Learning Objectives Students will be able to:	Corresponding Assessment Possibilities
1	**Grades 4-8** Apply a self-assessment baseline measurement to determine their personal stress level following a short meditation. **Standards** (CST-RR, CST-DHP, SST-PPE, SST-IDI, SST-IGI, CCSS.ELA-Literacy, CCRA.SL1, CCSS.ELA-Literacy.CCRA.W1)	**#47 Stress Check Log** • Students refer back to this worksheet to circle a Post-Stress Check number that best represents their level of stress following the meditation.
2	**Grades 4-8** Reflect on the meditation through journaling or drawing about their experience. **Standards** (CST-RR, CST-DHP, SST-PPE, SST-IDI, SST-IGI, CCSS.ELA-Literacy, CCRA.SL1, CCSS.ELA-Literacy.CCRA.W1)	**#52 Meditation 2 Journal 2** • Students use the worksheet to journal about their meditation experience. *Note: Copy these worksheets back to back to allow for student option.* **#53 PeaceScape Drawing 2** • Students draw an image of what peace means to them following the meditation.

Methodology

Activity 12 Meditation 2 incorporates all four self-care stress management strategies (*Skill #1: Stress Check, Skill #2: Breath Check, Skill #3: Tension Check and Skill #4: Balance Check*). Track 5 of the *Peace Be With You Audio Program* allows for an extended time to practice these skills and to experience a deeper state of relaxation. This exercise will reinforce and help to further integrate these essential life skills.

Three worksheets are utilized in this activity. First, direct students to a clean copy of *#47 Stress Check Log*, to record their *Pre-*and *Post-Stress Check* numbers following *Activity 12 Meditation 2*.

Following Track 5 of the *Peace Be With You Program Audio*, allow time for reflection, journaling or drawing, to further nurture the experience.

Second, the next two worksheets are copied as a double-sided handout for students to select between *#52 Meditation 2 Journal 2* and *#53 PeaceScape Drawing 2*, to help them best describe their meditation experience. Encouraging journaling and/or drawing helps to build empathy skills.

Third, refer students back to *#47 Stress Check Log*, to record their *Post-Stress Check* number following *Activity 15 Meditation 3*. The *Stress Check Log* can be kept in the Leader Folder.

Thank you for opening up your heart and classroom for this important work! Permit yourself to enjoy this *Peace Be With You Program Audio* track with your students. By doing so you will benefit; and they will too from your modeling.

Activity 12
Meditation 2

Facilitator Script

TIME/PREPARATION/LOGISTICS & PROCESS

10:00 PREPARATION/LOGISTICS
- Make copies of *#47 Stress Check Log, #52 Meditation 2 Journal 2, & #53 PeaceScape Drawing 2* for grades 4-8.
- Students sit quietly at their desks for the duration of this exercise. It is at the Teacher's discretion whether or not to permit students to lie down on the floor.
- If acceptable, permit students to lie down on carpeted floor and bring in a head pillow for this exercise.
- Listen to Track 5 prior to exercise.
- Room lights dimmed or off with enough natural light.
- Cue audio to Track 5.
- Settle students and begin playing Track 5.

TIME   PROCESS
00:00 Ask: "Class. Who can tell me the two important rules from our first meditation exercise?

> **Expected Response:** Rule # 1: No talking. Rule # 2: Do Not Disturb Your Neighbor. (If students do not remember either rule, reiterate these rules for them.

1:00   Say: "Raise your hand if you agree to these rules. Thank You."

Note: Hand out #47 Stress Check Log.

> **Say:** "Class. On the *Stress Check Log*, go to the *Pre-Stress Check* and circle your current level of stress. (Allow 10 seconds)

2:00 Say: "Thank you."

> **Say:** "The track you are about to hear is similar, but a little longer than the first meditation. Sit comfortably in your seats (or you can find a place on the floor to lie down.)"

3:00   Say: "There is no need to write during this exercise. Just relax and listen carefully to the audio track. When the track is over sit quietly without talking, until I give you the next direction."

(Play Track 5 of Audio Program—28:54 minutes)

32:00 Say: "Welcome back."

> **Say:** "Please refer back to your *Stress Check log* and on the *Post-Stress Check* circle your current level after this meditation." (Allow 10 seconds)

Activity 12 Facilitator Script (Continued)

<u>**TIME**</u> <u>**PROCESS**</u>

33:00 **Say:** "Please raise your hand if you were able to reduce your stress by at least one point. Good! Keep practicing."

34:00 **Say:** "Now, without talking, stand up. Stretch to the left. Stretch to the right." (Demonstrate this or some other movement.)

34:00 **Say:** "Good job everyone. I can see and feel God's Peace from all of you."

Say: "You now have two options for the remainder of the class. With Option #1 (#52) you will journal about your meditation experience. With Option #2, draw a *PeaceScape* of your experience with this meditation. Either option you choose can be completed on the handout on your desk."

50:00 **Say:** "Please complete the option of your choice in silence. You have until the end of the period. If you are finished before others, please sit quietly or find something to read or another assignment to complete."

*Note: If the teacher permits the entire class period for students to complete one of the two options, the 50:00 minute class period at the end of this script is arbitrary. Please adjust to match the actual timeframe of your scheduled class period.

Unit 2: Lesson Seven
Spiritual Formation through Prayer & Meditation

*"But He would withdraw
to deserted places and pray."*

Luke 5:16

Lesson Seven Purpose

To deepen students spiritual awareness through prayer and meditations by strengthening their relationship to Christ in order to build empathy and compassion for self and others.

Lesson Seven Overview

Unit 1 and the previous lessons and activities in *Unit 2* are a culmination of exercises in student formation. *Lesson Seven* takes students deeper into spiritual formation through the use of prayer and meditation to strengthen their relationship to Christ, by touching their hearts and minds to build empathy and compassion.

Lesson Seven begins with *Activity 13: Affirmations for the Heart*, to touch the hearts and minds of students as a reminder of Christ's love and compassion. *Activity 14*: *St. Francis of Assisi Prayer* is an examination of this profound prayer and the relevance of each element for our daily lives.

The *Peace Be With You Program Audio* completes *Unit 2* with *Activity 15: Meditation 3*. This meditation is a brief Christ-centered retreat to help students build and strengthen their relationship with Christ. Any and all of *Unit 2* can be revisited throughout the school year to reinforce and enhance the important concepts and principles in spiritual formation.

Again, it is important to note that any of the meditations or prayers offered in the *Peace Be With You Christ Centered Bullying Redirect* program are not intended to replace Mass or any other Christian worship services. Attendance to Mass in community is important for our faith journey to partake in the Eucharist as well as our own personal prayer and meditation throughout the week.

Overarching Goal

The overarching goal of this lesson is to deepen students' faith journey, by providing a safe and spiritual classroom as an invitation to open their heart and mind to Christ.

For further support in implementing the Peace Be With You Curriculum refer to:
Unit 2: Lesson Seven in the *Teacher Curriculum Guide* for a more in-depth understanding of the importance of contemplative and intrapersonal skill building for forming successful servant-leaders.

> ***"Call to me, and I will answer you; I will tell you great
> things beyond the reach of your knowledge."***
>
> ***Jeremiah 33:3***

> ***"Silence is the strength of our interior life....
> If we fill our lives with silence,
> then we will live with hope."***
>
> ***Thomas Merton***

Activity 13
Affirmations for the Heart

Activity 13 Purpose
To touch students hearts and minds by strengthening and affirming them in the love of Christ.

Activity 13 National Standards/Themes Correlation
Themes of Catholic Social Teachings: • Life and Dignity of the Human Person (CST-DHP) • Solidarity (CST-S) Social Studies Themes: • People, Places, and the Environment (SST-PPE) • Time, Continuity, and Change (SST-TCC) Language Arts Speaking and Listening Standards: • Prepare for and participate effectively in a range of conversations and collaborations with diverse partners, building on others' ideas and expressing their own clearly and persuasively. (CCSS.ELA-Literacy.CCRA.SL1) Language Arts Writing Standards: • Introduce claim(s) and organize the reasons and evidence clearly. (CCSS.ELA-Literacy.CCRA.W1)

	Learning Objectives Students will be able to:	Corresponding Assessment Possibilities
1	**Grades 4-8** Listen to affirmation to build empathy and strengthen their faith and hope in Christ. ***Standards*** (CST-S, CST-DHP, SST-TCC, SST-PPE, CCSS.ELA-Literacy.CCRA.SL.1, CCSS.ELA-Literacy.CCRA.W1)	***#54 Worksheet*** ***My Heart Affirmation*** • Students write down meaningful words recalled from listening to the meditation and craft a personal affirmation statement using the words chosen.

Methodology

Activity 13: Affirmations for the Heart, includes over 30 affirmations found on the *Peace Be With You Audio Program* and in written script (*See Appendix I: Affirmations for the Heart*). These Christ-centered affirmations are intended to touch the hearts and minds of students by strengthening and affirming them in the love of Christ. Each affirmation is stated in the first person and repeated in the third person to enhance listening and spiritual deepening from two different vantage points.

Following *Peace Be With You Program Audio* track 5, students are invited to write down on *#54 Worksheet My Heart Affirmation,* the most meaningful words they recall. Using their chosen words, students then craft a personal affirmation statement.

Students will receive the most benefit and have more ownership, by choosing and writing down words recalled from the meditation to create a personal affirmation statement.

A logical next step is to invite students to verbally share their personal heart affirmation with the class. This can be a powerful way to solidify the message and build student confidence in the process. However, such an exercise should only commence as voluntary and at teacher discretion.

Familiarizing yourself with your students' affirmations, can be a great way to make a personal connection with them. With student permission, a teacher can remind and reinforce the essence of his/her message, to offer hope and strength when needed.

Teachers are encouraged to repeat this audio track at any time throughout the school year, as a touchstone experience.

"Then the peace of God
that surpasses all understanding
will guard your hearts
and minds in Christ Jesus."

Philippians 4:7

Activity 13
Affirmations for the Heart

Facilitator Script

TIME/PREPARATION/LOGISTICS & PROCESS

30:00 PREPARATION/LOGISTICS
- Teacher is encouraged to listen to audio Track 6 ahead of time.
- Make copies of *#54 Worksheet: My Heart Affirmation.*
- Cue audio to Track 6.
- Settle students prior to playing Track 6.
- Room lights are dimmed or turned off if there is enough natural light.
- Hand out *#54 Worksheet: My Heart Affirmation* after students listen to Track 6.

TIME PROCESS

00:00 Ask: "Class, who can tell me our two rules when listening to an audio track?"

Expected Response: Rule # 1: No talking. Rule # 2: Do Not Disturb Your Neighbor.

1:00 Say: "Yes. Thank You."

Ask: "Does anyone know what an affirmation statement is?"

Possible Response: Don't know. A statement affirming something or someone.

2:00 Say: "Yes, the affirmation statements we are about to listen to are a kind and gentle reminder that we are all Children of God and to help affirm and strengthen us in our faith."

Say: "I invite you to open your hearts and minds to really take to heart what is said."

3:00 Say: "Please sit comfortably in your seats during this exercise. No need to write. Just let yourself relax and listen carefully to this audio track of a person calmly guiding you through the affirmation statements that are accompanied by gentle music. When the track is over please sit quietly without talking, until I give you the next direction."

*(Play Track 6 of Audio Program—12:40 minutes)

17:00 Say: "Welcome back. Without talking, please take a look at the worksheet that is being handed out. *(Pause until each student has received #54 Worksheet.)* Write down any words that stood out or touched you in some way during the affirmations. You do not have to recall the actual affirmation statement; only capture words that were meaningful for you." *(Allow 2-3 minutes for students to write their words.)*

28:00 Say: "Class, please take the words you have written down and put them together to craft your own personal affirmation statement. Write your special words and your affirmation on the worksheet." *(Allow 5 minutes for students to craft their affirmation.)*

TIME   PROCESS

33:00 Say: "This is a great starting point. Your heart affirmation may change over time. That's okay. Feel free to revise it whenever you like. Remember to create a decorative display, or simply write down your Heart Affirmation on a poster, post-it, or blank index card, so you can read it as often as you like for encouragement."

Optional: Ask: "Would anyone like to share their affirmation statement by reading it out loud to the class?"

*Note: You may get a handful of students to read and you may not get any volunteers at all. Whatever the outcome is okay.

35:00 Say: "Thank you (<u>name of student</u>) for sharing your very thoughtful affirmation statement with us."

*Note: Repeat the above script in your own words for any other students who share their affirmation statement.

36:00 Say: "So good to see you all working so hard on this! Please take your affirmation statement home to share it with your parents. Have a parent sign it and turn it in tomorrow so that I can read your work too."

*Note: The end time on this activity will depend on whether or not you use the option to have students share their affirmation statement.

Activity 14
The Peace Prayer of St. Francis

Activity 14 Purpose
To analyze and immerse students in *The Peace Prayer of St. Francis* through reading, reflecting, writing, and singing this prayer, to increase awareness of an actionable step they can take to be an instrument of peace at home and school.

Activity 14 National Standards/Themes Correlation
Themes of Catholic Social Teachings: • Life and Dignity of the Human Person (CST-DHP) • Solidarity (CST-S) Social Studies Themes: • People, Places, and the Environment (SST-PPE) • Individual Development and Identity (SST-IDI) • Individuals, Groups, and Institutions (SST-IGI) • Time, Continuity, and Change (SST-TCC) Language Arts Speaking and Listening Standards: • Prepare for and participate effectively in a range of conversations and collaborations with diverse partners, building on others' ideas and expressing their own clearly and persuasively. (CCSS.ELA-Literacy.CCRA.SL1) Language Arts Writing Standards: • Introduce claim(s) and organize the reasons and evidence clearly. (CCSS.ELA-Literacy.CCRA.W1)

	Learning Objectives **Students will be able to:**	**Corresponding Assessment Possibilities**
1	**Grades 4-8** Read, analyze and interpret *The Peace Prayer of St. Francis.* ***Standard*** CST-S, CST-DHP, SST-PPE, SST-IDI, CCSS.ELA-Literacy.CCRA.W1	***#55 The Peace Prayer*** • Students will check one prayer-line that holds the most meaning and use the verse to write a relevant example illustrating one way they can be an instrument of peace at home and school.
2	**Grades 4-8** Sing along to *The Peace Prayer of St. Francis.* ***Standard*** CST-S, CST-DHP, SST-PPE, SST-IDI, SST-IGI, SST-TCC, CCSS.ELA-Literacy.CCRA.SL.1, CCSS.ELA-Literacy.CCRA.W1	***#56 Peace Prayer Lyrics*** • Students will sing along to a YouTube video of *The Peace Prayer of St. Francis song.* **Note: To save paper, the lyrics can be placed on a Smartboard or another electronic medium for student access.*

Methodology
The Peace Prayer of St. Francis of Assisi is a profound and beautiful prayer, with a powerful spiritual resonance for all. This prayer is a central and integral message/theme, which is in the spirit of the *Peace Be With You Christ Centered Bullying Redirect* program.

Students will benefit by analyzing and immersing themselves in the *The Peace Prayer of St. Francis of Assisi* through reading, reflecting, writing and singing. Activity 14 utilizes two worksheets to support teacher instruction and student learning on this powerful prayer. *#55 The Peace Prayer*. Students read and reflect on the prayer and choose one line that holds the most meaning for them. Using their chosen prayer-line, students write a relevant example to illustrate an actionable step they can take to become an instrument of peace at home and school.

Hand out or display on a Smartboard or another electronic medium, *#56 Peace Prayer Lyrics*, for everyone to join in singing *The Peace Prayer of St. Francis* from this YouTube video; https://www.youtube.com/watch?v=ihhvm6eLWZI **(2:51 minutes).** The YouTube video also scrolls the lyrics, making it easy to follow along.

The Peace Prayer of St. Francis

Lord, make me an instrument of your peace:
where there is hatred, let me sow love;
where there is injury, pardon;
where there is doubt, faith;
where there is despair, hope;
where there is darkness, light;
where there is sadness, joy.

O divine Master, grant that I may not so much seek
to be consoled as to console,
to be understood as to understand,
to be loved as to love.
For it is in giving that we receive,
it is in pardoning that we are pardoned,
and it is in dying that we are born to eternal life.
Amen.

Activity 14
The Peace Prayer of St. Francis

Facilitator Script

TIME/PREPARATION/LOGISTICS & PROCESS

10:00 PREPARATION/LOGISTICS
- Make copies of *#55 The Peace Prayer* & *#56 Peace Prayer Lyrics*.
- Cue computer or another electronic device to:
  https://www.youtube.com/watch?v=ihhvm6eLWZI **(2:51 minutes)**
- Settle students prior to singing song.

TIME   PROCESS

00:00 Say: "Class, please silently read *The Peace Prayer of St. Francis* printed on the worksheet in front of you. Please look up to let me know when you have completed the reading."

2:00   Say: "Now let's read the prayer as a class." (*Teacher, begins to read, prompting students to join in.*)

3:00   Say: "Thank you class."

   Say: "In silence, please take one more look at the *Peace Prayer* and use a highlighter in the color of your choice on the lines that have the most meaning for you. Raise your hand to let me know when you have chosen your favorite lines in the prayer." (*Allow 1 minute*)

5:00   Say: "Now class, using one of the prayer-lines you have chosen, write an example to illustrate how you can be an instrument of peace. Quietly complete this exercise and look up when you are completed." (*Allow 5 minutes*)

10:00 Say: "Class, take this worksheet home tonight and share what you have written with your parents and have them sign it. Bring this back tomorrow so I can read it too. Thank you."

   Optional: Ask for students to volunteer sharing their written example with the class.

Note: You may get a handful of students to read and you may not get any volunteers at all. Whatever the outcome is okay.

12:00 Say: "Class, let's all join in together to sing the *Peace Prayer of St. Francis* by following along on this YouTube video."

*(Play https://www.youtube.com/watch?v=ihhvm6eLWZI **(2:51 minutes)**

15:00 Say: "Thank you. That was beautiful! I have full confidence that each of you are very capable of being instruments of peace both at home and school."

Note: The end time on this activity will depend on whether or not you use the option to have students share their written example with the class.

Activity 15
Meditation 3

Activity 15 Purpose
To deepen spiritual formation by listening to Meditation 3 to encourage students to be an instrument of peace and remain open in heart to hear God's call to servant-leadership.

Activity 15 National Standards/Themes Correlation
Themes of Catholic Social Teachings: • Life and Dignity of the Human Person (CST-DHP) • Solidarity (CST-S) Social Studies Themes: • People, Places, and the Environment (SST-PPE) • Individual Development and Identity (SST-IDI) • Individuals, Groups, and Institutions (SST-IGI) • Time, Continuity, and Change (SST-TCC) Language Arts Speaking and Listening Standards: • Prepare for and participate effectively in a range of conversations and collaborations with diverse partners, building on others' ideas and expressing their own clearly and persuasively. (CCSS.ELA-Literacy.CCRA.SL1) Language Arts Writing Standards: • Introduce claim(s) and organize the reasons and evidence clearly. (CCSS.ELA-Literacy.CCRA.W1)

	Learning Objectives Students will be able to:	Corresponding Assessment Possibilities
1	**Grades 4-8** Apply a self-assessment baseline measurement to determine their personal stress level following a short meditation. *Standards* (CST-RR, CST-DHP, SST-PPE, SST-IDI, SST-IGI, CCSS.ELA-Literacy, CCRA.SL1, CCSS.ELA-Literacy.CCRA.W1)	*#47 Stress Check Log* • Students refer back to this worksheet to circle a Post-Stress Check number that best represents their level of stress following the meditation.
2	**Grades 4-8** Listen to a Christ-centered meditation to deepen spiritually and strengthen faith and hope in Jesus. *Standards* CST-S, CST-DHP, SST-PPE, SST-IDI, SST-IGI, SST-TCC, CCSS.ELA-Literacy.CCRA.SL.1, CCSS.ELA-Literacy.CCRA.W1)	*#57 Meditation 3 Journal 3* • Students use the worksheet to journal about their meditation experience. *Note: Copy these worksheets back to back to allow for student option.* *#58 PeaceScape Drawing 3* • Students draw an image of what peace means to them following the meditation.

Methodology

This meditation is an invitation to draw students closer to Christ. In the process the exercise will help students to learn more about self-care, by taking time to nurture their body, mind and spirit. Self-care is essential to strengthen one's relationship to self, God, and others. The challenge for all of us is taking the necessary time to slow down long enough to rest for rejuvenation, to open our hearts, and to hear God's call. Each of the previous meditations build on the other to further develop one's inner life and to deepen spiritual formation.

Activity 15 utilizes three worksheets. First, direct students to a clean copy of *#47 Stress Check Log,* to record their *Pre-*and *Post-Stress Check* numbers following *Activity 15 Meditation 3.*

Following Track 7 of the *Peace Be With You Program Audio,* allow time for reflection, journaling or drawing, to further nurture the experience.

Second, the next two worksheets are copied as a double-sided handout for students to select between *#57 Meditation 3 Journal 3* and *#58 PeaceScape Drawing 3,* to help them best describe their meditation experience. Encouraging journaling and/or drawing helps to build student empathic skills.

Third, refer students back to *#47 Stress Check Log,* to record their *Post-Stress Check* number following *Activity 15 Meditation 3.* The *Stress Check Log* can be kept in the Leader Folder.

Thank you for opening up your heart and classroom for this important work! Permit yourself to enjoy this *Peace Be With You Program Audio* track with your students. By doing so you will benefit; and they will too from your modeling.

Activity 15
Meditation 3

Facilitator Script

TIME/PREPARATION/LOGISTICS & PROCESS

30:00 PREPARATION/LOGISTICS
- Make copies of the *#47Stress Check Log for each student.*
- Make copies of *#57 Meditation 3 Journal 3, & #58 PeaceScape Drawing 3* (back to back) for each student.
- Students sit quietly at their desks for the duration of this exercise. It is at the Teacher's discretion whether or not to permit students to lie down on the floor.
- If acceptable, permit students to lie down on carpeted floor and bring in a head pillow for this exercise.
- Listen to Track 7 prior to exercise.
- Room lights dimmed or off with enough natural light.
- Cue audio to Track 7.
- Settle students and begin playing Track 7.

TIME   PROCESS
00:00 Say: "Class. Let's remind each other of the two important rules when listening to an audio track.

Say: "Together, let's say the rules: (Teacher leads to prompt students to join in.)
Rule # 1: No talking.
Rule # 2: Do Not Disturb Your Neighbor."

1:00   Say: "Raise your hand if you agree to these rules. Thank You."

Note: Hand out #47 Stress Check Log.

Say: "Class. On the *Stress Check Log*, go to the *Pre-Stress Check* and circle your current level of stress. (Allow 10 seconds)

Say: "Thank you."

3:00   Say: "Sit comfortably in your seats during this exercise. No need to write. I invite you to just relax and listen carefully to this audio track of a person calmly guiding you through a peaceful and Christ-centered experience accompanied by gentle music. When the track is over please sit quietly without talking, until I give you the next direction."

*(Play Track 7 of Audio Program—20:25 minutes)

Activity 15 Facilitator Script (continued)

<u>**TIME**</u> <u>**PROCESS**</u>

24:00 **Say:** "Welcome back. Without talking, please refer back to the *Pre-Post-Stress Check* worksheet log, and make an entry on the *Post-Stress Check* line that reflects this meditation.

25:00 **Say:** "Now Class, without talking, refer to your worksheet and take time to journal or draw a *PeaceScape* of your experience during the meditation. (*Allow 15:00 minutes*)

38:00 **Say:** "I am very proud of you all. So good to see you journaling and drawing! Please take your journal entry and drawings home to share it with your parents. Have a parent sign it and turn it in tomorrow so that I can read your work too."

*Note: Teachers are encouraged to play gentle music of your choice as background when working on tasks following the audio tracks. The Peace Project: The Music, is an option.

Unit 2
Comprehensive Review and Four Agreements

Purpose	
To reinforce the concepts and principles learned to promote positive actions and encourage positive ripple effects in school and at home.	
Learning Objectives **Students will be able to:**	**Corresponding Assessment Possibilities**

	Learning Objectives **Students will be able to:**	**Corresponding Assessment Possibilities**
1	**Grades 4-8** Recall and recite *Unit 2* concepts by completing the comprehensive review. ***Standards*** *(CST-DHP, CST-CFCP, CST-RR, CST-S, SST-C, SST-PPE, SST-IDI, SST-IGI, CCSS.ELA-Literacy.CCRA.SL1, CCSS.ELA-Literacy.CCRA.W1)*	***#59 Unit 2: Comprehensive Review***
2	**Grades 4-8** Reflect, process, and agree to *Unit 2* principles by signing the Four Agreements. ***Standards*** *(CST-DHP, CST-RR, CST-S, SST-C, SST-PPE, SST-IDI, SST-IGI, CCSS.ELA-Literacy.CCRA.W1)*	***#60 Unit 2: Four Agreements*** • If the student agrees, he/she is to sign the *Pure in Heart Four Agreements* along with the teacher, principal and a parent.

Unit 2
Comprehensive Review and Four Agreements

Facilitator Script

TIME/PREPARATION/LOGISTICS & PROCESS

10:00 PREPARATION/LOGISTICS
- Make copies and hand out *#59 Unit 2: Comprehensive Review, and #60 Unit 2: Four Agreements (Grades 4-8)* to each student.
- Use *#59 Unit 2: Comprehensive Review* to work with students on reflection and writing about the entire unit.
- Invite students to take the completed *#59 Unit 2: Comprehensive Review and #60 Unit 2: Four Agreements* home to share both with a parent.
- Ask students to return the signed agreements to class and hand into the teacher.

TIME PROCESS

0:00 **Say:** "We have learned many new things in this third Unit. Let's review what we've learned by completing a student reflection activity. Please let me know you have finished, by giving me a thumbs-up."

5:00 **Say:** "Thank you for completing this reflection. Now that you have reviewed some of what you have learned, please look over the *Four Agreements* that have just been handed out."

Say: "Let's read the *Four Agreements* out loud together."

6:00 **Say:** "Thank you! Do you think you can agree to these statements?"

Expected Response: "Yes"

Say: "If you agree, please sign the *Pure in Heart Four Agreements (#60 Unit 2: Four Agreements).* I will come around and sign each of yours after you have signed it. Take the review worksheet and *Four Agreements* home to share with your parents. Return both tomorrow signed by a parent. Thank you for your commitment to working together to create positive ripples and build up our classroom and school community!"

*Note: Teachers are encouraged to revisit any of the Unit 2 lessons/activities throughout the school year.

Peace Be With You!

Unit 3
Love Your Neighbor

Jesus replied, "The first is this,
'Hear, O Israel! The Lord our god is
Lord alone! You shall love the Lord your
God with all your heart, with all your soul,
with all your mind,
and with all your strength.'
The second is this,
'You shall <u>love your neighbor</u>
as yourself.'
There is no other commandment
greater than these."

MARK 12: 29-31

Unit 3: Love Your Neighbor
Basic Premise

The basic premise of *Unit 3: Love Your Neighbor* is that students require essential life skills in how to get along with others. This does not mean one must agree on every topic or that one should consider everyone his/her friend. We should however, honor and respect the diversity of every human being. The message from the Gospel of Mark, and elsewhere in Scripture, is clear that we should love and accept each other as Children of God, in spite our differences.

Scripture tells us to "Love Our Neighbor" and Jesus is our perfect example for exactly how to do this. Everything we say and do should be in the manner of Christ. The school and classroom afford many opportunities to practice love for our neighbor. With authentic application of *Unit 3*, students will learn through practice, more about the compassion of Christ, and what it means to be more Christ-like in our actions. *Unit 3* challenges us to not just talk about concepts, but to whole-heartedly be more Christ-like in our actions. This is accomplished by actively demonstrating positive ripple contributions in our relationships to ultimately help build the Kingdom of God.

The primary focus of *Unit 3* is on building supportive peer relationships by developing healthy interpersonal skills. Good communication skills are essential for reducing conflict and mistreatment and building interpersonal bridges in getting along with one another.

> *"The most important single ingredient*
> *in the formula of success is*
> *knowing how to get along with people."*
>
> **Theodore Roosevelt**

Unit 3 teaches students two primary skills in effective communication. The *first*, which is often overlooked as a skill, and often undeveloped, is the skill of listening. Typically, listening translates into thinking how one will respond, which is not really listening to the other person. Not being heard can lead to a great deal of frustration, which has the potential to escalate when one is not heard. We have all "half-listened" and have also experienced the frustration of not being heard. "Surface listening" often leads to miscommunication, which can snowball into varying degrees of misunderstanding—what the person said and what was heard are not always in alignment.

The onset of electronic devices seems to have made it easier to "stay in touch;" however, this method of communication is missing one essential ingredient for effective human interaction—namely, face-to-face contact. *Unit 3* instructs students on how to truly listen and peacefully interact with others face to face and from the heart. Carefully designed communication exercises lead students in pairs, small groups, and large groups, for ample practice in the acquisition of these critical life skills.

The *second skill* is how to communicate clearly to help the listener be a better listener. *Unit 3* provides guidance for instruction on this skill, through the use of a five-step prescriptive communication tool called *"Clear Talk."* *Clear Talk* is a simple way to organize and communicate one's thoughts and feelings—making it less likely for the listener to become defensive and more likely to truly hear what is being said.

Combined, *CLEAR Listening* and *Clear Talk* provide a safe context and structure to fully engage students in the practice of active compassionate listening. Practice time is essential for students to make progress in development of these skills. Skills are acquired primarily through Scripture on the Good Samaritan. Students practice listening from the perspective of the biblical characters found in Luke 10: 25-37, while utilizing the *CLEAR Listening* and *Clear Talk* methods. Working toward building and improving student communication skills is vital for building trust and supportive peer relationships.

Living out the true nature of God's desire for us to hold each other in sacred-esteem, the encouraged setting for each of the lessons in this unit shifts from the "traditional" classroom to a *"Peace Circle."* The *Peace Circle* is intended to create a climate of inclusiveness and support, while actively engaging students in building community.

In *Unit 3* the *Peace Circle* is to be upheld as a sacred space that promotes reverence and respect. Although ideal, these conditions are achievable and optimal for your students to learn how to love our neighbor, love our classmates, love our teacher and love our school.

Unit 3: Love Your Neighbor

Scope and Sequence

Overview				
Authentic application of the Peace Be With You curriculum ideally follows the detailed lesson plans. Each activity requires approximately 30-45 minutes of classroom teacher instruction per week. Any special student assignments completed either in or outside of class do not align with the specified timetable below and are based on teacher discretion.				
Academic Calendar	February Thru May (Weeks 16-20)			Teacher discretion on revisiting lessons/activities throughout school year.
	Week 16	Week 17	Week 18	Week 19	Week 20+
Grade 4	Lesson 8 Activities 16a & 16b	Lesson 9 Activity 17 Special Assignment Possibilities	Lesson 10 Activity 18 Grades 4-8	Unit 3 Comp. Review Grades 4-8 — Unit 3 4 Agreements	*Peace Circle* and *Clear Talk* processes through the end of the School Year Grades 4-8
Grade 5					
Grade 6					
Grade 7					
Grade 8					

Unit 3: Lesson Eight
Harvesting Our Growth

*"Let us not lose heart of doing good,
for in due time we shall reap our harvest,
if we do not give up."*

Galatians 6:9

Lesson Eight Purpose

To review, reflect and harvest the learning from the two previous units to engage students in actively practicing the acquired skills to further reinforce and use as a springboard for developing effective communication skills and a stronger sense of community.

Lesson Eight Overview

Lesson Eight: Activity 16a: Harvesting Our Growth, begins with a comprehensive review of *Units 1* and *2* to help reinforce and integrate significant concepts and principles. Following this point of review students begin a seamless transition from intrapersonal to interpersonal skill building. The transition in *Activity 16b* is purposeful as students ceremoniously are introduced by way of invitation to enter the *Peace Circle* for the first time. The teacher is integral in setting the tone for the *Peace Circle* to be a safe, respectful and sacred space for students to practice peace building support strategies among peers—working toward building a stronger sense of Christian community.

Overarching Goal

The overarching goal is for students to transition from intrapersonal to interpersonal skill development, by laying the groundwork for them to feel safe and respected in peace building among each other, building a more fortified sense of community and ultimately the Kingdom of God.

For further support with implementing the Peace Be With You Curriculum refer to:
Unit 3: Lesson Eight in the *Teacher Curriculum Guide* for a more in depth understanding of the importance of interpersonal skill development and the significance of the *Peace Circle* and *Peace Stick for skill acquisition.*

Activity 16a
Harvesting the Growth

Activity 16a Purpose	
To review, reflect and harvest the learning from the previous two units and make a transition to interpersonal skill building.	

Activity 16a National Standards/Themes Correlation	

Themes of Catholic Social Teachings:
- Life and Dignity of the Human Person (CST-DHP)
- Call to Family, Community and Participation (CST-CFCP)

Social Studies Themes:
- Individual Development and Identity (SST-IDI)
- Individuals, Groups, and Institutions (SST-IGI)

Language Arts Speaking and Listening Standards:
- Prepare for and participate effectively in a range of conversations and collaborations with diverse partners, building on others' ideas and expressing their own clearly and persuasively. (CCSS.ELA-Literacy.CCRA.SL.1)

	Learning Objectives Students will be able to:	Corresponding Assessment Possibilities
1	**Grades 4-8** Examine and evaluate personal growth as servant-leaders, measure progress in personal safety and in the positive ripples created in school and at home. **Standards** CST-DHP, CST-CFCP, SST-IDI, SST-IGI, CCSS-ELA-Literacy.CCRA-SL.1	***#61 Worksheet*** ***Harvesting the Growth*** • Units 1 & 2 review to affirm progress in student learning. This worksheet also acts as a ceremonious guide for transitioning to interpersonal skill development.
2	**Grades 4-8** Ceremoniously recognize and offer their personal harvesting growth gifts in the Peace Circle. **Standards** **CST-DHP, CST-CFCP, SST-IDI, SST-IGI, CCSS.ELA-Literacy.CCRA.SL.1**	• Students use their completed *#61 Worksheet* for this exercise.

Methodology

Lesson Eight: Activity *16a: Harvesting Our Growth* and *Activity 16b: Entering the Peace Circle* are two concurrent activities implemented in the context of one class period. *Harvesting Our Growth* provides a point of review that helps to connect the dots with the previous two units, while simultaneously affirming students for their newly acquired skills. Many key elements about servant-leadership, being pure in heart, personal safety, and peer support are intentionally woven into Activity 16a to further reinforce and reexamine these important concepts and principles. Activity 16b builds on 16a with a ritual to recognize student skill development and also to introduce the *Peace Circle*.

> *"There are different kinds of spiritual gifts but the same Spirit;*
> *there are different forms of service but the same Lord;*
> *there are different workings but the same God*
> *who produces all of them in everyone.*
> *To each individual the manifestation of the Spirit*
> *is given for some benefit."*
>
> *1 CORINTHIANS 12:4-7*

> *"Striving to preserve the unity of the spirit*
> *through the bond of peace."*
>
> *Ephesians 4:3*

Activity 16a
Harvesting Our Growth

Facilitator Script

TIME/PREPARATION/LOGISTICS & PROCESS

2:00 PREPARATION
- Use Servant-Leader words from student folders, or make enough copies for each student.
- *Post #18 Poster: YVP Peer Support Strategies* on (Smart board image, flipchart or chalk/marker board).
- Make copies of *#61 Worksheet: Harvesting the Growth for students and teacher.*

SUPPLIES
- Container large enough to hold students completed worksheets.
- One "*Peace Stick*" (Natural wood if possible approximately 4'-5' high & 2"-3" in diameter).
- Strips of multi-colored paper for each student approximately 2" wide and 12" long.
- Stapler.
- Optional: To sing the song (with accompanying taped music) "We are many parts, we are all one Body" by Marty Haugen

LOGISTICS
- Students take out servant-leader words list from their folders or if a copy is provided for them.
- Post the Peer Support Strategies.
- Teacher is encouraged to participate in the review worksheet with students to model positive actions.
- On one strip of colored paper, students and teacher write down one of their answers from the worksheet that they are willing to share with the class in the *Peace Circle*.
- Begin this activity in the usual classroom seating arrangement.

TIME   PROCESS
00:00 Say: "Today we begin the final part of the *Peace Be With You* faith journey. It is important that we respect and understand what gifts each of us is able to bring to our classroom. Take out your Servant-leader Word List while I hand out a worksheet for us to use today."

*Note: Hand out worksheet #61 Worksheet: Harvesting the Growth to each student.

1:00   Say: "Please take a look at the Servant-Leader Word List and choose one word that best describes your strongest quality."

Say: "Using the skills from the last unit on prayer and meditation, close your eyes, take a deep breath, and imagine how pleased God is with you and your special quality." (Allow 30 seconds for silence.)

2:00   Say: "Thank you. Open your eyes and write your best leader quality as the answer to question #1 on the worksheet."

TIME   PROCESS

2:00   **Say:** "Thank you. Open your eyes and write your best leader quality as the answer to question #1 on the worksheet."

3:00   **Say:** "I invite you to recall what it means to be safe. Again, please close your eyes and take a moment to reflect on your personal *Safety Check* number for today. With prayerfulness, see yourself presenting your number to our loving God. With God's blessing make a promise to daily grow stronger to strive to reach for a 10 on the *Safety Check Line*. Add to your promise to help others grow stronger in their *Safety Check* number and ask for God's blessings on our efforts to support one another every day in striving to reach for a 10." (Allow 30 seconds to guide students through this.)

4:00   **Say:** "Thank you for reflecting on your *Safety Check* number and your promise to help yourself and others strive to reach a daily 10. On your worksheet, place your number in question #2."

5:00   **Say:** "Let's take a look up front and read over the *Peer Support Strategies Poster* (flipchart, Smartboard, chalkboard) as an important reminder."

6:00   **Say:** "Now, close your eyes and silently recall a time when you recently carried out one of these strategies with a classmate. In stillness, bring to mind the experience of the positive ripples you helped create with your caring support." (Allow 30 seconds of silence.)

7:00   **Say:** "With eyes remaining closed, recall the two Scripture role-plays and the virtuous actions of Jesus. Bring to mind how Jesus was able to remain calm, compassionate and supportive in some very tough situations. Know that each time you support and care for another person, your actions mirror the compassion of Christ." (Allow 30 seconds of silence.)

8:00   **Say:** "Thank you. Now open your eyes and answer question #3 about being supportive to another and question #4 about the positive ripples you help create with your compassionate support."

9:00   **Say:** "Class. Take a few moments to look at your answers. Take a deep breath and take in the gift that you are. Notice this awesome person—you—stepping into our classroom and school each day. Each of you is prayerfully entering into a circle of caring and compassionate support to make us all safer, stronger and more beautiful because of the unique gifts you bring to the circle."

Note: Hand out a strip of colored strip of paper to each student.

10:00 **Say:** "Look at the answers you wrote on your *Harvesting the Growth Worksheet*. Pick one answer that you are willing to share with the class and write that answer on the colored strip of paper being handed out."

11:00 **Say:** "Class. Fold your worksheet paper in half. Now, bring the folded worksheet, your colored paper strip with your gift written on it, and your chair to form a circle. (Pause until all students are seated in a circle formation.)

Activity 16b
Entering the Peace Circle

"And the fruit of righteousness
is sown in peace for those who cultivate peace."

James 3:18

Activity 16b Purpose
To begin the process of making a powerful connection with servant-leadership in the manner of Christ and set the stage for practicing Christ-like compassion to discover what it truly means to "Love Our Neighbor."

Activity 16b National Standards/Themes Correlation
Themes of Catholic Social Teachings: <ul><li>Life and Dignity of the Human Person (CST-DHP)</li><li>Call to Family, Community and Participation (CST-CFCP)</li><li>Rights and Responsibilities (CST-RR)</li><li>Solidarity (CST-S)</li></ul> Social Studies Themes: <ul><li>People, Places, and the Environment (SST-PPE)</li><li>Individual Development and Identity (SST-IDI)</li><li>Individuals, Groups, and Institutions (SST-IGI)</li></ul> Language Arts Speaking and Listening Standards: <ul><li>Prepare for and participate effectively in a range of conversations and collaborations with diverse partners, building on others' ideas and expressing their own clearly and persuasively. (CCSS.ELA-Literacy.CCRA.SL.1)</li><li>Evaluate a speaker's point of view, reasoning, and use of evidence and rhetoric. (CCSS.ELA-Literacy.CCRA.SL.3)</li><li>Present information, findings, and supporting evidence such that listeners can follow the line of reasoning and the organization, development, and style are appropriate to task, purpose, and audience. (CCSS.ELA-Literacy.CCRA.SL.4)</li></ul>

1	**Grades 4-8** Collaboratively collect, create and share a personal gift in a communal setting to strengthen the classroom community. **Standards** CST-DHP, CST-CFCP, CST-RR, CST-S, SST-PPE, SST-IDI, SST-IGI, CCSS.ELA-Literacy.CCRA.SL.1, CCSS.ELA-Literacy.CCRA.SL.3, CCRA.SL.1-Literacy.CCRA.SL.4	***Colored Paper Strip*** ***(No Worksheet)*** • Each student and the Teacher receive one colored paper strip to write their personal gift on. The end result of this exercise is an assembled *Peace Chain* that can be displayed in the classroom throughout the year as a symbol of supportive connection and class unity in the manner of Christ.

Methodology

Activity 16b: Entering the Peace Circle actively introduces students to the *Peace Circle* and *Peace Stick*. This is key in laying important groundwork to prepare students for upcoming practice in *CLEAR Listening* and *Clear Talk*.

Use of a *"Peace Stick"* and sitting in a circle formation may be foreign to many students and the traditional classroom. A reverent ritual structure is used to introduce these elements to create a safe and sacred space toward building a stronger sense of community among the class. Again, the Teacher is key in setting a loving and accepting tone for the *Peace Circle*.

"At the time, all discipline seems a cause
not for joy but for pain,
yet later it brings the peaceful fruit
of righteousness to those
who are trained by it."

Hebrews 12:11

Activity 16b
Entering the Peace Circle

Facilitator Script

TIME   PROCESS

13:00 Say: "Thank you. Welcome to our *Peace Circle.*"

Note: Teacher reverently places the empty container in the center of the Peace Circle.

14:00 Say: "Now class. One at a time, with reverence and silence, place only your folded paper into the container in the center of our circle and return to your seat in the *Peace Circle.* As you do this, please keep your colored strip of paper at your seat."

Note: Teacher sets the tone as to how students are to place their worksheet into the container. Model and encourage reverence with slow, deliberate actions during this process.

17:00 Say: "Thank you for taking your seat in the circle and placing your harvest worksheet into the container. Let's look at the container and respect all the gifts and richness that each of you bring to the *Peace Circle.*"

18:00 Say: "Close your eyes for a moment, imagine God's joy at the gifts each of you bring and ask Him to bless us as we begin our *Peace Circle.*"

Say: "Thank you."

Ask: "Can anyone tell me why sitting in a circle is so important?"

Note: As the teacher asks this, she/he should be seated in the circle with the students. Whatever a student shares (if respectful), honor the response.

Possible Responses: Everyone is equal. No one is first or last. Can see everyone. Can make eye contact with everyone. Symbol of unity and support. (Echo student responses)

19:00 Say: "Thank you for your responses."

Note: Teacher places the Peace Stick in the center of the Peace Circle.

20:00 Ask: "What have I added to the center of our *Peace Circle* alongside of the container?"

Expected response: A stick.

Ask: "Do you have any idea what this stick represents or why it is in our *Peace Circle*?"

Expected response: It's a talking stick. It's a listening stick. Only the person that holds the stick can speak.

Activity 16b Facilitator Script (continued)

Note: Teacher walks into circle and picks up the Peace Stick. Holding the Peace Stick, the teacher continues with the script. While speaking the teacher is making caring eye contact with students seated in the Peace Circle.

TIME   PROCESS

21:00   Say: "We will call this a *Peace Stick*. The *Peace Stick* symbolically represents the living tree from which it came. Imagine deep roots at the base of the *Peace Stick*, like a tree, creating a solid, secure and safe foundation for our classroom and school. Imagine from the top of the *Peace Stick* is an array of branches and leaves creating a canopy or umbrella over our *Peace Circle* and school to create a covering of inclusion and dignity for all."

Note: Teacher joins the Peace Circle holding the Peace Stick. Teacher picks up her/his colored paper strip and continuing to hold the Peace Stick asks students to stand with their colored paper strip.

TIME   PROCESS

22:00   Say: "The person holding the *Peace Stick* for this exercise is the only one permitted to speak. The role of the rest of us is to listen in silence and with respect."

Say: "I will start us off by sharing the gift I bring to our *Peace Circle*. After I share my gift, I will pass the *Peace Stick* to (student name) on my left. When (repeat student name) has shared her/his gift, I will then connect our colored paper strips like a chain. When our two *Peace Chain* links are connected, the *Peace Stick* is passed to (student name) on the left. We will go around the *Peace Circle* to share our gifts and form a *Peace Chain* until we've completed the circle."

Note: When everyone has shared his/her gift and the Peace Chain is completely formed, the teacher returns the Peace Stick to the center of the Peace Circle and returns to her/his seat.

32:00   Say: "Thank you class. Our *Peace Circle* and *Peace Chain* are now fully formed for us to continue to grow in the goodness that God has blessed us with."

33:00   Say: "At Mass you have heard the song 'We are many parts, yet one Body.' This song refers to all of us belonging to The Body of Christ. Our *Peace Circle* and *Peace Chain* represent that we are all interconnected. Each one of us is a part of the *One Body of Christ*."

Optional: To sing along to the song "We are many parts, we are all one Body" by Marty Haugen, go to this YouTube site: https://www.youtube.com/watch?v=zQP0RMfs8Vg (3:17)

Note: Script time is allotted here if you decide to use the YouTube option.

37:00   Say: "Quietly, exit the *Peace Circle* and gently carry our *Peace Chain* to the bulletin board (or other visual place) to pin it up together."

40:00   Say: "Please return to your seats in our *Peace Circle*."

Activity 16b Facilitator Script (continued)

TIME PROCESS

37:00 **Say:** "Thank you Class. Let our *Peace Chain* and *Peace Circle* be loving reminders of our interconnectedness as the One body of Christ."

Say: "For the remainder of the school year, all of the activities from this unit on *Love Your Neighbor* will be in held in our *Peace Circle*. Whenever you enter the *Peace Circle* and our classroom, I invite you to practice bringing your best qualities of respect and love for your neighbor."

Say: "Quietly exit our circle now and take your chairs with you to be seated in our usual classroom arrangement."

Do You Want To Fast
This Lent?

Fast from hurting words.......and say kind words.

Fast from sadness.................and be filled with gratitude.

Fast from anger.....................and be filled with patience.

Fast from pessimism..............and be filled with hope.

Fast from worries...................and be filled with trust in God.

Fast from complaints.............and contemplate simplicity.

Fast from pressures...............and be prayerful.

Fast from bitterness...............and fill your heart with joy.

Fast from selfishness......and be compassionate toward others.

Fast from grudges.................and be reconciled.

Fast from words.....................and be silent so you can listen.

Pope Francis
Lent 2017

Unit 3: Lesson Nine
CLEAR Listening

Lesson Nine Purpose

To actively engage youth in developing good listening skills through the use of Scripture and communication tools.

Lesson Nine Overview

Lesson Nine is key in the development of good listening skills to cultivate a safe learning environment and build supportive peer relationships and strengthen the classroom community. Making the *CLEAR Listening Poster* visible to students gives them some of the fundamental elements of good listening.

The *Good Listener/Poor Listener* exercise is a fun way for students to learn about the consequences and benefits of the two different listening styles through compare and contrast. This exercise is a warm up for the connection to Scripture from Luke 10: 25-37. The Scripture is used as the backdrop for the Good Samaritan Role-Reflection, which is an interactive activity that encourages student collaboration. This approach also serves as an empathy building strategy with students—sensitizing them to the role of each of the biblical characters.

Activity 17 closes with the *Role-Play 3: Inn Keeper/Good Samaritan,* which requires critical thinking hypothesis on how the Inn Keeper might have respond to the Good Samaritan. The role-play opts for a positive "put-up" approach by the Inn Keeper with the Good Samaritan, to demonstrate how students should treat each other during the *Clear Talk* process (and at all times) featured in Lessons 10 & 11. Teachers are encouraged to post *#62 CLEAR Listening Poster for student reference through the remainder of the school year.*

Overarching Goal

The overarching goal is for students to develop a strong foundation in interpersonal skills from which to build peace among peers and strengthen a sense of community in the classroom.

For further support with implementing the Peace Be With You Curriculum refer to:
Unit 3: Lesson Nine in the *Teacher Curriculum Guide* for a more in depth understanding of the significance of the *CLEAR Listening* as a key element to effective communication.

Activity 17
Good Listener/Poor Listener

Activity 17 Purpose
To actively engage students in compare and contrast between good and poor listening and to introduce active listening in an environment of respect and gratitude for self and others.
Activity 17 National Standards/Themes Correlation
Themes of Catholic Social Teachings: • Life and Dignity of the Human Person (CST-DHP) • Call to Family, Community and Participation (CST-CFCP) • Rights and Responsibilities (CST-RR) Social Studies Themes: • People, Places, and the Environment (SST-PPE) • Individual Development and Identity (SST-IDI) • Individuals, Groups, and Institutions (SST-IGI) Language Arts Speaking and Listening Standards: • Prepare for and participate effectively in a range of conversations and collaborations with diverse partners, building on others' ideas and expressing their own clearly and persuasively. (CCSS.ELA-Literacy.CCRA.SL.1) • Evaluate a speaker's point of view, reasoning, and use of evidence and rhetoric. (CCSS.ELA-Literacy.CCRA.SL.3) • Present information, findings, and supporting evidence such that listeners can follow the line of reasoning and the organization, development, and style are appropriate to task, purpose, and audience. (CCSS.ELA-Literacy.CCRA.SL.4) Language Arts Writing Standards: • Write arguments to support claims in an analysis of substantive topics or texts using valid reasoning and relevant and sufficient evidence.

	Learning Objectives **Students will be able to:**	**Corresponding Assessment Possibilities**
1	**Grades 4-8** Use of a visual to reflect on the elements involved with effective *CLEAR Listening and reference during a compare and contrast exercise.* ***Standards*** CST-DHP, CST-RR, SST-PPE, SST-IDI, CCSS.ELA-Literacy.CCRA.SL.3, CCSS.ELA-Literacy.CCRA.SL.4,	*#62 Poster* ***CLEAR Listening*** • Display this visual aid of the *CLEAR Listening* acronym for reference. ***No Worksheet*** ***Good Listener/Poor Listener Game*** • A fun exercise to stimulate compare and contrast discussion on the consequences of poor listening and the relational benefits of good listening.

2	**Grades 4-8** Read and engage in Scripture to set the stage for listening processes. **_Standards_** CST-RR, SST-PPE, CCSS.ELA-Literacy.CCRA.SL.1, CCSS.ELA-Literacy.CCRA.SL.3, CCSS.ELA-Literacy.CCRA.SL.4	**_#63 Scripture Connection 3_** **Luke 10: 25-37**
3	**Grades 4-8** Practice collaboration and communication skills through reflection on the biblical characters from the Good Samaritan Scripture passage. **_Standards_** CST-DHP, CST-CFCP, CST-RR, SST-PPE, SST-IDI, SST-IGI, CCSS.ELA-Literacy.CCRA.SL.1, CCSS.ELA-Literacy.CCRA.SL.3, CCSS.ELA-Literacy.CCRA.SL.4	**_#64a-#64b Role-Reflection & Directions_** **_The Good Samaritan_** • Practice collaboration and communication skills, as well as, empathy skills to understand the possible thoughts and feelings of each of the biblical characters from the Good Samaritan Scripture passage. ***Note: #'s 64a & 64b are to be copied back to back.**
4	**Grades 4-8** Role-play to actively engage in Scripture and to introduce and practice listening skills. **_Standards_** CST-DHP, CST-CFCP, CST-RR, SST-PPE, SST-IDI, SST-IGI, CCSS.ELA-Literacy.CCRA.SL.1, CCSS.ELA-Literacy.CCRA.SL.3, CCSS.ELA-Literacy.CCRA.SL.4	**_#65 Role-Play 3_** **_Inn Keeper/Good Samaritan_** • Use Role-Play 3 script for *CLEAR Listening* practice and to introduce to nonverbal and active listening skills.
5	**Grades 4-8** Further integrate and develop effective listening skills. **_Standards_** CST-DHP, CST-CFCP, CST-RR, SST-PPE, SST-IDI, SST-IGI, CCSS.ELA-Literacy.CCRA.SL.1, CCSS.ELA-Literacy.CCRA.SL.3, CCSS.ELA-Literacy.CCRA.SL.4	**_#66 Worksheet_** **_CLEAR Listening_** • Students complete the *CLEAR Listening* worksheet as homework and are encouraged to share with parents.

| 6 | **Grades 4/5**
Increase their knowledge of the importance of good listening.

Standards
CST-DHP, CST-CFCP, CST-RR, SST-PPE, SST-IDI, CCSS.ELA-Literacy.CCRA.SL.1, CCSS.ELA-Literacy.CCRA.SL.3, CCSS.ELA-Literacy.CCRA.SL.4, CCSS.ELA-Literacy.CCRA.W.1

Grades 6-8
Identify and write about 5 blocks to listening & 5 Tips to effective listening.

Standards
CST-DHP, CST-CFCP, CST-RR, SST-PPE, SST-IDI, CCSS.ELA-Literacy.CCRA.SL.1, CCSS.ELA-Literacy.CCRA.SL.3, CCSS.ELA-Literacy.CCRA.SL.4, CCSS.ELA-Lieracy.CCRA.W.1 | ***Activity 17: Optional Homework Assignment**

View with a parent:
"*How to be a Good Listener*" (1:36 minutes)

https://www.youtube.com/watch?v=8XUE3urz3Fc

• Write one paragraph to describe what was learned.

View with a parent:
"*Active Listening: 5 Blocks to Effective Listening and 5 Tips for Better Listening*" (4:37 minutes)

https://www.youtube.com/watch?v=y7gHLSK6zcY&list=PLq0hB4Em-o9uXWjSrsH6xtJsMoKhg0Q7y

• Write the 5 blocks on the left half of a sheet of paper and the 5 tips on the right half. Then write a paragraph on the one "Tip" that you will work to make improvement. |

Methodology

Activity 17 begins with a fun activity (*Good Listener/Poor Listener*) to compare and contrast two very different communication styles. As the title suggest the first round of this exercise begins by exaggerating what poor listening looks like. Although contrived, sadly this often reflects how distracted we are in real life and that giving someone our full attention is not the norm.

The second round of *Good Listener/Poor Listener* juxtaposes the first, by asking students to focus on good listening skills and noticing the distinct differences between the two communication styles. This exercise is an important segue for immersing students in the Good Samaritan Scripture story and for continued focus on virtuous Christ-like actions.

Activity 17 continues by asking students to speculate the thoughts and feelings of certain biblical characters (Inn Keeper) who do not seem to play a prominent role in this scriptural story. This is an opportunity to build empathy by encouraging students to think more inclusively and expansively about the dynamic of mistreatment, but more importantly about the kind actions of others. Each sequential element in this activity is carefully designed to encourage interpersonal skill development and promote a safe learning community.

#66 Worksheet CLEAR Listening is given as homework for continued integration and to bridge school with home about the importance of good listening skills for the family.

An additional option (Teacher discretion) is to assign the YouTube Videos contained in the last Learning Objective/Assessment Possibilities on good listening and effective listening as homework for the respective grades.

For further support with implementation of the Peace Be With You Curriculum refer to:
Unit 3: Love Your Neighbor in the *Teacher Curriculum Guide* for a more in-depth understanding of effective communication skill development through the use of *CLEAR Listening* and *Clear Talk.*

"Whoever has ears ought to hear."

MATTHEW 11:15

"When you talk,
you are only repeating
what you already know.
But if you listen,
you may learn something new."

HH DALAI LAMA XIV

Activity 17
Good listener/Poor listener

Facilitator Script

TIME, PREPARATION, LOGISTICS, & PROCESS

5:00 PREPARATION
- *#62 Poster: CLEAR Listening as a visual for class reference.*
- Familiarize yourself with the *Good Listener/Poor Listener* activity.
- Make copies of *#63 Scripture Connection 3, #64a Role-Reflection & #64b Role-Reflection Directions (back to back), #65 Role-Play 3 & #66 Worksheets* for each student.

SUPPLIES
- One *"Peace Stick"* (Natural wood if possible approx. 4'-5' high and 2"-3" diameter).
- One Container (basket or bowl) to hold Good Samaritan roles written on slips of paper.

LOGISTICS
- On blackboard, Smartboard or wall post *#62 Poster: CLEAR Listening.*
- Arrange students in a *Peace Circle.*
- Place the *"Peace Stick"* on floor in the center of the *Peace Circle* at the appropriate time in the script.
- Place Good Samaritan roles on written slips of paper in the container.

SUPPLIES
- One *"Peace Stick"* (Natural wood if possible approximately 4'-5' high & 2"-3" diameter).
- Container (basket or bowl) to hold Good Samaritan roles written on slips of paper.

LOGISTICS
- On blackboard, Smartboard or wall post *#62 Poster: CLEAR Listening.*
- Arrange students in a *Peace Circle.*
- Place the *"Peace Stick"* in the center of the *Peace Circle* on the floor at the appropriate time in the script.
- Place Good Samaritan roles on written slips of paper in the container.

TIME PROCESS
00:00 Say: "Welcome back to our *Peace Circle.*"

Say: "Thank you for bringing your best personal qualities and harvested knowledge with you to our *Peace Circle.*"

1:00 Say: "Count off one, two, one, two, one, two starting with (student name) on my left. The first one and two are a team. The second one and two are a team, and so forth."

*Note: If the number is uneven, the teacher pairs with the last student.

TIME PROCESS

2:00 **Say:** "We are going to play a game called '*Good Listener/Poor Listener.*' "

Say: "For this first part of the game, all #1's will talk to their partner about a great movie they have recently seen and all #2's will be poor listeners."

3:00 **Say:** "When I say time, wait quietly to hear the next set of directions. #1's, you may begin." (Allow 1 minute)

4:00 **Say:** "Time. #1's you are now poor listeners and #2's you share a great movie you have recently seen with #1's. You may begin." (Allow 1 minute)

5:00 **Say:** "Time.

Ask: "Class. What was this experience of trying to share with a poor listener like for you?"

Possible Responses: Horrible. Awful. Frustrating. Rude. Distracting. Didn't like it. Wanted to walk/run away. (Echo student responses.)

6:00 **Say:** "Thank you."

Ask: "Has anyone ever experienced in real life what it's like to not be heard, given attention or taken seriously?"

Expected Response: YES!

7:00 **Say:** "Me too! We have all experienced this and know how awful it is to not have someone listen to us. It doesn't feel good at all!"

Ask: "What was it like to be the poor listener during the game?"

Possible Responses: Fun. Easy. Felt bad for him/her because I could see he/she didn't like it.

8:00 **Ask:** "In real life, does it seem easy to let ourselves get distracted and not focus on what the other person is saying?"

Expected Response: YES!

Say: "Class. Let's do this exercise over by practicing good listening."

9:00 **Say:** "#1's will share with your partner about whatever you would like and #2's will practice being the best listeners possible."

Say: "When I say 'Time,' wait quietly to hear the next set of directions. #1's, you may begin." (Allow 1 minute)

Activity 17 Facilitator Script (continued)

<u>TIME</u> <u>PROCESS</u>

10:00 **Say:** "Time. #1's it's your turn to practice being the best possible listeners and #2's share whatever you would like with your partner. You may begin."
(Allow 1 minute)

11:00 **Say:** "Time."

Ask: "Class. What was this experience like having a good listener?"

Possible Responses: Person was attentive. Didn't talk, disrupt, or interrupt me. Looked at me. Smiled. Nodded head. Valued. Important. Understood. Comforted. Took me seriously. I wanted to talk more. (Echo student responses.)

12:00 **Say:** "Thank you class. All of these things that you have pointed out, (i.e., eye contact, smiling, not interrupting, nodding head, being attentive, etc.) are excellent *CLEAR Listening* skills that we will spend time practicing throughout the year."

Ask: "Has anyone ever experienced in real life what it's like to be heard, given attention and taken seriously?"

Expected Response: YES!

13:00 **Say:** "Me too! What an amazing experience! Having someone truly listen is a gift, not only from the listener, but a gift from God."

Ask: "What was it like to be a good listener during the game?"

Possible Responses: Fun. Meaningful. Lots of work to stay focused. Hard not to interrupt or talk when the person is talking. (Echo student responses.)

14:00 **Ask:** "Class. Which approach—poor listening or good listening, is more likely to cause conflicts and misunderstanding?"

Expected Response: Poor listening.

Ask: "And which approach—good listening or poor listening, is more likely to build trust and create peace in our relationships?"

Expected Response: Good listening.

15:00 **Say:** "Thank you class! I agree with you. We are all both good listeners and poor listeners in real life. Poor listening is easy, but there is a price to pay. Good listening may require more of our time and focus, but is much more fruitful—makes lots of positive ripples!"

TIME PROCESS

Say: "Let's take a closer look some of the key ingredients of face-to-face communications using the acronym C-L-E-A-R. This acronym will help us better understand the important elements of effective listening. If you look up here at the (Smartboard, wall), I have posted a *CLEAR Listening Poster* that we can all refer to throughout the year."

*Note: Teacher discretion for instruction on CLEAR Listening, i.e., one or more students recite the acronym, teacher reads.

16:00 Say: "C is for Connect: Connecting face to face is an important part of building relationships. By connecting with others and using good listening skills we both (speaker and listener) become better people. "

Ask: "Why might there be less face-to-face communication today?"

Possible Responses: Use of electronic devices. Social media. Less time.

17:00 Say: "I agree. There is a lot of upside about technology and electronic devices, but as we discussed in *Living in "Fast Forward"* there are also a lot of downside. Face-to-face communication, including how we listen, is rapidly becoming a lost art, but still is a very important art."

18:00 Say: "L is for Listen: Listen with your eyes, ears, and heart. A good listener is open, still, and does not disrupt or interrupt the speaker."

Say: "E is for Eye Contact. When we make eye contact we tune into what a person is saying."

Say: "A is for Attention. When we give the speaker our full attention it helps them feel valued and important."

19:00 Say: "R is for Respect. Respect means to be kind and considerate of what the person is saying. You don't have to agree or disagree, just listen! The letter R also stands for Relaxed. Stay as relaxed as possible, especially if there is a conflict, to hear the person out."

20:00 Ask: "What *Servant Leader Words* from our list might remind us of being good listeners?"

Possible Responses: Respectful. Caring. Attentive. Kind. (Echo student responses.)

21:00 Say: "Thank you. Let us always remind ourselves to make every effort to be (student responses) with each other every day."

Say: "Class. Before we LISTEN to the Scripture from Luke about the Good Samaritan, it's important for us to understand who a Samaritan is. At the time of Jesus, Samaritans were considered by the Jews to be a low class of people because they intermarried with non-Jews and did not keep all the Jewish laws. Therefore, Samaritans were considered outcast and not people to be associated with."

Activity 17 Facilitator Script *(continued)*

Note: Hand out #63 Scripture Connection 3 (Luke 10: 25-37) or post on Smartboard.

TIME   PROCESS

22:00   Say: "Class. As you **LISTEN** with open hearts and minds, let yourself imagine what each character in this Scripture reading might be feeling, thinking, or saying."

Note: Teacher reads or asks students to volunteer to read the Scripture from Luke.

23:00   Say: "Thank you for reading and listening to the Scripture."

Say: "Take a look at *#64a Role-Reflection: The Good Samaritan* being handed out. On the back is *#64b Role-Play Directions* for the role-reflection. Let's read the directions out loud together."

24:00   Say: "Thank you."

Note: Teacher hands the container with roles written on slips of paper to a student seated at the front of the class and asks him/her to take one slip of paper and pass the container to the next student.

Say: "As this container comes around, take one slip of paper to discover the role you will play in this next activity."

25:00   Say: "I see that everyone has a role. You may begin." (Allow at least 5 minutes)

Note: Teacher calls students back to their seats in the Peace Circle.

30:00   Say: "Thank you for doing this exercise."

Ask: "Could you imagine yourself being in the role you played during the activity?"

Note: Teacher discretion on whether or not you take this discussion further with the class.

Expected answer: Yes!

Note: Hand out #65 Role Play 3: Inn Keeper/Good Samaritan to each student.

31:00   Say: "Class. Let's take the good listening skills we are learning a step further."

Say: "When everyone has a role-play script handout, please return to your pairs and wait for directions."

33:00   Say: "Okay Class. Let's practice *CLEAR Listening* with our partner. #1's you will begin from the script as the Inn Keeper and #2's you will be the Good Samaritan. Everyone look up when I say 'Time.' Inn Keeper's you may begin." (Allow 30 seconds)

Activity 17 Facilitator Script (continued)

TIME PROCESS

34:00 Say: "Time. Using the same script #2's you will be the Inn Keeper this round and #1's you are the Good Samaritan." (Allow 30 seconds)

35:00 Ask: "Good Samaritans. Were you able to do *CLEAR Listening* with the Inn Keeper?"

Possible Responses: No. Yes. Made eye contact. Gave the person attention. Wasn't sure what to say.

36:00 Say: "Class. When someone is speaking in an excited, rapid, hurried (abrupt, angry) manner it is really difficult for the listener to hear the person."

37:00 Say: "Taking time to use good nonverbal listening skills can really help and we don't have to say anything at all. Nonverbal communication is about 85% of all communication."

Ask: "Which of the skills on the *CLEAR Listening Poster* are nonverbal skills?"

Expected Response: Connect. Listening with your eyes, ears and heart. Using good eye contact. Paying full attention. Respecting and Relaxing.

38:00 Say: "Good. You're right, all of them! Using good nonverbal skills makes a huge difference in helping someone to feel heard and valued, and we don't have to say anything at all."

Say: "At the end of the Good Samaritan script, it asks the Samaritan to say; 'what I hear you saying is...........'"

Ask: "What happened when you did this?"

Possible Responses: Wasn't sure what to do/say. Helped. Didn't help. Person was talking too fast. Couldn't understand the person.

39:00 Say: "Thank you. Another listening skill we'll be working on is called 'active listening' or 'paraphrasing.' This is another skill in building trust. When the person is finished speaking, if we share back with them what was said, it helps them trust we truly did hear them. More on this later."

40:00 Say: "Class. Next week I am very excited to share with you a 5-step communication tool called '*Clear Talk.*'" *Clear Talk* is a way to help the speaker better communicate what she/he is trying to say, which in turn helps the listener be an even better CLEAR Listener."

Say: "Class. Listening is vital to everything we do. I invite you to spend time tonight reflecting on *CLEAR Listening by* completing *#66 Worksheet CLEAR Listening* being handed out to you now. Please do share this worksheet with a parent and turn it in signed tomorrow."

Optional: See Activity 17 "Methodology" for optional YouTube viewing assignment.

41:00 Say: "Thank you class for all of your hard work today!"

Unit 3: Lesson Ten
Clear Talk

*"Let us then pursue what
leads to peace
and to build up one another."*

ROMANS 14:19

Unit 3: Lesson Ten Purpose

To increase peer support and enhance relational skills by practicing good interpersonal communications for further skill acquisition in an effort to build trust, a stronger sense of classroom community and a safe and thriving learning environment.

Lesson Ten Overview

Unit 3: Lesson Ten shifts from intrapersonal skill development to interpersonal skill development. Unit 3 engages students in interactive communication processes to develop effective skills in positive communication. Interpersonal skills are essential for building supportive peer relationships, strengthening the classroom community, and cultivating a safe learning environment.

Lesson Nine is a fundamental building block to *Lesson Ten.* Key elements, such as *CLEAR Listening* and the *Good Samaritan Scripture* passage, are reintroduced to reinforce concepts and principles for further content integration. *Lesson Ten* strengthens *CLEAR Listening* skills by introducing students to a 5-step method of communication called *"Clear Talk."* Students voluntarily enter the *Peace Circle*, inviting another student to receive a put-up using each of the five steps in sequential order.

In Activity 18, grades 4-8 practice building interpersonal skills by using put-ups to express gratitude toward peers using the *Clear Talk* framework. A spirit of gratitude sets the tone for an important foundational message—peer support is built on respect, kindness, and compassion toward others. In turn, the compassion of Christ is how we build a strong Christian community and ultimately, the Kingdom of God.

The *Clear Talk* process is kept very basic for all grades to practice using this communication tool. *More advanced training in applying Clear Talk and peace-building skills with grades 6-8 will be available to educators in the near future. Lesson Ten: Activity 18* is the program end-point for grades 4-8, followed by the comprehensive program wrap up. *Clear Talk practice is highly encouraged through the remainder of the school year.*

Overarching Goal

The overarching goal is to enhance interpersonal skills, by building peace and positive peer support to strengthen the classroom, and building school community to create a safe and thriving learning environment.

For further support with implementing the Peace Be With You Curriculum refer to:
Unit 3: Lesson Nine & Ten in the *Teacher Curriculum Guide* for a more in depth understanding of the significance of *Clear Talk and CLEAR Listening* as key elements to effective communication.

"Finally, brothers, rejoice. Mend your ways,
Encourage one another,
agree with one another, live in peace,
and the God of love and peace with be with you."

2 Corinthians 13:11

"May the Lord of peace himself
give you peace at all times
and in every way.
The Lord be with all of you."

2 Thessalonians 3:16

"May the God of hope fill you
with all joy and peace in believing,
so that you will abound in hope
by the power of the Holy Spirit."

Romans 15:13

Activity 18
Clear Talk

Activity 18 Purpose
To introduce and practice a method communication for further interpersonal skill development in an environment of respect and gratitude to build trust and community.
Activity 18 National Standards/Themes Correlation
Social Studies Themes:

Social Studies Themes:
- People, Places, and the Environment (SST-PPE)
- Individual Development and Identity (SST-IDI)
- Individuals, Groups, and Institutions (SST-IGI)

Language Arts Speaking and Listening Standards:
- Prepare for and participate effectively in a range of conversations and collaborations with diverse partners, building on others' ideas and expressing their own clearly and persuasively. (CCSS.ELA-Literacy.CCRA.SL.1)
- Evaluate a speaker's point of view, reasoning, and use of evidence and rhetoric. (CCSS.ELA-Literacy.CCRA.SL.3)
- Present information, findings, and supporting evidence such that listeners can follow the line of reasoning and the organization, development, and style are appropriate to task, purpose, and audience. (CCSS.ELA-Literacy.CCRA.SL.4)

	Learning Objectives **Students will be able to:**	**Corresponding Assessment Possibilities**
1	**Grades 4-8** Playfully mix up the seating arrangement as a fun exercise to encourage inclusiveness. **Standards** CST-DHP, CST-CFCP, SST-PPE, SST-IDI, CCSS.ELA-Literacy.CCRA.SL.1, CCSS.ELA-Literacy.CCRA.SL.3, CCSS.ELA-Literacy.CCRA.SL.4	***No Worksheet*** • Students participate in an Ice Breaker to help them step out of their comfort zone and think more inclusively.
2	**Grades 4-8** Describe, practice and demonstrate *Clear Listening* through active participation in *Peace Circle* processes. **Standards** CST-DHP, CST-CFCP, SST-PPE, SST-IDI, CCSS.ELA-Literacy.CCRA.SL.1, CCSS.ELA-Literacy.CCRA.SL.3, CCSS.ELA-Literacy.CCRA.SL.4	***#67 Teacher Reference*** ***Clear Talk Observation Rubric*** • This rubric is used to critique student progress on listening skills, level of participation in the process, and to help determine if and where re-teaching is needed.

3	**Grades 4-8** Understand and practice a 5-step method of communication. **Standards** CST-DHP, CST-CFCP, SST-PPE, SST-IDI, CCSS.ELA-Literacy.CCRA.SL.1, CCSS.ELA-Literacy.CCRA.SL.3, CCSS.ELA-Literacy.CCRA.SL.4.	**#68 Poster** ***Clear Talk*** • Display this visual aid on *CLEAR Talk* for reference. **#69 Role-Play 4** ***Person Who Was Mistreated*** **#70 Worksheet** ***Peer Support Practice***

Methodology

Activity 18: Clear Talk begins by welcoming students back to the *Peace Circle* and a quick review of *CLEAR Listening*. Students and teacher then engage in a fun active icebreaker exercise to get everyone moving. Students commonly sit next to friends or congregate in cliques and are not always thinking inclusively. In a very fun and nonthreatening way, the icebreaker mixes up the seating arrangement so students end up sitting next to someone they may not usually sit next to. Please do emphasize the three rules of 1. Play hard. 2. Play fair. And 3. Nobody hurt. We do want this to be fun and do not want to have the fun spoiled by someone getting injured during the process. We have never had a student get hurt during this activity and want to keep it that way.

The activity then transitions to teacher instruction of the five steps in the *Clear Talk* method of communication. Please familiarize yourself with the five steps in *Clear Talk* prior to instruction. Each step is important, as is the sequential order of the steps. *Clear Talk* is a helpful organizational framework for the speaker to effectively communicate thoughts and feelings. The process is also helpful in reducing blame and/or a defensive reaction in the listener.

Activity 18 is a brief, but important introduction to *Clear Talk*. Grades 4-8 learn the foundations of this framework as an effective tool for building healthy relationships through positive communication with peers and adults. *Activity 18* only uses "put-ups" to keep the process simple, build rapport and to promote positive peer support. Teacher instruction on *Clear Talk* is best demonstrated in the center of the *Peace Circle* with a student. For this demonstration, only select a student with whom you are willing to share put-ups, to model the desired approach. Following *Activity 18, Unit 3: Comprehensive Review and Unit 3: Four Agreements* is the end point in the curriculum for all grades.

Lessons Eight and *Nine* are a great starting point; however, these two lessons alone will most likely not make a significant difference in how students communicate. Therefore we strongly suggest additional practice opportunities beyond *Activity 18 and Activity 19* for grades 4-8, through the remainder of the school year.

Activity 18
Clear Talk

Facilitator Script

TIME, PREPARATION, LOGISTICS, & PROCESS

5:00   PREPARATION
- Preview Icebreaker exercise.
- Make two copies of *#69 Role Play 4: Person who was Mistreated.*

SUPPLIES
- *#62 Poster: CLEAR Listening*
- *#68 Poster: Clear Talk*
- *Peace Stick*

LOGISTICS
- Post *#62 Poster: CLEAR Listening* and *#68 Poster: Clear Talk* for visual reference.
- Students are in a *Peace Circle* seating arrangement.
- Remove teacher chair from circle just prior to entering the circle to explain the Ice Breaker. Return teacher chair and sit down during the last round to end the Ice Breaker.
- Place *Peace Stick* in center of *Peace Circle* after the Icebreaker.

TIME/PROCESS
00:00 Say: "Welcome back to our *Peace Circle*."

Ask: "Again, I invite you to be mindful of the personal qualities and increased knowledge you bring into our circle?" (Pause for brief reflection)

Ask: "Who can tell me what the acronym *CLEAR* stands for in *CLEAR Listening* without looking at the poster?" (Connect, Listen, Eye Contact, Attention, Respect)

1:00 Say: "Thank you (Student Name)."

Note: If the student gets hung up on any of the acronym, ask if he/she would like help from the class.

Say: "You've got it! Thank you (Student Name) for being a *CLEAR Listener*."

Say: "I invite everyone to practice being *CLEAR Listeners* within and outside of the *Peace Circle* on a daily basis. We're going to practice this skill throughout the year so we can get better and better at it."

Say: "Before we begin practicing *CLEAR Listening*, let's have some fun!"

Activity 18 Facilitator Script (continued)

<u>**TIME**</u> <u>**PROCESS**</u>

2:00 **Say:** "For this activity there are three rules:
1. Play Hard
2. Play Fair
3. Nobody Hurt."

Say: "Raise your hand if you agree to these rules."

Say: "Thank you all for agreeing to these important rules."

3:00 **Say:** "Class. This game is called, "I Like to....? The person standing in the center says, "I like to ... ? and finishes the sentence with what he or she likes."

Note: This is an exercise on inclusion. Encourage students to say something that would include as many people as possible. The object is to unwittingly get students to mix up the seating arrangement they began with.

Say: "If what the person in the center says fits (you like the same thing they do) leave your chair and quickly and safely find another chair in the circle, but not a chair on your immediate right or left (has to be at least two chairs to the right or two to the left)."

Ask: "Now class. When I step into the center and say 'I like to.....?' what's is going to happen?"

Expected Response: Everyone is going to rush around to get a chair.

Say: "That's right! There will be a lot of mayhem in the center of the circle and I'm not going to play traffic cop."

4:00 **Say:** "Turn to the person on your right and say: PLAY HARD, PLAY FAIR and NOBODY HURT! Now, turn to the person on your left and say: PLAY HARD, PLAY FAIR and NOBODY HURT!"

Say: "Thank you class!"

Note: Teacher enters center of the circle to demonstrate what the person in the center is to do, while removing her/his chair and placing it outside of the circle. Similar to musical chairs, removing the chair causes someone to not have a seat for the icebreaker to proceed.

Say: "Okay. Here we go! I'll start us off. I like to.......eat pizza!"

Note: Teacher sits down soon after saying "pizza." All students and teacher will be seated at this point except for one student who remains standing in the center of the circle.

5:00 **Say:** "Okay, (Student Name), it's your turn to say, 'I like to _ !' and finish the sentence."

Activity 18 Facilitator Script (continued)

<u>TIME</u>   <u>PROCESS</u>

Note: Allow 5-10 students to have a turn getting in the center of the circle. The icebreaker ends at teacher discretion by returning your chair and sitting down in the circle.

10:00 Say: "It is great to see everyone laughing and having fun! Thank you all for playing hard, playing fair and I am really glad nobody was hurt!"

Say: "Class. Tell me again, why sitting in a circle is so important?" (Echo responses)

Possible Responses: Everyone is equal. No first or last. Can see everyone. Can make eye contact with everyone. Sign or symbol of unity and support.

Say: "Thank you for your thoughtful responses."

11:00 Ask: "When we first started our *Peace Circle* what did everyone place in the container (basket, bowl) in the center of the circle?"

Expected response: Personal gifts we bring to circle.

Say: "Thank you all for continuing to bring your personal gifts to our *Peace Circle*, classroom, school and your homes."

12:00 Say: "I want to teach you *Clear Talk* which is a communication tool that will help us practice good listening skills. Good listening is also a gift we can give to others and makes us better servant-leaders."

Note: Teacher places Peace Stick on the floor in the center of the Peace Circle and returns to seat.

Ask: "Class. What did I just place in the center of the circle?"

Expected Response: Peace Stick.

13:00 Say: "Thank you. Just as the (basket, bowl) holding all of our personal gifts had special meaning, the *Peace Stick* also has special meaning for our *Peace Circle*."

Note: Teacher enters circle, picks up the Peace Stick and holds it up right. From the center of the Peace Circle, the teacher continues with the facilitator script, turning clockwise to make eye contact with each student.

Say: "The *Peace Stick* symbolically represents the tree from which it came. Imagine the *Peace Stick* has deep roots, like a strong oak tree, creating a secure and safe foundation for our classroom. Further imagine an array of branches and leaves coming out of the top of the *Peace Stick* that create a canopy or umbrella over our *Peace Circle*. This canopy covering represents inclusion and dignity for all. It is with this kind of respect and spirit of gratitude from below and above that we will do *Clear Talk* with each other."

Note: Teacher places Peace Stick on the floor in the center of the Peace Circle and returns to seat.

TIME   PROCESS

14:00 Say: "Class. *Clear Talk* is a way of organizing and communicating our thoughts and feelings so that what we say is clearer for the listener to hear. There are five easy steps to *Clear Talk*."

Note: Teacher selects a student that she/he has observed modeling positive peer support.

> **Ask:** "(Student Name-A) will you come up to help me demonstrate the five steps in Clear Talk?"

> **Expected Response:** Yes. (If for any reason this student says he/she passes, ask another student.)

Note: Teacher discretion whether students in the Peace Circle stand or remain seated during your demonstration.

> **Say:** "Thank You (Student Name-A) for coming into the *Peace Circle* with me."

> **Expected Response:** You're welcome.

> **Say:** "Class. This first step in *Clear Talk* is saying 'Thank you!' to the person. Saying 'Thank You!' is so simple, yet so important."

> **Ask:** "Why do we say 'thank you' to someone for anything?"

15:00 Possible Responses: We're grateful. Good manners. Out of respect. Shows kindness. Shows we Care. (Echo Student Responses)

> **Say:** "All of your answers are correct. Let's take 'Thank You!' a step further. Thank you in our *Peace Circle* means, "I see the Christ in you and I invite you to see the Christ in me. This means we are all children of God, created in God's image. Each of us is a good person at our core."

> **Say:** "Step 2 in *Clear Talk* is 'Data.' *Data* simply means I just describe what happened or what I observed or how the other person's actions affected me."

Note: The script below gives a contrived example of an observation. The most powerful observation you can share with the student assisting you is a real and recent example, where their action(s) had a positive ripple effect.

16:00 Say: "The *Data* is.....I noticed that (Student Name-A) reached out to (Student Name-B), who was sitting all by himself in the cafeteria, and you went over and sat down with him."

Activity 18 Facilitator Script (continued)

<u>TIME</u> <u>PROCESS</u>

Say: "Step 3 are my *Feelings* about what (Student Name-A) did. Feelings are so important; and it is so important that we communicate what we feel with others in a clear way. There are *Five Basic Feelings—Mad, Sad, Glad, Afraid and Ashamed.* There are many variations of these five basic feelings. For instance, I may not be mad, but I am frustrated or irritated. I may not be ashamed, but I am embarrassed."

Say: "(Student Name-A), I feel joy about your actions toward (<u>Student Name-B</u>) and very proud of you for what you did!"

17:00 **Say:** "Step 4 is what I notice or observe about what the person did. There are two incomplete sentences that help to express this: 'Your actions said?' and 'My actions said?'"

Say: "(<u>Student Name-A</u>), your actions said you really care about others and that you demonstrated positive peer support to (<u>Student Name-B</u>) and, you are a good model for us in what it means to be a servant-leader."

Say: "In Step 5 I share what I '*Want.*' There may be more than one '*Want*' that we want to share. I ask myself a question: 'What do I want the person to know about how their actions impacted me?' "

Say: "(<u>Student Name-A</u>), my first *Want* is to let you know I noticed the positive ripples you made. My second *Want* is that you continue to be a good Christian servant-leader and a Christ-like example of how to make positive ripples in our school."

Note: After Step 5, transition to CLEAR Listening (Active Listening).

18:00 **Say:** "Now (<u>Student Name-B</u>), it's your turn to practice active listening. Start by saying to me, 'What I heard you say is....' "

Note: Encourage the student to repeat (paraphrase) what you said, using each Clear Talk step as a guide for what was heard, i.e., "What I heard you say is 'Thank You!" "What I heard you say is the data is".....etc. If the student gets stuck, ask him/her to get help from the class.

19:00 **Ask:** "Class. Do you think (<u>Student Name-B</u>) listened and heard what I said?"

Expected Response: Yes.

Ask: "What did you see or hear (<u>Student Name-B</u>) do that demonstrated good listening?"

Possible Response: Made good eye contact. Nodded head. Didn't interrupt. Didn't fidget or disrupt. Looked interested. Was attentive. Repeated back what you said.

TIME   PROCESS

Say: "I agree. Let's give (<u>Student Name-B</u>) one clap… two claps… three claps…! Thank you (Student Name-A) for being willing to help me with the *Clear Talk* demonstration. Thank you class for also being *CLEAR Listeners* as I presented *Clear Talk*."

20:00 Say: "Class. Let's do a role-play to demonstrate another example of *Clear Talk* using the *Good Samaritan Scripture*."

Ask: "Who would like to play the role of the person who was mistreated?"

Say: "Thank you (<u>Student Name—1</u>) for volunteering to be the person who was mistreated."

Say: "Hypothetically, as you sit there in our *Peace Circle*, you have thoughts as the mistreated person that you would like to do a *Clear Talk* with the Good Samaritan."

Say: "Class. There is a difference between 'thoughts' (sitting on them) and the courage to take positive action on those thoughts. So now (<u>Student Name—1</u>) your thoughts shift into an action. You get up from your seat and enter the *Peace Circle*. Good; welcome (<u>Student Name—1</u>) to the center of the *Peace Circle*."

21:00 Say: "(<u>Student Name—1</u>), please pick up the *Peace Stick* and hold it upright, just as I did when I demonstrated. Good! Thank you."

Say: "Class. In *Clear Talk*, the person who initiates entering the center of the *Peace Circle*, is the person who picks up the *Peace Stick*, and is the one who will speak to the person invited into the circle. The person invited into the center is the *CLEAR Listener*."

22:00 Ask: "Who would like to play the role of the Good Samaritan?"

Say: "Thank you (<u>Student Name—2</u>) for volunteering to be the Good Samaritan!"

Say: "Now (<u>Student Name—1</u>) please invite (<u>Student Name—2</u>), the Good Samaritan and 'CLEAR Listener' into the center of the circle to hold the *Peace Stick* with you."
(Pause as Student 2 enters the Peace Circle)

23:00 Say: "Thank you both for coming into our *Peace Circle*!"

Note: Give the two students in the center of the circle each a copy of #69 Role-Play 4: Person Who was Mistreated.

TIME   PROCESS

Say: "(Student Name—1), you may begin with the role-play script."

Student A says:
Step 1: Thank you!: "<u>*Thank you*</u> Good Samaritan for coming into the circle and into my life."

Step 2: Data: "I was robbed and beaten very badly. I was lying there alone. The priest and Levite walked passed me to the other side of the road. You passed by, saw me, and tended to me."

24:00 *Step 3: Feelings:* "I was very scared. I was in deep pain. I was afraid. I felt alone. I was hopeful when you stopped. I felt loved and cared for when you tended to my wounds and brought me to the Inn."

Step 4: Your actions said.... "Your actions said that you are a very kind and compassionate person."

25:00 *Step 5: Wants:* "I want you to know that I have deep respect and gratitude for your compassion and how you cared for me."

Say: "Thank you (Student Name—1) for demonstrating *Clear Talk* as the person who was mistreated might say to the Good Samaritan."

Say: "Now, (Student Name—2), as the Good Samaritan, it's your turn to demonstrate *Active Listening* with (Student Name—1), by repeating what you heard."

25:00 Say: "Remember class. This does not have to be word for word. The easiest way to do this is to go through each of the *Clear Talk* steps and paraphrase what you heard the person say. Also remember that the Peace Circle is here if you would like help."

*Note: If (Student Name—2) has trouble recalling what was said, invite the student to ask for help from students' in the Peace Circle.

Student A says:
Step 1: Thank you!: "What I heard you say is '<u>*Thank you*</u> for coming into the circle and into my life."

Step 2: Data: "What I heard you say is that you were robbed and beaten very badly and lying all alone. A priest and Levite walked by and to the other side of the road. I saw you, and tended to you."

26:00 *Step 3: Feelings:* "What I heard you say is that you felt very scared, alone and in lots of pain. I also heard you say that when I stopped it gave you hope, and that you felt loved and cared for when I tended to your wounds and brought you to the Inn."

Step 4: Your actions said.... "What I heard you say is that my actions said that I am a very kind and compassionate person."

TIME   PROCESS

Step 5: Wants: "What I heard you say is that you want me to know that your have deep respect and gratitude for my compassion and how I cared for you."

27:00 **Ask:** "(Student Name—1) do you feel heard and are you complete?"

Expected Response: Yes.

Say: "Class. When both the speaker and listener are complete they conclude with some mutual sign of peace. This could be a *hand-shake, fist tap, hug, or some other positive gesture of gratitude.*"

Say: "Thank you both for doing a great job demonstrating *Clear Talk* and *CLEAR Listening*. Let's give (Student Name—1) and (Student Name—2) one clap......two claps....three claps!"

*Note: Teacher and students return to their seats in the Peace Circle.

28:00 **Ask:** "Class. What did you notice about the *Clear Talk* and *CLEAR Listening* that we just witnessed?"

Expected Responses: (Student Name—1) spoke in a clear way. (Student Name—2) repeated what was heard. Used good eye contact. Didn't interrupt.

Ask: "Class. Are you ready to practice *Clear Talk* and *CLEAR Listening*?"

Expected Response: Yes.

29:00 **Say:** "Awesome! Please close your eyes. Think about a person in this circle that you would like to give a put-up." (Allow 1 minute)

Say: "Okay...Open your eyes. Thank you."

Ask: "Who would like to start?"

*Note: Invite any student that would like to acknowledge another student with a put-up into the center of the circle to practice using the 5 steps of Clear Talk. In turn, have this student invite in the other student as CLEAR Listener.

**Note: Teacher steps into the center of the circle with the two students for support and guidance, at least for the initial Clear Talk practices.

30:00 **Say:** "Thank you (Student Name-1) for being the first one to step in our *Peace Circle*!"

Ask: "Class what leader word(s) would describe (Student Name-1) for being the first to step into our circle?"

Activity 18 Facilitator Script (continued)

TIME PROCESS

 Possible Responses: Courageous. Brave. Willing to take action. Caring. Thoughtful. Initiator.

31:00 Ask: "(Student Name-1), do you hear the positive leader qualities being used to describe your actions?"

 Expected Response: Yes.

 Ask: "(Student Name-1), who would you like to invite into our *Peace Circle*?"

32:00 Say: "Good choice! Welcome (Student Name-2) into the circle."

Note: Use #67 Teacher Reference: Clear Talk Observation Rubric to take notes and give feedback. The rubric not intended to be a grading tool. It is best to be transparent about your use of the rubric with the class if you choose to use it.

 Say: "(Student Name-1), as you begin your *Clear Talk*, you can use the *Clear Talk Poster* on the wall (or on the Smartboard). I'm here along with the rest of the class to help guide you if you need any help."

Note: Most Clear Talks and CLEAR Listening processes are fairly brief (2-3 minutes); however, some may last a little longer.

33:00 Say: "(Student Name-1), are you complete?"
 (After the student speaking has gone through the five steps.)

 Expected Response: Yes.

 Say: "(Student Name-2), it's your turn to practice active listening."

34:00 Ask: "(Student Name-1), do you feel heard by (Student Name-2)?"
 (When the student listening has completed.)

 Expected Response: Yes.

 Ask: "(Student Name-1), how difficult or easy was it for (Student Name-2) to hear your put-up?" (Echo the response).

 Ask: "(Student Name-2) does that describe your experience?"

 Expected Response: Yes.

35:00 Say: "Thank you both for being our first (ever) *Clear Talk* speaker and CLEAR Listener. Please give each other some mutual sign of peace. Thank you. You may be seated in our *Peace Circle*."

 Say: "Class. Let's give (Student Name-1) and (Student Name-2) one clap...two claps...three claps..."

Activity 18 Facilitator Script (continued)

TIME   PROCESS

36:00 Say: "Class. What did you observe about the *Clear Talk* and *Clear Listening* between (<u>Student Name-1</u>) and (<u>Student Name-2</u>) that we just witnessed?"

*Note: Encourage students' seated in the circle to give direct positive feedback to the two students that just completed the process.

**Note: Repeat the process by inviting another student in the center of the circle to do a Clear Talk. That student in turn, invites a student with whom he/she would like to do the Clear Talk. Teacher discretion and class time determine how many Clear Talks will take place during the class period.

37:00 Say: "Class. Let's stand and hold hands (if appropriate) and close our *Peace Circle* for today in prayer. Our Father......"

*Note: Let students know that Clear Talk and CLEAR Listening practice will continue throughout the school year.

Unit 3
Comprehensive Review and Four Agreements

Purpose	
To reinforce the concepts and principles learned to promote positive actions and encourage positive ripple effects in school and at home.	
Learning Objectives **Students will be able to:**	**Corresponding Assessment Possibilities**
1 **Grades 4-8** Recall and recite *Unit 3* concepts by completing a comprehensive review. ***Standards*** *(CST-DHP, CST-CFCP, CST-RR, CST-S, SST-C, SST-PPE, SST-IDI, SST-IGI, CCSS.ELA-Literacy.CCRA.SL1, CCSS.ELA-Literacy.CCRA.W1)*	***#71 Unit 3: Comprehensive Review***
2 **Grades 4-8** Reflect, process, and agree to *Unit 3* principles by signing the Four Agreements. ***Standards*** *(CST-DHP, CST-RR, CST-S, SST-C, SST-PPE, SST-IDI, SST-IGI, CCSS.ELA-Literacy.CCRA.W1)*	***#72 Unit 3: Four Agreements*** • If the student agrees, he/she is to sign the *Love Your Neighbor Four Agreements* along with the teacher, principal and a parent.

Unit 3
Comprehensive Review and Four Agreements

Facilitator Script

TIME/PREPARATION/LOGISTICS & PROCESS

10:00 PREPARATION/LOGISTICS
- Make copies and hand out *#71 Unit 3: Comprehensive Review, and #72 Unit 3: Four Agreements* to each *(Grades 4/5)* student.
- Use *#71 Unit 3: Comprehensive Review* to work with students on reflection and writing about the entire unit.
- Invite students to take the completed *#71 Unit 3: Comprehensive Review and #72 Unit 3: Four Agreements* home to share both with a parent.
- Ask students to return the signed agreements to class and hand into the teacher.

TIME PROCESS
0:00   **Say:** "We have learned many new things in this third Unit. Let's review what we've learned by completing a student reflection activity. Please let me know you have finished, by giving me a thumbs-up."

5:00   **Say:** "Thank you for completing this reflection. Now that you have reviewed some of what you have learned, please look over the *Four Agreements* that have just been handed out."

Say: "Let's read the *Four Agreements* out loud together."

6:00   **Say:** "Thank you! Do you think you can agree to these statements?"

Expected Response: "Yes"

Say: "If you agree, please sign the *Love Your Neighbor Four Agreements (#72 Unit 3: Four Agreements)*. I will come around and sign each of yours after you have signed it. Take the worksheet and four agreements home to share with your parents. Return them both tomorrow, signed by a parent. Thank you for your commitment to working together to create positive ripples and build up our classroom and school community!"

*Note: Teachers are encouraged to revisit any of the Unit 3 lessons/activities throughout the school year.

Peace Be With You!

Appendix A
Unit 1: Student Worksheets

Table of Contents

Name: _____ Date: _____

Which Servant Leader Word Fits Me Best?

1. Choose one servant leader word from our class list that best describes you and write it here: _____

2. Explain why that servant-leader word best describes you.

_____
_____
_____
_____
_____
_____
_____

#1 Worksheet-Unit 1-Lesson 1-Activity 1

Name: _____ Date: _____

Which Servant Leader Word Fits Me Best?

1. Choose one servant leader word from our class list that best describes you and write it here: _____

2. Explain why that servant leader word best describes you.

_____
_____
_____
_____
_____
_____

#1 Worksheet-Unit 1-Lesson 1-Activity 1

Name: _____ **Date:** _____

What Do You Know About Servant Leader Words?

Choose *Option 1* or *Option 2* below. Follow the directions for the option of your choice.

Option 1—One-Page Essay	Option 2—Oral Presentation
• Using correct paragraph structure and mechanics, write a description about why the servant-leader words are important. • The essay should be a minimum of one-page. • Include examples to clarify and personalize your ideas.	• Use index cards to create a 30 second to 1 minute oral presentation describing why the servant-leader words are important. • Use the index cards as a guide to help keep track of your ideas. • During the oral presentation, remember to make eye contact and express enthusiasm using your voice and gestures to help engage your audience.

Name: _____ **Date:** _____

Exit Ticket
New Servant-Leader Word

Directions: Write one new servant-leader word and why you think this word should be added to our class list on the Exit Ticket below.

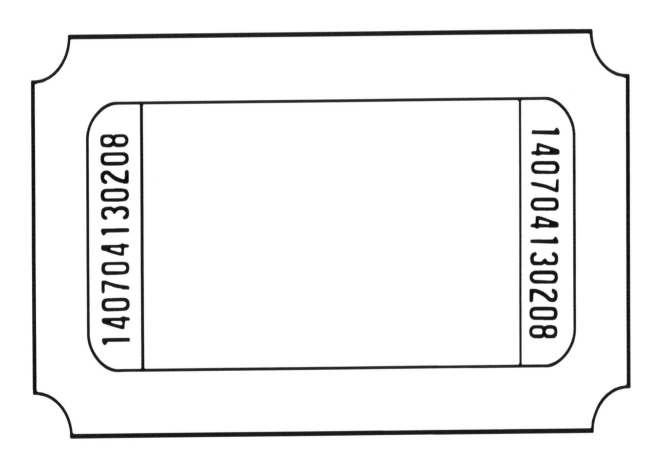

Name: _____ **Date:** _____

Whom Do I Admire?

Directions: Think of a person that you admire. Reflect and write on the following questions:

1. Who is the person you chose? (Pick someone other than a parent)

_____

_____

_____

_____

2. What positive qualities do you admire in this person and why?

_____

_____

_____

_____

3. Which of these positive qualities are similar to Jesus' actions and why?

_____

_____

_____

_____

4. What specific practice steps can you take to model for others the same servant-leader qualities that you admire in this person?

_____

_____

_____

_____

#4 Worksheet-Unit 1-Lesson 1-Activity 1

Name: _____ Date: _____

Servant-Leader and Servant-Follower

Directions: In the Venn diagram below, compare and contrast the qualities of a Servant-Leader with those of a Servant-Follower. Be as detailed as possible.

Servant-Leader   Servant-Follower

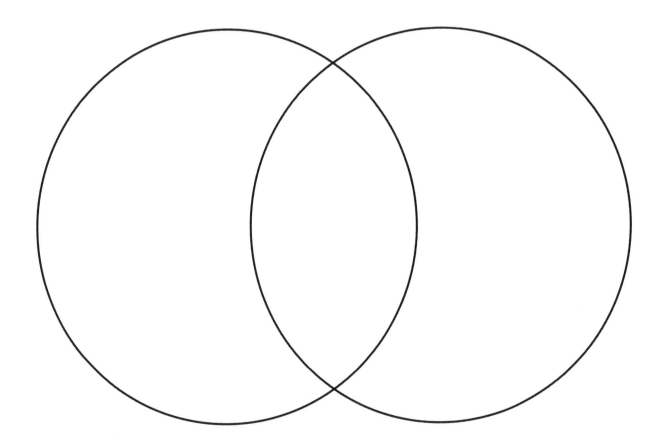

Name: _____ **Date:** _____

Real World Servant-Leader

Directions: Choose a real-world servant-leader and follow the steps below to create a PowerPoint to present to the class on why and how you believe this person models the qualities of a servant-leader.

Step 1: Create a Title Slide
*Include the following:
- Name and image of the servant-leader chosen
- Your name

Step 2: Background Information Slide
*Include details such as:
- Where was he/she born?
- Family history
- Interesting hobbies or unique facts?
- Where does this servant leader currently live?

Step 3: Career or Vocation Slide
*Include details such as:
- What is the career or vocation (ministry) of this servant-leader?
- What does their career path (job) or vocation (ministry) require them to do?
- What events led to him/her becoming a servant-leader?

Step 4: Servant-Leader Justification
- Why do you think this person a servant-leader?
- What qualities of a servant-leader do they model?

Step 5: Modeling Servant Leader Behaviors
- What qualities of this person are you or would you like to model for others?
- Why are these qualities important to you?
- How do you or will you model these qualities?

Step 6: Like Jesus
- What qualities does this person model in the manner of Jesus?
- What similar positive ripples does this real-world servant-leader make to Jesus?

Step 7: Anything Else?
- Be creative with graphics and any other interesting information you want to add about this person.

Name: _____ Date: _____

<u>Servant-Leadership</u>
Reflection 1

Write how your view of yourself as servant-leader has changed since the beginning of this program.

_____
_____
_____
_____
_____
_____
_____
_____
_____
_____
_____
_____
_____
_____
_____
_____
_____
_____
_____
_____
_____
_____
_____

#7 Reflection 1-Unit 1-Lesson 1

Teacher Reference
Negative Ripples

The following are the four negative ripple questions:
1. In general, have you ever been putdown?
2. In general, have you ever putdown anyone?
3. Have you ever been putdown by someone in the class?
4. Have you ever putdown someone in the class?

Why do we ask these four questions?
- Asking the class to respond to the four negative ripple questions with a show of hands is a non-threatening way to engage students in taking a close communal examination of how they treat one another.
- When the vast majority of students raise their hands for all four negative ripple questions, there is a stark collective reality that putdowns are pervasive.
- Asking the four negative ripple questions purposefully exposes the low standard created among students and an opportunity for them to recognize and understand that this form of mistreatment inhibits positive servant-leadership.
- A stark view of the current reality ("Wow, there is a lot of mistreatment going on here.") is necessary in order to create a dissatisfaction with the current state (I don't like that we treat each other like this and want something better!"). The tension between the current reality and dissatisfaction with the current state is purposeful in order to motivate students to make a shift toward a higher standard of conduct.

#8 Teacher Reference Unit 1-Lesson 2-Activity 2

Name: _____ **Date:** _____

Negative Actions = Negative Ripples

Write on the following:

A time when you put someone down at school or at home:

_____

_____

_____

What was wrong with what you did? How do you know that?

_____

_____

_____

What did you notice going on for the other person when you did that?

_____

_____

_____

What was your goal? Next time you have that goal, what will you do differently?

_____

_____

_____

How did your actions prevent others from becoming their best selves?

_____

_____

_____

What did your words and attitude say to others about you?

_____

_____

_____

If in a similar situation, what would be some better choices you could make?

_____

_____

_____

What next steps can you take to make amends—to right any wrongs caused by your actions?

_____

_____

_____

What support do you need to help restore trust and make these amends?

_____

_____

_____

#9 Worksheet-Unit 1-Lesson 2-Activity 2

Name: _____ **Date:** _____

Negative Actions = Negative Ripples

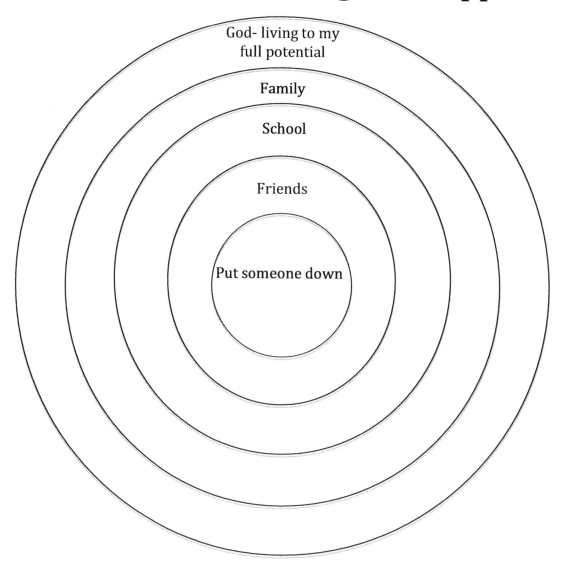

God- living to my
full potential

Family

School

Friends

Put someone down

Directions:
1. In the center circle write an example of when you put someone down at school or home.
2. In each circle from the center circle, write what negative ripples your negative actions may have caused. Only fill-in the circles that apply.

#10 Worksheet-Unit 1-Lesson 2-Activity 2

Name: _____ **Date:** _____

Triangle Talk
Triangle 1

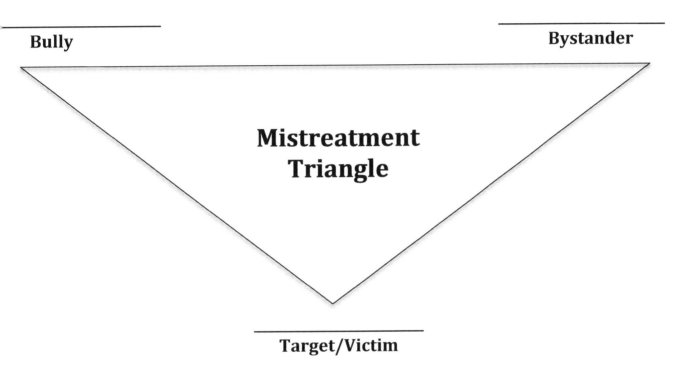

Bully

Bystander

Mistreatment Triangle

Target/Victim

Group Discussion:
1. What weaknesses do you notice about the above Mistreatment Triangle?
2. Why are the terms like bully, bystander, and victim that describe people not helpful?
3. What suggestions do you have for more helpful and hopeful language to replace these terms?
4. How and why do you think this new language will make things better?

#11a Worksheet-Unit 1-Lesson 2-Activity 2

Name: _____ **Date:** _____

Triangle Talk
Triangle 2

Servant Leadership
(God)

Peace Be With You
Triangle

Self-Care (Skills for Inner Strength)   **Supportive Peer Relationships**
(Holy Spirit)   **(Son-Jesus)**

Group Discussion:
1. What strengths do you notice about the above *Peace Be With You* Triangle? 2. What about this triangle is helpful and hopeful? 3. What specific servant-leader actions could bring *Peace Be With You* into our classroom? 4. What next steps could we take together to put these actions into motion?

#11b Worksheet-Unit 1-Lesson 2-Activity 2

Name: _____ **Date:** _____

Poor Choice Cartoon

Directions: In the boxes below create a cartoon strip using drawings, speech bubbles, and/or captions to describe a poor choice you made that may have caused negative ripples. At the end of your cartoon show how you could turn the negative ripple choice into a positive ripple choice.

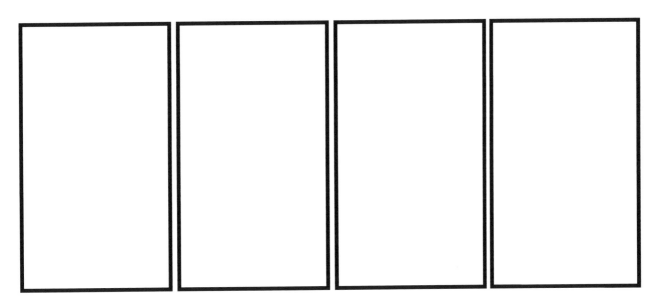

*Student: When you have completed this worksheet, please share it with a parent. Ask one or both parents for an example of a poor choice or negative attitude in which they were able to turn their poor choice or negative attitude into something positive.

#12 Worksheet-Unit 1-Lesson 2-Activity 2

Name: _____ **Date:** _____

Attitude Adjustment

Directions: In the left column titled "Negative Attitude" list five different ways your attitude can discourage others. Next, follow the arrows across to the box in the column titled "Positive Attitude" and list five ways you can make an "Attitude Adjustment" to be encouraging and supportive of others.

Negative Attitude		Positive Attitude
1.		1.
2.		2.
3.		3.
4.		4.
5.		5.

*Student: When you have completed this worksheet, please share it with a parent. Ask one or both parents for an example of a poor choice or negative attitude in which they were able to turn their poor choice or negative attitude into something positive.

#13 Worksheet-Unit 1-Lesson 2-Activity 2

Teacher Reference
Positive Ripples

Four Positive Ripple Questions:
1. In general, have you ever received a put-up (felt complimented, encouraged and supported by someone)?
2. In general, have you ever given a put-up (complimented, encouraged and supported someone)?
3. Have you ever received a put-up (complimented, encouraged, supported) from someone in our class?
4. Have you ever given a put-up (complimented, etc.) to someone in our class?

Why Do We Ask These Four Questions?
*   Asking the class to respond to the four positive ripple questions with a show of hands is a non-threatening way to engage students in taking a close communal examination of how capable they are of treating one another well.
*   When the vast majority of students raise their hands for all four of the positive ripple questions, this is an opportunity to reinforce that put-ups do exist among students and are the preferred method of treatment.
*   Asking the four positive ripple questions purposefully exposes that a high standard is possible and challenges students to raise the bar even higher by building on the current level of put-ups to promote positive servant-leadership.
*   The purpose of the positive ripple questions is to generate positive emotions (Joy, happiness) to recall recent and past fond memories to contrast the putdown sequence, to inspire and motivate a new reality.
*   By juxtaposing these two views through the negative and positive ripple questions, students are presented with an opportunity to collectively "Choose Your Flavor," giving the class permission, motivation, and ownership in a more hopeful reality.
*   A mutual agreement for a more desirable state (put-ups, positive emotions, compliments, and supportive statements) empowers and motivates students to make a fundamental shift from putdowns to put-ups inspiring them to collectively create a positive ripple and thriving school climate.
*   Students are now able to create a new reality ("Wow, we can and do treat each other well!") and ("I want to build on being a part of something positive").

#14 Teacher Reference Unit 1-Lesson 2-Activity 3

My Definition of Attitude

Directions: Use each letter in the acrostic below to write a positive word that is associated with have a positive attitude. The first one has a sample for you!

Letter	Positive Word
A	**Example: Achieve**
T	
T	
I	
T	
U	
D	
E	

Name: _____ **Date:** _____

Cool Compliments

Put-up (compliment) 3-5 classmates today!

Write on the following:

How do you feel when you give put-ups to others?

_____
_____
_____
_____
_____
_____

How do people respond when you put them up?

_____
_____
_____
_____
_____

What ripple effects do you make when you put-up others?

_____
_____
_____
_____
_____
_____

How will you encourage more put-ups among your peers?

_____
_____
_____
_____
_____

#16 Worksheet-Unit 1-Lesson 2-Activity 3

Name_____ Date_____

<u>Peer Support Strategies</u>
Youth Voice Project

Check any of the strategies below you have done to support another student:
1. ___ Spent time, sat with them, hung out with them.
2. ___ Talked to them at school to encourage them.
3. ___ Listened to them.
4. ___ Gave them advice (hope).
5. ___ Helped them tell an adult (about a problem).
6. ___ Helped them get away; made a distraction.
7. ___ Called (or texted) them at home to encourage them.

Write on the following:
1. Choose one checked action strategies. I choose #_____.

2. How did the other student respond when you did that?

   _____
   _____
   _____

3. How did you feel after you did that?

   _____
   _____
   _____
   _____

4. What Servant-Leader word(s) did you demonstrate when you did that?

   _____

Bonus: Choose an unchecked action strategy that you would be willing to try in the future. How would you go about carry out this strategy?

   _____
   _____
   _____
   _____

#17 Worksheet-Unit 1-Lesson 2-Activity 3

Teacher Reference

Youth Voice Project
Peer Support Strategies

Most helpful support actions:

__Spent time, sat with me, hung out with me.

__Talked to me at school to encourage me.

__Listened to me.

__Gave me advice (hope).

__Helped me tell an adult (about a problem).

__Helped me get away; made a distraction.

__Called (or texted) me at home to encourage me.

My Dream School

Write on the following:

Describe what your school would be like with only positive ripples.

_____
_____
_____
_____
_____
_____

How would everyone be treating each other?

_____
_____
_____
_____
_____
_____

What would everyone be saying? What would everyone be doing?

_____
_____
_____
_____
_____
_____

What would your school look like if it were the most amazing school (Dream School) on the planet?

_____
_____
_____
_____
_____
_____

#19 Worksheet-Unit 1-Lesson 2-Activity 3

Name: _____ **Date:** _____

Positive Ripples in the Bible

Directions: In the chart below are two passages from Scripture that describe the positive actions by two different people in the Bible. Read the passages and list the positive ripple effects in the space provided for both Biblical characters. Using the guidelines below the chart, choose one of the two Biblical characters and create a power point presentation to present to the class.

Scripture Passages and Biblical Persons	Positive Ripple Actions
Luke 10: 25-37—The Good Samaritan	The Good Samaritan
Luke 15: 11-32—The Prodigal Son (focus on verses 13-21)	The Prodigal Son

Choose one of the above Biblical characters. Create a PowerPoint slide presentation include the following:

Slide 1: Biblical person's name, the scripture passage, and a photo image if possible.

Answer these questions:
Slide 2: What impact did the biblical characters' choices and actions have on himself?
Slide 3: What impact did the biblical characters' choices and actions have on others?
Slide 4: What impact did the biblical characters' choices and actions have on me?
Slide 5: What choices and actions has the biblical character inspired in me to make me want to create positive ripples?

#20 Worksheet-Unit 1-Lesson 2-Activity 3

Name: _____ **Date:** _____

Choose Your Flavor

Directions: Things happen every day that I can and cannot control. Whatever the situation, I am faced with a choice or flavor of attitude—Positive or Negative. Think about a situation that could have caused a negative attitude and negative ripples, but instead you made the choice to stay positive—turning a negative situation into positive ripples with a positive attitude.

Situation examples:
- You received a failing grade on a test.
- Your best friend decided not to sit with you at lunch.
- A field trip you were looking forward to was cancelled due to weather.

Situation:

_____
_____
_____
_____
_____
_____
_____

Positive Attitude	Positive Ripple Effects
What I did to stay positive in a negative situation is….	I chose to make positive ripples by….

In a similar situation, my best choice for creating positive ripples in the future is to….

#21 Worksheet-Unit 1-Lesson 2-Activity 3

Name: _____ **Date:** _____

Positive Actions = Positive Ripples

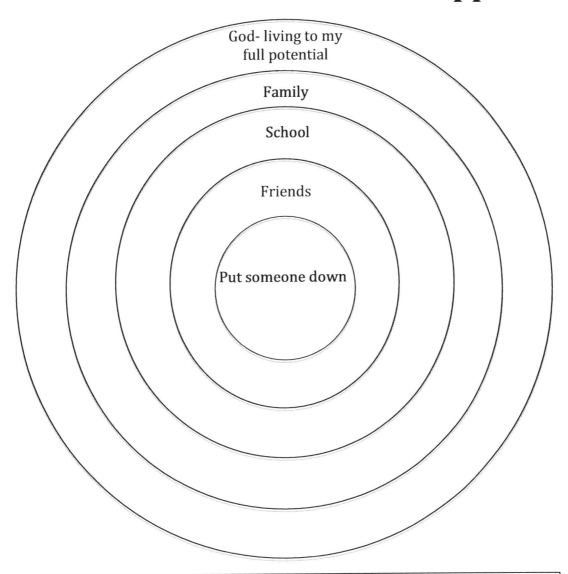

God- living to my
full potential

Family

School

Friends

Put someone down

Directions:
1. **In the center circle write a positive servant-leader action you will do to encourage positive ripples in our school.**
2. **In each circle from the center circle, write what positive ripples you believe you will make by your action.**
3. **Also include in each circle how you will involve other students in this same action to increase the ripple effects.**

#22 Worksheet-Unit 1-Lesson 2-Activity 3

Name: _____ **Date:** _____

Safe to Be Me

Directions: In the space below, fill-in the blank circles with words, phrases, ideas, etc. that are important for you to feel safe to be yourself. Draw extra lines and circles to your web to include any additional words, phrases, ideas, etc.

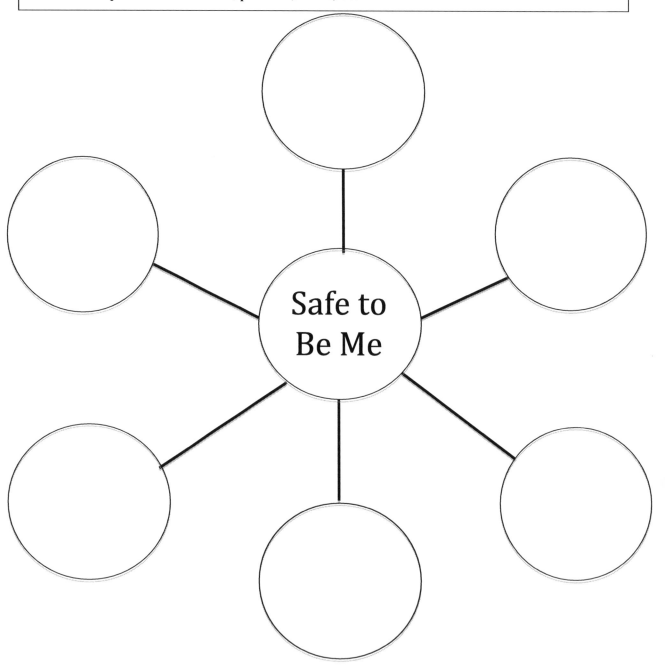

#23 Worksheet-Unit 1-Lesson 3-Activity 4

Four Areas of Safety

Physical Safety	Everyone should be reasonably free from any type of physical harm or threat of harm. No adult or student should enter another's personal space in a way that causes physical harm or threatens to cause physical harm, or interfere with learning. *Physical Safety* at a "10" means a student feels confident that our school is free from the following actions: punch, push, pinch, kick, slap, scratch, poke, choke, trip, bite, pull hair, flick, or any other form of physical mistreatment. *Physical Safety* at a "10" also means there is a presence of respect for the personal space of all.
Mental/ Emotional Safety	Everyone should make reasonable efforts to protect the mental and emotional wellbeing of each person. Together we create a school climate where students feel comfortable being themselves and expressing their views, without fear of being judged. A school where all students feel respected and accepted. *Mental/Emotional Safety* at a "10" means a student feels confident that our school is free from the following actions: verbal/nonverbal put downs for any reason, ostracized for appearance, demeaned, ridiculed, or humiliated. *Mental/Emotional Safety* at a "10" also means there is a presence of respect for the dignity of all.
Social Safety	Everyone should make reasonable efforts to protect others from relational harm or threat of harm in face-to-face settings and in all electronic communications. *Social Safety* at a "10" means a student feels confident that our school is free from the following actions: starting or keeping rumors going, negative texts or social media posts, talking behind someone's back, laughing at, or ridiculing, ignoring or excluding. *Social Safety* at a "10" also means there is a presence of respect for the dignity of all.
Spiritual Safety	Everyone should be reasonably free from any type of harm or threat of harm when praying, worshiping or expressing their religious beliefs. *Spiritual Safety* at a "10" means a student feels confident that our school is free from the following actions: Any form of racial or cultural prejudice, racial, cultural or religious slurs, ridicule, or ostracized for participation in worship. *Spiritual Safety* at a "10" also means there is a presence of respect for the dignity of all.

#24 Teacher Reference-Unit 1-Lesson 3-Activity 4

Name: _____ **Date:** _____

Four Areas of Safety Defined

Directions: Identify and write in the remaining letters filling in the blanks spaces to complete the words that describe the four areas of safety. In the right column write a definition for each of the four areas of safety. Hint: Think about the *Safety Check* talked about in class.

Area of Safety	Definition
P_ _ _ _ _ _	
M_ _ _ _/**E**_ _ _ _ _ _ _ _	
S_ _ _ _ _	
S_ _ _ _ _ _ _	

Name: _____ Date: _____

Examples of Four Areas of Safety

Directions: Write one or more examples for each of the four key areas of safety listed below.

Area of Safety	Example
Physical	
Mental/Emotional	
Social	
Spiritual	

Name: _____ **Date:** _____

Safety Check Line

Directions: Place an X on the Safety Check Line where it best represents your current level of safety at school. Next, in the space below, write the steps you will take to help yourself get closer to a 10.

0   1   2   3   4   5   6   7   8   9   10

LEAST SAFE   **SAFEST**

What steps will I take to get closer to a 10?

_____
_____
_____
_____
_____
_____

List those who can support you in getting closer to a 10?

_____
_____
_____
_____
_____
_____

"Every Christian community should be an oasis of charity and warmth in the midst of a desert of solitude and indifference."

POPE FRANCIS

#27 Worksheet-Unit 1-Lesson 3-Activity 4

360° Safety Diagram

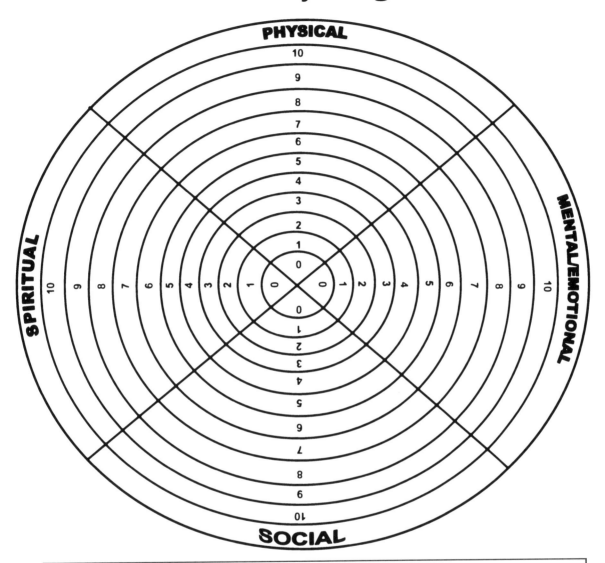

Directions:

1. Color each of the four quadrants in the *360° Safety Diagram* (on the next page) to a number that best represents you.

2. Use a different color for each quadrant (Physical, Mental/Emotional, Social, and Spiritual).

3. On separate paper, write down the number you chose for each of the four quadrants. Add and divide by 4 to get your Safety Check number.

Example: *Physical quadrant= 6, Mental/Emotional= 8, Social= 3 and Spiritual= 7,*

Add each quadrant: 6 + 8 + 3 + 7 = 24, then divide 24 ÷ 4 = 6

The 360° Safety number in this example is 6.

#28 Worksheet-Unit I-Lesson 3-Activity 5

Name: _____ **Date:** _____

<u>360° Safety Reflection</u>

Directions: Below write about your personal 360° Safety.

What can I do to increase my current level of safety in each of the four safety categories?

_____
_____
_____
_____
_____
_____
_____

What steps can I take to help myself strengthen my overall 360° Safety number?

_____
_____
_____
_____
_____
_____
_____

What can I do to help my classmates get closer to a "10"?

_____
_____
_____
_____
_____
_____
_____

#29 Reflection 2-Unit 1-Lesson 3

Jesus Models Dignity for One
Scripture Connection 1

A reading from the Gospel of Luke 19: 1-10:

He (Jesus) came to Jericho and intended to pass through the town. Now a man there named Zacchaeus, who was a chief tax collector and also a wealthy man, was seeking to see who Jesus was; but he could not see him because of the crowd, for he was short in stature. So he ran ahead and climbed a sycamore tree in order to see Jesus, who was about to pass that way. When he reached the place, Jesus looked up and said to him, "Zacchaeus, come down quickly, for today I must stay at your house." And he came down quickly and received him with joy. When they all saw this, they began to grumble, saying, "He has gone to stay at the house of a sinner." But Zacchaeus stood there and said to the Lord, "Behold, half of my possessions, Lord, I shall give to the poor, and if I have extorted anything from anyone I shall repay it four times over." And Jesus said to him, "Today salvation has come to this house because this man too is a descendant of Abraham. For the Son of Man has come to seek and to save what was lost.

#30 Scripture Connection 1-Unit 1-Lesson 4-Activity 6

Jesus Models Dignity for One
Role-Play 1

Narrator: "This story is from the Gospel of Luke chapter 19 verses 1 to 9. Jesus entered Jericho and was passing through. A man was there by the name of Zacchaeus; he was a chief tax collector and was wealthy. He wanted to see who Jesus was, but because he was short he could not see over the crowd. So he ran ahead and climbed a sycamore-fig tree to see him, since Jesus was coming that way. When Jesus reached the spot, he looked up and said to him:

Jesus: "Zacchaeus, come down immediately. I must stay at your house today."

Narrator: So he came down at once and welcomed him gladly. All the people saw this and began to mutter,

Grumbling Crowd: "He has gone to be the guest of a sinner."

Narrator: But when he met Jesus face to face, Zacchaeus stood up and said to the Lord,

Zacchaeus: "Look, Lord! (Grateful for His kindness) Here and now I give half of my possessions to the poor, and if I have cheated anybody out of anything I will pay back four times the amount."

Jesus: "Today salvation has come to this house, because this man, too, is a son of Abraham.

#31 Role-Play 1-Unit 1-Lesson 4-Activity 6

Name: _____ Date: _____

Jesus Models Dignity for One
Scripture Analysis 1

Directions: 1. Read Luke 19: 1-10 and reflect on this passage.
2. Work in assigned groups to answer the questions below.
3. Prepare to discuss your answers with the class.

List Group Members: _____

_____

1. Who is being mistreated?_____
   A. How? _____
   B. Why? _____
   C. Identify the person's feelings: _____
2. Who is mistreating? _____

   _____
   A. How? _____
   B. Why? _____
   C. Identify the person's feelings: _____
3. Who is witnessing mistreatment?_____
   A. How _____
   B. Why? _____
   C. Identify the person's feelings: _____
4. Which character(s) caused a negative ripple? _____
   A. How? _____
   B. Why?_____
   C. What was the result? _____
5. Which character(s) caused a positive ripple? _____
   A. How?_____
   B. Why?_____
   C. What was the result? _____

"Strive not to be a success, but to be of value."

Albert Einstein

#32 Scripture Analysis 1-Unit 1-Lesson 4-Activity 6

<u>Debate (Grades 6-8)</u>
The Virtuous Actions of Jesus versus Peer Mistreatment

Directions: Based on the Luke 19: 1-10 Scripture passage, you and your partner will debate the actions of Jesus with those of people participating in peer mistreatment.

Follow the debate guidelines below:

1. Decide who will be discussing the actions of Jesus and who will discuss peer mistreatment.
2. Take 8 minutes to develop your point of view. As you do this reflect on the following questions:
   - What are the actions of those involved in peer mistreatment?
   - What are Jesus' actions?
   - Which actions should change?
   - What actions can I model?
   - What did I learn?
3. Use an index card to help record and organize your thoughts.
4. Each person will have one minute to debate their thoughts with their partner.
5. After each person has presented, take 1-2 minutes to ask each other any clarification questions.

<u>Grading Rubric Points</u>
Did the debater:
- Successfully argue their point of view?
- Stay on topic?
- Focus their ideas on demonstrating an understanding of the different actions?
- Ask questions that helped further clarify the topic or argument?
- Ask questions that helped generate further discussion?
- Use good presentation and communication skills?
- Look at their audience?
- Speak loud enough and clear enough to be heard?

#33 Debate (Grades 6-8)-Unit 1-Lesson 4-Activity 6

Name: _____ Date: _____

<u>Jesus Models Dignity for One</u>
Reflection

Directions: After reading the passage from Luke 19:1-10 and the group discussion activity, answer the following questions to reflect on how this scripture passage personally relates to your life.

1. How is this Scripture relevant to my personal life?

   _____
   _____
   _____
   _____
   _____

2. What biblical character(s) in this Scripture passage do I identify with?

   _____
   _____
   _____
   _____
   _____

3. Apply two or more servant-leader words to this biblical character. How does he/she demonstrate one or more of the servant leader words? What is the result (positive ripple) of his/her virtuous actions?

   _____
   _____
   _____
   _____
   _____

4. How does this Scripture personally impact me? How am I inspired by this Scripture passage?

   _____
   _____
   _____
   _____
   _____

"Spread love everywhere you go.
Let no one ever come to you
without leaving happier"
   Mother Teresa   *#34 Reflection 3-Unit 1-Lesson 4-Activity 6*

Jesus Models Dignity for All
Scripture Connection 2

A reading from the Gospel of John 8: 1-11:

But Jesus went to the Mount of Olives. Early in the morning He came again into the temple, and all the people were coming to Him; and He sat down and began to teach them. The Scribes and the Pharisees brought a woman caught in adultery, and having set her in the center of the court they said to Him, "Teacher, this woman has been caught in adultery, in the very act. "Now in the Law Moses commanded us to stone such women; what then do You say?" They were saying this, testing Him, so that they might have grounds for accusing Him. But Jesus stooped down and with His finger wrote on the ground. But when they persisted in asking Him, He straightened up, and said to them, "He who is without sin among you, let him be the first to throw a stone at her." Again He stooped down and wrote on the ground. When they heard it, they began to go out one by one, beginning with the older ones, and He was left alone, and the woman, where she was, in the center of the court. Straightening up, Jesus said to her, "Woman, where are they? Did no one condemn you?" She said, "No one, Lord." And Jesus said, "I do not condemn you, either. Go. From now on sin no more."

#35 Scripture Connection 2-Unit 1-Lesson 4-Activity 7

Jesus Models Dignity for All
Role-Play 2

Narrator: "This story is from the Gospel of John chapter 8 verses 1 to 11. Jesus had gone up to the Mount of Olives for a night. Early the next morning he returned to the Temple and all the people gathered around Him and He sat down to teach them. (The people approach Jesus. He sits down and those gathered around sit down with Him). The teachers of the Law (Scribes) and the Pharisees brought in a woman accused of adultery (Enter Pharisees and woman). They made her stand before the crowd gathered and the Leader said to Jesus:

Leader: "Teacher, this woman was caught in the act of adultery. Now in the Law, Moses commanded us to stone such a woman. What then do you say?

[When the leader says this, the students acting as the crowd will stand up and collect a "stone" preparing to "stone" the woman as indicated by the leader's words.]

Narrator: "The Pharisees were asking this question as a test, so that they might have grounds for accusing Him. But Jesus bent down and started to write on the ground with his finger. When they kept questioning Him…"

Leader: "Teacher, what do you say?"

Members of the crowd: "Teacher, what do you say we should do?"

Narrator: "Then Jesus stooped down and with His finger wrote on the ground. But when they persisted in asking Him, He straightened up, and said to them…."

Jesus: "If any one of you is without sin, let him be the first to throw a stone at her."

Narrator: "Again Jesus stooped down and wrote on the ground. At this, those who heard Him began to drop their stone and go away one at a time, the older ones first, until only Jesus was left with the woman still standing there. Jesus straightened up and asked her…"

[As the narrator reads about the people leaving one at a time, the students will drop their "stones/rocks" and walk to the back of the room until only Jesus is left with the woman.]

Jesus: "Woman, where are they? Has no one condemned you?"

Woman: "No one, Sir!"

Narrator: "And Jesus said….."

Jesus: "Then neither do I condemn you. Go now and sin no more!"

#36 Role-Play 2-Unit 1-Lesson 4-Activity 7

Name: _____ **Date:** _____

<u>Jesus Models Dignity for All</u>
Scripture Analysis 2

Directions: Read John 8: 1-11 and reflect on this passage.
Work in assigned groups to answer the questions below.
Prepare to discuss your answers with the class.

List Group Members: _____
_____

1. Who is being mistreated? _____
   A. How? _____
   B. Why? _____
   C. Identify the person's feelings: _____

2. Who is mistreating? _____
   A. How? _____
   B. Why? _____
   C. Identify the person's feelings:_____

3. Who is witnessing mistreatment? _____
   A. How? _____
   B. Why? _____
   C. Identify the person's feelings: _____

4. Which character(s) caused a negative ripple? _____
   A. How? _____
   B. Why? _____
   C. What was the result? _____

5. Which character(s) caused a positive ripple? _____
   A. How? _____
   B. Why? _____
   C. What was the result? _____

#37 Scripture Analysis 2-Unit 1-Lesson 4-Activity 7

Jesus Models Dignity for All
Reflection

Directions: After reading the passage from John 8: 1-11 and the group discussion activity, answer the following questions to reflect on how this scripture passage personally relates to your life.

1. How is this Scripture relevant to my personal life?

_____
_____
_____
_____

2. What biblical character(s) in this Scripture passage do I identify with?

_____
_____
_____
_____

3. Apply two or more servant-leader words to this biblical character? How does he/she demonstrate one or more of the servant-leader words? What is the result (positive ripple) of his/her virtuous actions?

_____
_____
_____
_____

4. How does this Scripture personally impact me? How am I inspired by this Scripture passage?

_____
_____
_____
_____

"Respect cannot be inherited,
respect is the result of right actions."
Amit Kalantri

Unit 1
Comprehensive Review

"My goal is not to be better than anyone else, but to be better than I used to be."
Wayne Dyer

Way to go! You have completed Unit One. With all the work done, take this time to reflect
and *harvest the goodness* of your efforts.

Reflect and write on the following sentences:

The best servant-leader word to describe me is _____

I make good choices. One example of a good choice I made is when…
_____

I have a positive attitude. One example of a positive ripple I created is when…
_____

I create a safe and positive school for others and myself. Right now, I think our class is
at a (pick a number between 0-10) _____ on the *Safety Check Line*. Together we are
working toward getting to a "10" by
_____
_____

I understand the harm of the *Mistreatment Triangle* (1), but do my part to help create
the Peace Be With You Triangle (2) to support my classmates' by _____
_____

The Scripture from the two role-plays that helped me to better know the compassion of
Christ is… _____
_____

Why?_____

I celebrate what I am learning. One area in *Peace Be With You* where I have grown the
most is…
_____
_____

Thank you God for inviting me to be an instrument of Your peace!

#39 Unit 1-Comprehensive Review

Name_____ **Date**_____

Unit One
Four Agreements

After reflecting on Unit One of Peace Be With You:

I agree to be kind to my classmates with positive support and encouragement.

I agree to make choices that make positive ripples.

I agree to be open to learning more about Jesus as a servant-leader.

I agree to seek out a trusted adult if I need help.

Student Signature: _____   Date: _____

Parent Signature: _____   Date: _____

Teacher Signature: _____   Date: _____

Principal Signature: _____   Date: _____

- Sign & date this agreement if you agree.
- Take this agreement home.
- Read this agreement with your parent(s) and ask one of them to sign it.
- Ask your teacher to sign your agreement.

#40 Unit 1-Four Agreements

Appendix B
Unit 2: Student Worksheets

Table of Contents

Activity 15: Meditation 3

Team Member Name: 1._____ Date: _____
Team Member Name: 2._____ Date: _____

Living in "Fast Forward"

"There is more to life than increasing its speed."
Mahatma Gandhi

Directions:
- List your responses to the prompts in the column under "My Thoughts."
- Discuss with your partner the prompts and list "How We are Similar" and "How We are Different."
- Use this chart to help you and your partner share what you have learned during class discussion time.

#	Prompts	My Thoughts	How We are Similar	How We are Different
1	Jot down a few words to help you recall a time when you hurried or rushed to get somewhere or do something. Also jot down, who was with you and how you were treating each other at the time.			
2	List some words to describe what was physically happening inside of you while you were hurrying.			
3	List some words to describe what you were thinking while your were rushing around.			
4	List some words to describe what were you feeling emotionally during this hurried state.			
5	List some words to describe what the consequences of this hurried pace might have been for you and everyone else.			
6	List some words to describe how does the technology (phone, tablet, computer, etc.) you use affect the hurried pace of your life.			
7	List some words to describe how do advertisements and commercials play on how we feel about ourselves.			

#41 Worksheet-Unit 2-Lesson-5 Activity 8

Prayer and Poem Options
Activity 8: Living in "Fast Forward"

Prayer for a Peaceful Internet

Good and gracious God, thank You for the good gift of electronic devices through which we can create, communicate, learn, and praise You. Thank you for the many ways You bless our world by making our lives easier with technology and the Internet. Praise You for giving us the good gifts of creativity and compassion that we can reflect Your image online. Give me the strength and courage to always spread love, peace and joy with a pure heart when using all my electronic devices. Grant me self-control to thoughtfully and creatively use social media to post and say only what builds others up. Help me to always remember to use the Internet as a powerful instrument of Your peace. In my relationships through technology, may I always communicate deep care and compassion, reflecting Your love through my every thought, word and action with others. Amen.

Serenity Prayer on Technology
Please grant me the
Serenity to accept the technology I have
Courage to use it mindfully, and the
Wisdom to know when to turn it off. Amen.

Christ Has No Online Presence but Yours
Christ has no online presence but yours,
No blog, no Facebook page but yours,
Yours are the tweets through which love touches this world,
Yours are the posts through which the Gospel is shared,
Yours are the updates through which hope is revealed.
Christ has no online presence but yours,
No blog, no Facebook page but yours.

Poem by Meredith Gould

#42 Prayers and Poem Options

Jesus & Technology

Directions: With your assigned partner, choose 4 of the discussion starters below. You and your partner will have 10 minutes to discuss the 4 topics. Bring your thoughts back to the whole class discussion when time is called. Tonight, discuss 2 different discussion topics with your parents/family members. Write a brief summary of the discussion you had at home on the lines provided. Return this worksheet to school tomorrow. In the boxes provided before the discussion starters, place an X in the ones chosen for class and an ✓in the ones chosen for home.

Discussion Starters:

☐ Do you think Jesus would use electronic devices if He were physically with us today?

☐ What would He use technology for?

☐ Do you think He would refer Facebook, Twitter, Instagram, Snapchat, email, texting, YouTube, or a combination of these? Why?

☐ Do you think Jesus would have a preference? What would it be?

☐ If Jesus used Twitter, what would His #Hashtag be?

☐ How many followers would you guess He would have?

☐ Would He respond to the Tweets of others or would He only have followers?

☐ Give one or more examples of what a Tweet from Jesus might say.

☐ What might Jesus Tweet to our President?

☐ What might Jesus Tweet to other world leaders?

☐ What might Jesus Tweet to religious or spiritual leaders?

☐ What might Jesus Tweet to ordinary people like you and me?

☐ Would His message be the same to all or different?

☐ What would Jesus post on social media sites?

☐ Would Jesus take Selfies? Why?

☐ Who would be in His Selfies or other photo posts?

☐ What might Jesus tell us about love and compassion through His electronic devices?

☐ How do you imagine things would be in our world today, if technology was available when Jesus was here on Earth? Would his message be any different or would His message be the same no matter what?

☐ We know that Jesus only communicated face-to-face or to His Heavenly Father through prayer. If Jesus only used electronic devices to get His message out, how do you think His love and compassion would still get through to people?

Partner Discussion Summary:

_____

_____

_____

Summary of family discussion:

_____

_____

_____

#43 Worksheet-Unit 2-Lesson 5-Activity 8

Name_____ Date_____

Poster Directions
Negative/Positive Stress

1. Choose and cut out 5 negative stress pictures and 5 positive stress pictures from the classroom magazine supply.
2. Title your poster at the top (ex., Negative/Positive Stress, Stress in My Life, etc.)
3. Divide the poster into two halves:
    a. Label one half Negative Stress
    b. Label one half Positive Stress
4. Arrange and glue the negative and positive stress pictures on the appropriate half.
5. For each picture, create a short caption that describes how that item creates positive or negative stress for you. (ex., a clock under Negative Stress, with the caption: I feel rushed by all I have to do in a short amount of time each day.)
6. When finished, place your poster on the classroom wall at eye level.
7. Please be creative, colorful, and neat in creating your poster.

#44 Poster Directions-Unit 2-Lesson Five-Activity 9

Name_____ Date_____

Poster Directions
Negative/Positive Stress

1. Choose and cut out 5 negative stress pictures and 5 positive stress pictures from the classroom magazine supply.
2. Title your poster at the top (ex., Negative/Positive Stress, Stress in My Life, etc.)
3. Divide the poster into two halves:
    a. Label one half Negative Stress
    b. Label one half Positive Stress
4. Arrange and glue the negative and positive stress pictures on the appropriate half of the poster.
5. For each picture, create a short caption that describes how that item creates positive or negative stress for you. (ex.,, a clock under Negative Stress, with the caption: I feel rushed by all I have to do in a short amount of time each day.)
6. When finished, place your poster on the classroom wall at eye level.
7. Please be creative, colorful, and neat in creating your poster.

#44 Poster Directions-Unit 2-Lesson Five-Activity 9

Grading Rubric
Negative/Positive Stress Poster

Name: _____

Date Poster Graded: _____

___ out of 5   Poster Titled

___ out of 5   Poster Divided into Negative and Positive sections

___ out of 10   5 pictures in each section

___ out of 20   Caption for each picture

___ out of 10   Correct use of CUPS

___ out of 5   Creativity

___ out of 5   Neatness

___ out of 60   Final Grade

Comments: _____

_____

_____

_____

_____

_____

Name: _____

Date Poster Graded: _____

___ out of 5   Poster Titled

___ out of 5   Poster Divided into Negative and Positive sections

___ out of 10   5 pictures in each section

___ out of 20   Caption for each picture

___ out of 10   Correct use of CUPS

___ out of 5   Creativity

___ out of 5   Neatness

___ out of 60   Final Grade

Comments: _____

_____

_____

_____

_____

_____

#45 Grading Rubric-Lesson 5-Activity 9

Team Member(s):_____Date_____

Guitar Analogy Video

Video Production

Directions:
- With your assigned group, create a video outside of class time that is no longer than 3 minutes of viewing time.
- Save the video to an electronic device you can bring to class.
- The video is to be shared with the parents of each group member.
- Each parent must approve the video on the permission form for viewing by the class.
- Videos will be graded for creativity, originality and positivity.
- This group project is due in two weeks from today.
- Have fun!

Please consider the following questions when producing your video:
1. If you were to turn the tuning keys at the top of a guitar to loosen the strings, what would happen?
2. What would be the effect of guitar strings with no tension?
3. What might be the ripple effect of no tension or stress in your life?
4. If you were to turn the tuning keys at the top of a guitar to tighten the strings as tight as possible, what might happen?
5. What would be the effect of guitar strings with too much tension or even a broken string?
6. What might be the ripple effect of high tension or stress in your life?
7. If you were to tune the strings to perfect pitch, what would happen?
8. What would be the effect of a tuned guitar?
9. What might be the ripple effect if your life were perfectly tuned?

I have viewed the video: _____(Parent's Signature)

#46 Video Production-Unit 2-Lesson-5-Activity 9

Name_____ Date_____

Directions: Log your progress by circling your Pre- and Post Stress Check numbers and answering the formula below.

PRE-STRESS CHECK

0   1   2   3   4   5   6   7   8   9   10

LOW   HIGH

POST-STRESS CHECK

0   1   2   3   4   5   6   7   8   9   10

LOW   HIGH

STRESS CHECK FORMULA
Pre-Stress Check (___) – Post-Stress Check (___) = Stress Reduction Score (___)

#47 Stress Check Log

Name_____ Date_____

Directions: Log your progress by circling your Pre- and Post Stress Check numbers and answering the formula below.

PRE-STRESS CHECK

0   1   2   3   4   5   6   7   8   9   10

LOW   HIGH

POST-STRESS CHECK

0   1   2   3   4   5   6   7   8   9   10

LOW   HIGH

STRESS CHECK FORMULA
Pre-Stress Check (___) – Post-Stress Check (___) = Stress Reduction Score (___)

#47 Stress Check Log

Name_____ Date_____

Meditation 1 Journal 1

Journal below your thoughts and feelings about the meditation experience. Consider the following questions in your journal entry: Did your Post-Stress Check reveal a reduction in stress? If so, by how many numbers? Why do you think you were able to achieve reduced stress? If not, why do you think you weren't able to reduce stress with this activity? Where, when and how could you use this self-care strategy in the future?

_____

_____

_____

_____

_____

_____

_____

_____

_____

_____

_____

_____

_____

_____

_____

_____

_____

_____

_____

_____

#48 Meditation 1 Journal 1-Activity 10b

Name_____ Date_____

PeaceScape Drawing 1

Draw a PeaceScape to represent your image of peace after the meditation.

Write a description of the story your Peacescape is telling.

_____
_____
_____
_____
_____
_____
_____
_____
_____
_____
_____

#49 PeaceScape 1-Activity-10b

Name: _____ Date: _____

Stress Management Skills

Directions: For each of the four stress management skills listed below, write how you will develop them. Also, describe how that strategy will help you to manage your stress.

Stress Management Skills	How I will develop this skill.	How will this strategy help me manage stress?
Stress Check		
Breath Check		
Tension Check		
Balance Check		

Name: _____ Date: _____

Taking Good Care of Myself

Directions:
- List four self-care strategies that you can use in your daily life to reduce stress.
- Choose one strategy and describe how you will use it in your daily life to support inner peace.

4 Self-Care Strategies I can use in my Daily Life:

1. _____

2. _____

3. _____

4. _____

I will use the _____ strategy on

a daily basis by _____

_____

Using this strategy will help me to achieve inner peace by _____

_____

***If helpful, discuss a second strategy you will use daily.

I will use the _____ strategy on

a daily basis by _____

_____

Using this strategy will help me to achieve inner peace by _____

_____

#51 Worksheet-Unit 2 Lesson 6 Activity 11

Name_____ Date_____

Meditation 2 Journal 2

Journal below your thoughts and feelings about the meditation experience. Consider the following questions in your journal entry: Did your Post-Stress Check reveal a reduction in stress? If so, by how many numbers? Why do you think you were able to achieve reduced stress? If not, why do you think you weren't able to reduce stress with this activity? Where, when and how could you use this self-care strategy in the future?

_____

_____

_____

_____

_____

_____

_____

_____

_____

_____

_____

_____

_____

_____

_____

_____

_____

_____

_____

_____

#52 Meditation Journal 2-Activity-12

Name_____ Date_____

PeaceScape Drawing 2

Draw a PeaceScape to represent your image of peace after the meditation.

Write a description of the story your Peacescape is telling.

_____
_____
_____
_____
_____
_____
_____
_____
_____

#53 PeaceScape 2-Activity-12

Name: _____ Date: _____

My Heart Affirmation

Directions 1: After listening to the audio track, write down the most meaningful, encouraging or inspiring words that touched your heart.

Word: _____

Word: _____

Word: _____

Word: _____

Word: _____

Word: _____

Word: _____

Word: _____

Word: _____

Word: _____

Directions 2: Use your word list above to write a Heart Affirmation for yourself in the box below.

My Heart Affirmation:

Directions 3: Create a decorative display of your Heart Affirmation on a poster, post-it or blank index card. Place your creation in a prominent place so you can read it every day for encouragement.

#54 My Heart Affirmation-Activity 13

Name_____ Date_____

Peace Prayer of St. Francis

Lord, make me an instrument of your peace:
where there is hatred, let me sow love;
where there is injury, pardon;
where there is doubt, faith;
where there is despair, hope;
where there is darkness, light;
where there is sadness, joy.

O divine Master, grant that I may not so much seek
to be consoled as to console,
to be understood as to understand,
to be loved as to love.
For it is in giving that we receive,
it is in pardoning that we are pardoned,
and it is in dying that we are born to eternal life.
Amen.

Directions 2: Choose one highlighted word and give an example of your struggle in the box below labeled "I need support." Choose two other highlighted words and give examples of how you can offer support to your classmates in the box below labeled "I can give support."

I Need Support: _____ (Example)	I Can Give Support: _____ (Examples)

Bonus: List at least one *Youth Voice Project Peer Support Strategy* that you could add to support

classmates: _____

#55 The Peace Prayer-Unit 2-Lesson 7-Activity 14

Appendix B   239

The Peace Prayer of St. Francis
(Lyrics)

"Make me a channel of your peace.
Where there is hatred let me bring your love,
Where there is injury your pardon Lord,
And where there's doubt true faith in you.

Make me a channel of your peace,
Where there's despair in life, let me bring hope,
Where there is darkness, only light,
And where there's sadness, every joy.

O Master grant that I may never seek,
So much to be consoled as to console,
To be understood as to understand,
To be loved as to love with all my soul.

Make me a channel of your peace.
It is in the pardoning that we are pardoned,
In giving of ourselves that we receive.
And in the dying that we're born to eternal life.

O Master grant that I may never seek,
So much to be consoled as to console,
To be understood as to understand,
And to love as to love with all my soul.

Make me a channel of your peace.
It is in pardoning that we are pardoned,
In giving of ourselves that we receive.
And in dying that we're born to eternal life.

Make me a channel of your peace."

#56 Peace Prayer Lyrics-Unit 2-Activity 14

Name_____ Date_____

Meditation 3 Journal 3

Journal below your thoughts and feelings about the meditation experience. Consider the following questions in your journal entry: Did your Post-Stress Check reveal a reduction in stress? If so, by how many numbers? Why do you think you were able to achieve reduced stress? If not, why do you think you weren't able to reduce stress with this activity? Where, when and how could you use this self-care strategy in the future?

_____

_____

_____

_____

_____

_____

_____

_____

_____

_____

_____

_____

_____

_____

_____

_____

_____

_____

_____

#57 Meditation 3 Journal 3-Activity-15

Name_____ Date_____

PeaceScape Drawing 3

Draw a PeaceScape to represent your image of peace after the meditation.

Write a description of the story your Peacescape is telling.

_____
_____
_____
_____
_____
_____
_____
_____
_____

#58 PeaceScape 3-Activity-15

Pure in Heart
Unit 2 Comprehensive Review

Nothing in all creation is so like God as stillness.
Meister Eckhart

Congratulations on completing Unit 2: Pure in Heart! This is a time to pause and use your new reflective skills. Reflect on your personal growth during this unit and your school year so far.

Complete the following sentences:

Being more aware of my fast pace, I take steps to slow down and become mindful of my breathing and when I do the results have been _____
_____
_____
_____

After the *Peace Be With You* audio mediations I feel _____
_____
_____
_____

Scripture tells us that Jesus went off by himself to pray. My perception on prayer and the importance of quiet and stillness has changed in the following ways
_____
_____
_____
_____

I celebrate all that I am learning. The greatest personal growth on my faith journey that I have achieved by using prayer and meditation or any of the other self-care strategies is _____
_____
_____
_____
_____

#59 Unit 2–Comprehensive Review

Pure In Heart
Four Agreements

1. I agree to practice at least one of the self-care strategies.

2. I agree to write down my affirmation statement and refer to it as often as I like.

3. I agree to practice being quiet and still—opening my heart to listen to God through prayer and meditation.

4. I agree to seek out a trusted adult if I need help.

Student Signature: _____ Date: _____

Parent Signature: _____ Date: _____

Teacher Signature: _____ Date: _____

Principal Signature: _____ Date: _____

- Take this agreement home.
- Read this agreement with your parent(s).
- Sign this agreement with a parent.
- Show this signed agreement to your teacher and principal to sign.

#60 Unit 2-Four Agreements

Appendix C
Unit 3: Student Worksheets

Table of Contents

Harvesting Our Growth

1. From the rich list of Servant leader words and the Gifts and Fruits of the Holy Spirit, I live out and model the gift of _____ In my life.

2. Today, in the presence of my teacher and classmates I am a _____ on the Safety Check Line. I commit to helping myself and my classmates progress closer to a "10."

3. I recall with joy the time I provided a Peer Support Strategy by

   _____

   _____

   _____

   _____

   _____

4. The positive ripple effect(s) from my peer support was

   _____

   _____

   _____

   _____

   _____

5. These are my qualities and the gift of safety, and compassion that I bring to my class. God Bless Me and Our Class!

   _____

   _____

   _____

   _____

   _____

Name_____ Date _____

#61 Worksheet-Unit 3-Lesson 8-Activity 16a&b

CLEAR Listening Poster

C Connect	***Connect*** face to face. This is an important part of building relationships. By connecting with others and using good communication, we become better people.
L Listen	***Listen*** with your eyes, ears, and heart. A good listener is open, still, and does not disrupt or interrupt the speaker.
E Eyes	***Eye Contact*** is a great way to tune into what the speaker is saying
A Attention	Attentive focus on what the speaker is saying. Give them your full ***Attention***. Look interested!
R Respect	***Respect*** means being kind and considerate of what the person is saying. You don't have to agree or disagree, just listen. The letter R also stands for ***Relaxed***. Stay as relaxed as you can and just hear the person out.

Scripture Connection 3
Luke 10: 25-37

There was a scholar of the law who stood up to test him and said, "Teacher, what must I do to inherit eternal life?" Jesus said to him, "What is written in the law? How do you read it?" He said in reply, "You shall love the Lord, your God, with all your heart, with all your being, with all your strength, and with all your mind, and your neighbor as yourself."

He replied to him, "You have answered correctly; do this and you will live." But because he wished to justify himself, he said to Jesus, "And who is my neighbor?"

Jesus replied, "A man fell victim to robbers as he went down from Jerusalem to Jericho. They stripped and beat him and went off leaving him half-dead. A priest happened to be going down that road, but when he saw him, he passed by on the opposite side.

Likewise a Levite came to the place, and when he saw him, he passed by on the opposite side. But a Samaritan traveler who came upon him was moved with compassion at the sight.

He approached the victim, poured oil and wine over his wounds and bandaged them. Then he lifted him up on his own animal, took him to an inn and cared for him.

The next day he took out two silver coins and gave them to the innkeeper with the instruction, 'Take care of him. If you spend more than what I have given you, I shall repay you on my way back.'

Which of these three, in your opinion, was neighbor to the robbers' victim?" He answered, "The one who treated him with mercy." Jesus said to him, "Go and do likewise."

#63 Scripture Connection 3-Unit 3-Lesson 9-10-Activity 17-18

Name: _____ Date: _____

The Good Samaritan Role Reflection

Levite	Injured Person	Good Samaritan	Priest	Robber	Innkeeper
You are a person of importance. Did your actions demonstrate positive servant leadership? Why or why not? Initials: _____	How did you feel when the Levite and the Priest passed you? Initials: _____	Why did you stop to help the injured person? Initials: _____	You are a person of importance. Did your actions demonstrate positive servant leadership? Why or why not? Initials: _____	Why did you rob the man on the road? Initials: _____	How did you feel when the wounded man was brought to your inn and all his care was paid for? Initials: _____
What did your actions say when you saw the wounded man and moved to the opposite side of the road? Initials: _____	How did you feel when no one stopped to help you? Initials: _____	How did you care for the wounded man and for so long? Initials? _____	What did your actions say when you saw the injured person and moved to the opposite side of the road? Initials: _____	What were your thoughts and feelings when you left the man alone on the side of the road? Initials: _____	Why did you care for the wounded man? Initials: _____
Why didn't you help the injured person? Initials: _____	How did you feel when the Good Samaritan stopped to help you? Initials: _____	How did you care for the injured person even when you were not there? Initials: _____	Why didn't you help the injured person? Initials: _____	What would you do differently if you could go back before you robbed the man? Initials: _____	What were your feelings toward the Good Samaritan and his care of the wounded man? Initials: _____

#64a Role Reflection-Unit 3-Lesson 9-Activity 17

*Directions for Role Reflection (next page-#64b) can be printed on back or posted on Smartboard.

The Good Samaritan Role Reflection

<u>Directions</u>

1. You will be assigned a role (Injured Person, Robber, Levite, Priest, Good Samaritan, or Innkeeper) by your teacher.

2. Move around the room to find different classmates who have been assigned the different roles and ask them the questions listed for their specific role below.

3. Have your classmate initial the box after you have discussed the question!

4. Try to find a different classmate for each question!

5. Continue to move around the room until time is called or you have completely filled in the chart.

#64b Directions-Unit 3-Lesson 9-Activity 17

Inn Keeper/Good Samaritan
Role-Play 3

Directions:
1. #1's are Character 1: Inn Keeper & #2's are Character 2: Good Samaritan.
2. Use the prompts written below your role.
3. Roles switch—#2's become Character 1: Inn Keeper & #1's become Character 2: Good Samaritan.

#1 Character 1: Inn Keeper
#2 Character 2: Good Samaritan

Role-Play Script

Innkeeper:
Innkeeper speaking in an excited, hurried voice to the Good Samaritan.

Hey, what happened? Here. Let me hold the door open while you carry this injured person inside. What can I do to help? Here. Set him in this side room. I will get a basin of water for you to take care of his wounds. Thank you for the money you paid for my expenses in taking care of this person to stay here. Are a Samaritan? I do not get many Samaritans at my Inn. I promise to tend to the needs of this person until you return.

Good Samaritan
Good Samaritan says nothing until the Inn Keeper is finished speaking.

Ask yourself:
Being the best listener possible, what do you hear the Inn Keeper saying?

Say:
What I hear you (Inn Keeper) saying is………

#65 Role-Play 3-Lesson 9-Activity 17

Name: _____ Date: _____

CLEAR LISTENING

C **Connect**	List 3 things I can do to **Connect** when listening to a friend without using an electronic device: 1. _____ 2._____ 3. _____
L **Listen**	When I actively **Listen**, what do I notice happening for the other person I am listening to? _____ _____ _____ _____
E **Eyes**	Why is **Eye** contact important and how can I improve on this when listening to others? _____ _____ _____ _____
A **Attentio** **n**	When I give someone my full **Attention**, what do I notice happening for the other person? _____ _____ _____ _____
R **Respect**	How can I demonstrate **Respect** when I am listening to others? _____ _____ How can I be **Relaxed** when I am listening to others? _____ _____

#66 Worksheet-Unit 3-Lesson 9-Activity 17

Teacher Reference
Clear Talk Observation Rubric

Peace Circle Date: _____

Students who participated in Clear Talk:

Student 1 (Speaker): _____

Student 2 (Listener): _____

Student 1 Observations:
- ☐ Demonstrated eye contact   Notes: _____
- ☐ Used appropriate volume   Notes: _____
- ☐ Followed Clear Talk Steps   Notes: _____
- ☐ Demonstrated CLEAR Listening Notes: _____
- ☐ Other: _____

Student 2 Observations:
- ☐ Demonstrated eye contact   Notes: _____
- ☐ Used appropriate volume   Notes: _____
- ☐ Followed Clear Talk Steps   Notes: _____
- ☐ Demonstrated CLEAR Listening Notes: _____

Other: _____

Students in the Peace Circle:
- ☐ Listened attentively   Notes: _____
- ☐ Actively Participated Notes: _____
- ☐ Other: _____

Concerns:
_____
_____
_____
_____

#67 Teacher Reference -Unit 3-Lessons 10-Activity 18

<u>Clear Talk</u>

1. Thank you

2. Data

3. Feelings

4. Actions said...

5. Want(s)

Clear Talk Script
Person Who was Mistreated

Script: Person Who was Mistreated says:

Thank you: "Thank you Good Samaritan for coming into circle and into my life."

Data: "I was robbed and beaten very badly. I was laying alone on the road. The priest and Levite walked to the other side of the road and walked passed me. You passed by, saw me, and attended to me."

Feelings: "I was very scared. I was in deep pain. I was afraid I was going to die. I felt alone. I was hope with you stopped. I felt loved and cared for when you started attending to my wounds and bring me to the Inn."

Your actions said: "The using wine and oil to attend to my wounds gave me comfort. Taking me to the Inn took away fear of what was I going to do. Your actions spoke of compassion and care."

Want: "I want you to know that I so grateful that you saved my life. Thank you."

#69 Role Play 4-Unit 3-Lesson 10-Activity-18

Name: _____ Date: _____

Peer Support Practice

Directions: Write out a Clear Talk (Using Put-Ups) you want to do with a classmate. If you would like to follow through with the Clear Talk in a Peace Circle, let your teacher know so they can support you with the process.

Steps   **Actions**

1   **Thank You!**

2   **Data** (What happened?)
_____
_____

3   **Feelings** (Glad, Comforted, Gratitude, etc.)
I feel/felt _____.

4   **Your actions said .....?**
Your actions said _____
_____

5   **Wants**
I want _____
_____

What positive ripples might you create if you follow through with this Clear Talk? _____
_____

What could happen if you don't follow through with the Clear Talk?
_____
_____

#70 Worksheet-Unit 3-Lesson 10-Activity-18

Unit 3 Comprehensive Review
Grades 4-8

"My peace I leave with you; my peace I give you."
John 14:27

Congratulations on completing Unit 3! You can be very proud of all the work that you have done and all that you have accomplished. Take this time to reflect and write about the ripple effects you have made from your efforts.

After reflecting, complete the following sentences.

As a leader, the best word to describe myself from the Servant-Leader Word List is_____

One example of a positive ripple I created as a good listener is_____
_____
_____

I understand the importance of CLEAR Listening and I practice it by_____
_____
_____

I am creating a stronger, safer environment for myself and others. Right now, I am working toward getting closer to a "**10**" by using Clear Talk in the following ways_____
_____

I understand the importance of giving Peer Support in the form of put-ups. I am practicing to build up my classmates and school community by_____
_____

I celebrate what I am learning. One area where I have grown the most from Peace Be With You is_____
_____

Thank you God for inviting me to be an instrument of Your peace!

Name_____ Date_____

Love Your Neighbor
<u>Four Agreements</u>
Grades 4-8

1. I agree to practice CLEAR Listening when I am with another person.

2. I agree to practice Clear Talk, thinking through all 5 steps before I speak.

3. I agree to use put-ups whenever possible to strengthen my relationships with peers, and the family of God.

4. I agree I will seek out a trusted adult if I need help.

Student's Signature:_____ Date: _____

Parent's Signature: _____ Date: _____

Teacher's Signature: _____ Date: _____

Principal's Signature: _____ Date: _____

- Take this agreement home and read it with your parent(s).
- If you agree, sign this agreement with a parent.
- Show this signed agreement to your teacher and have her/him and your Principal to sign it too.

#72 Unit 3-Four Agreements

About the Author

Frank A. DiLallo is employed with the Diocese of Toledo since 1990 and currently is Director of the Office of Child & Youth Protection. As an educator and consultant for over 30 years, Frank has extensive experience in the prevention, intervention and a Catholic response to bullying. He earned a B.A. in sociology and Master of Education degree in Guidance & Counseling. He is also a Licensed Professional Counselor, Licensed Independent Chemical Dependency Counselor-CS, and Certified Prevention Specialist-II in the state of Ohio.

Frank is the published co-author of *Peace Be With You Christ Centered Bullying Solution* and author of *Peace2U: Three Phase Bullying Solution*. He is a contributing author to numerous books and has produced two audio CD's—*The Peace Project: Meditations for Young Adults,* and *Make Me an Instrument of Your Peace: Inspiration for Strength, Hope and Healing.*

Frank frequently facilitates professional development with educators on bullying prevention, intervention and response and parent trainings on creating a successful bridge between home and school. He is a frequent regional, state, and national conference speaker and consults with educators and parents around the country on the topic. As a professional educator, Frank is passionate about promoting peace and compassion in Catholic schools.

To his writing Frank brings the additional perspective of being a husband, proud father of four children, two grandchildren, and practicing Catholic.

Acknowledgements

This book could not have been accomplished if not for the tremendous commitment of time, energy, and support of many people to whom I am eternally grateful. **THANK YOU TO:**
-My wife, Michelle for her love, feedback, and many sacrifices in loving support of me and my work.
-My daughter Joy, son Josh and daughter-in-law Danielle, son Andrew and daughter-in-law Alis, and two grandsons, Ezra and Shiloh, for their inspiration and support along the way.
-Our son David who passed away in November 2016—I love you son with all my heart.
-My family by marriage, Carol Fadell, Dr.'s Michael Jr. & Melody Fadell & Dr. Michael Fadell Sr.
-Dr. Steve Cady for helping me formulate the original model for Peace Be With You.
-Ernie Lewis for his many helpful consultations in visioning the Bullying Redirect series.
I am the man I am today, and truly blessed because of the tremendous network of support in my life—
Steve Cady, Denny Corathers, Tom Kapacinskas, Andy Lyke, Warren Parsons, Tony Packo Jr., Tony Packo III, brother Bill Phillips & sister-in-law Shirley Phillips, Thom Powers, Joe Schmidbauer, Dennis Shackley and Joe Sparks.
-Co-authors Thom Powers, and Lisa Bartholomew (The Peace Team) for the many hours of tireless reviews, meetings, email exchanges (at all hours of the day and night), comments, feedback, suggestions and revisions—resulting in a much grander vision than I could have ever thought of on my own.
-Carolyn Price for her very helpful and meticulous editing.
-Rae Bechtel for the finishing touches on formatting.
-Stan Davis for the powerful impact he has had in influencing my current view of bullying.
-Christian Educators across the U.S. for their meaningful feedback on the original Peace Be With You program—to whom I give much credit for the fruitful outcome of this current book.
-Parents for the mutual learning and trust in my consultation on this topic.
-Keith Tarjanyi for his creative and inspiring cover design for the Bullying Redirect series. The image represents a bullying redirect toward a mindset of growth, resiliency, and hopeful promise.
-Chris Knight for believing in me and being such an incredible advocate of my work.
-Ric Stuecker, for his inspiring work and many literary contributions for a better world.
-My father Frank DiLallo and mother Ruth DiLallo, my hero's and #1 supporters!

-Frank A. DiLallo

About the Author

Thom Powers attended the former St. Mary's College Seminary in Kentucky and St. Maur's School of Theology in Indianapolis, Indiana. Leaving prior to receiving orders in 1969, he entered the workforce, yet never lost touch with religious education. Working in industry, he picked up the titles of "padre" and "unofficial chaplain' among co-workers. From this experience, Thom realized the deep hunger for richer spirituality among adults, especially for men.

Having served as a speaker on the diocesan speaker's roster for Sacramental preparation, Thom's specialty has been adult education. Along with his wife Dianne, Thom spent over twenty years co-coordinating religious education with an inner-city parish in the Diocese of Toledo, Ohio. He was the first lay president for the Board of Trustees of Our Lady of the Pines Retreat Center in Fremont, Ohio.

More recently, Thom has been working with pastoral councils and the spiritual dimension of their ministries. Some of this work has been directed towards merging or closing of parishes. Thom and his daughter Krista Powers have done workshops in caring for the soul of caregivers.

Thom and Dianne have been married 48 years, parents to two daughters, a son through marriage, four grandchildren, and a delightful new great grandson.

Acknowledgments

I continued to be filled with deep gratitude, wonder and awe. Our first book, *Peace Be With You: Christ-Centered Bullying Solution* was an incredible journey, not to be topped, so I thought. This book of *Peace Be With You: Christ-Centered Bullying Redirect* has expanded my work with Frank DiLallo.

The opportunity to continue my friendship with Frank DiLallo and bring it to a deeper collaborative dimension continues to be a gift of gold. Welcoming the newest member of our team, Lisa Bartholomew, has provided well-roundedness and a strong classroom tie. Weaving our different academic traditions together and support for one another has brought out the best in each of us.

Peace Be With You: Christ-Centered Bullying Redirect has invited me to enter more deeply into the process of making peace in a wounded world. I have profound appreciation for the dialogue with, and feedback from teacher evaluations, and I am honored to have witnessed many of the *Peace Be With You* activities with students in many classrooms. I am also grateful for quiet self-reflection, and prayer, to help understand where the Spirit is calling me in this work. This new book has created a spiritual harvesting process unlike anything I could have ever imagined.

To my wife Dianne for her support, her wisdom as a parent and educator, her editing and tremendous enduring patience, I am lovingly indebted. Likewise, my gratitude extends to our two daughters, Patrice Powers-Barker and Krista Marie Powers, and to our son through marriage, Jim Barker for encouragement, interest and remarkable dialogues around the topic of bullying within schools and beyond into the workforce and daily life.

To family members and friends who have died and in their lives shared their suffering wounds from mistreatments, I pray the pain is now fully healed in the loving arms of Our God through Resurrection.

For us, who remain to celebrate daily life, may this work contribute to making all lives more Christ-centered, peaceful, supportive and loving.

To our grandchildren: Taylor, Jordan, Nathan; our grandson through marriage, Christopher, our newest addition, great grandson Dalton James and all children, Peace be with you.

-Thom Powers

About the Author

Lisa Bartholomew has been an educator at Regina Coeli Catholic School in Toledo, Ohio for 24 years. She has a Bachelors in Education degree from the University of Toledo and a Masters in the Art of Teaching from Bowling Green State University. Lisa has taught students in grades 4-8 throughout her career in all subject areas.

Lisa has been a member of the Peace Be With You team for the past 5 years and has used the curriculum since it's very beginning. She joined the team, first, as a presenter of the curriculum, then as a co-author.

Lisa has been married to Gary for 26 years and has two daughter, Caryn and Annie.

Acknowledgments

Each and every day, as an educator, I am shocked and devastated by the continued stories of violence and hurtful actions in our schools. I pray that the curriculum that has been developed by our team will bring change and encourage a loving and compassionate heart in each and every person who is introduced to it. I truly believe it is an ever-important need in our ever-changing world.

As an educator, I am awed and amazed that I am an author of this marvelous curriculum. I have been a proud advocate of the use of this curriculum since it's beginning. I feel continually privileged to have been included in the *Peace Be With You* curriculum and movement. I am honored to be working with my mentors, brothers in Christ, and dear friends, Frank DiLallo and Thom Powers. They continue to ground me and guide my work in the classroom.

To my husband, Gary, for his questions, his support, and his guiding spirit, I am blessed every day that you are in my life. To my daughter, Caryn and Annie, I thank you for your continued love and support. Your lives have guided me on the very importance of this work! To my aunt, Jan McNichol, for always pushing me to keep at it and do my best work, I am forever grateful! To my family, thank you for your continued love and support!

-Lisa Bartholomew

Readership Acknowledgements

Greetings in Christ!

As a school administrator you work tirelessly to address volumes of multilayered concerns. You maintain a vigilant focus to ensure safety and dignity for all in your school building. As ministers of the Gospel you are the guardian of Catholic identity and vanguard for academic excellence, while simultaneously keeping the "big picture" in clear view. With unwavering support of your staff, you provide the necessary tools and resources for them to be at their best. Always striving to be in partnership with your parents and the greater community, you work tirelessly to remain patient, kind, fair and flexible. We recognize you are constantly stretched with many overwhelming demands simultaneously requiring your time and attention. With total admiration for you and your God given abilities, we thank you for all you do and for your dedication to Catholic schools! You are our my prayers.

As a teacher, your ministry extends far beyond lesson plans. Your primary objective is to educate the whole person. You try out innovative approaches in an effort to creatively capture the attention and sustain the interest of your students. You have the unique ability to listen and get to know and recognize each of your students as the gifted person they can be. You deeply understand how essential it is to build rapport, while continuously nurturing mutual trust and respect with your students. At times, the dynamic constellation of student personalities can be overwhelming with a fascinating array of multiple intelligences that create endless challenges in your classroom. We recognize your enormous stretch to juggle academics, integrate formation and exercise classroom management. You painstakingly communicate with and make every effort to engage parents in the learning process. With total admiration for you and your God given abilities, we thank you for all you do and for your dedication to Catholic schools! You are in our prayers.

As a school counselor, the school is very blessed to have you. You are an invaluable resource and support person for students, teachers, parents and administrators. Your ministry extends far beyond preparing academic schedules, sharing compassion and accounting for academic credits. You are gifted with a unique skill set, the core of which is to empathically listen to others (students, parents and even staff). With tremendous understanding, you reach out to reconcile a myriad of interpersonal and intrapersonal struggles to help those in need find balance and peace. You also have an uncanny way of intuitively noticing the general health of the school "spirit." You are skillfully apt at making significant contributions to improve the overall school climate by implementing individual, group, classroom and whole-building strategies. With total admiration for your God given abilities, we thank you for all you do and for your dedication to Catholic schools! You are in our prayers.

We are humbled by your tremendous dedication to the school community and Catholic education. Your commitment to provide a safe, positive, disciplined school and caring Christ-centered classrooms is commendable. As rewarding as education is, we also acknowledge the many seemingly insurmountable challenges that exist today in creating the optimal conditions necessary to establish a flourishing learning environment. We sincerely hope this book is a helpful resource for all staff in your school toward sustaining a safe, threat free Christ-filled environment. If there is anything we can do to support you in your Christ centered bullying prevention efforts, please feel free to contact us at: *https://www.peacebewithyou.world*

Peace Be With You!

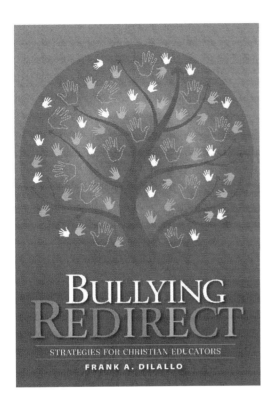

Purchase Online at: Peacebewithyou.world

"There are no 'easy answers' and no simple solutions in addressing the often destructive and hurtful ways in which children engage with each other, but the insights Bullying Redirect offers in this series are invaluable and potentially life changing. I urge you to read and consider this seminal work."

Chris Knight
Secretary For Catechetical
Formation And Education
Superintendent of Schools
Diocese of Cleveland

"Bully Redirect brings much-needed clarity to parents when trying to address the difficult challenges of bullying. Parents will gain insight into how to appropriately support youth who engage in mistreatment, youth who experience mistreatment, and youth who witness mistreatment, while at the same time encouraging actions that increase resiliency and self-efficacy. Grounded in the research of the Youth Voice Project, this book is a welcome addition for parents and caregivers in their efforts to promote empathy and kindness."

Patti Agatston, Ph.D.
Co-Author, Cyberbullying: Bullying
In The Digital Age

Made in the USA
Lexington, KY
15 September 2019